Writing between the Lines

The University of Georgia Press *Athens & London*

Writing

between the Lines

Race and Intertextuality

ALDON L. NIELSEN

© 1994 by the University of Georgia Press
Athens, Georgia 30602
All rights reserved
Designed by Richard Hendel
Set in Baskerville and Gill types
by Tseng Information Systems, Inc.
Printed and bound by Thomson-Shore, Inc.
The paper in this book meets the guidelines
for permanence and durability of the Committee
on Production Guidelines for Book Longevity of
the Council on Library Resources.

Printed in the United States of America
98 97 96 95 94 C 5 4 3 2 1

Library of Congress Cataloging in Publication Data
Nielsen, Aldon Lynn.
  Writing between the lines : race and intertextuality /
Aldon L. Nielsen.
      p. cm.
    Includes bibliographical references and index.
    ISBN 0-8203-1603-2 (alk. paper)
    1. American literature—Afro-American authors—History and
criticism.   2. American literature—White authors—History and
criticism.   3. American literature—20th century—History
and criticism.   4. Afro-Americans in literature.   5. Whites in
literature.   6. Race in literature.   7. Intertextuality.   I. Title.
PS153.N5N54   1994
810.9'355—dc20   93-23000

British Library Cataloging in Publication Data available

FOR ANNA EVERETT

All this I have ended with a tale twice told

but seldom written, and a chapter of song. . . .

Thus in Thy good time may infinite reason turn the

tangle straight, and these crooked marks on a fragile

leaf be not indeed

THE END

—W. E. B. Du Bois

Contents

Acknowledgments

I begin where I ended *Reading Race,* by acknowledging once again the care and encouragement of Anna Everett. May our revisionary company continue.

I have at times been tempted to title this work *How I Spent My Summer Vacations.* This time I have had help, and for making my breaks so productive I must thank many. Two summer research stipends from the California State University and one from the National Endowment for the Humanities made it possible for me to conduct the extensive research required in this project. I was also fortunate enough to be selected for participation in the NEH Summer Seminar on the Problems of Race in American Literature 1865–1930, which was held on the Berkeley campus of the University of California under the direction of Eric Sundquist. The dedicated scholars I worked with that season gave me much to think about, and our continuing postal seminars have been invaluable to the evolution of my thinking.

My colleagues in the departments of English and American Studies at San Jose State University may recognize some of their own fingerprints in the margins of this text, and I thank them all for their patience and kindness. I particularly want to acknowledge the influence of Grey Osterud and Roy Christman. The weekly meetings of our American Studies teaching team in the early stages of this book were a refuge from the other demands of university life. Jack Haeger, chair of the San Jose State Department of English, deserves special mention for his dedication to the future of the untenured. Jack has always found ways to make the examined life possible for faculty working under what one outside evaluator has called "an unusually oppressive work load." While seeing this book through press, and beginning the next project, I have enjoyed the support of a fellowship from the UCLA Institute of American Cultures for research and writing at the Center for Afro-American Studies.

Much of this book has been road tested at conferences around the country, and I want to note the support of conference organizers and panel chairs at the Twentieth Century Literature Conference, the

Modern Language Association, the Philological Association of the Pacific Coast, the Midwest Modern Language Association, the Society for the Study of the Multiethnic Literatures of the United States and the Louisiana State University Conference on Intertextuality in the Americas. Excerpts from earlier versions of some chapters appeared in the following journals: the *African American Review,* the *Arkansas Quarterly, Emergences, Pacific Coast Philology,* and the *William Carlos Williams Review.*

I am, as always, deeply appreciative of the work done on my behalf by Karen Orchard and the staff at the University of Georgia Press. Karen's early interest and her words of encouragement when we met at conferences kept me going; her anonymous readers and her attentive staff kept me running.

Eric Sundquist, Richard Flynn, and Jerry Ward have each cast a cold eye across portions of my prose or offered important suggestions; any remaining infelicities are entirely my own responsibility.

Finally, I want to acknowledge the centrality to my mission in this work of my students at San Jose State University. In an era when they *are* the diversity that others want to manage, these fine students manage time and again to remind me of what a commitment to scholarship and social responsibility might really mean.

Writing between the Lines

[T]he presence and predicaments
of black people are neither additions
to nor defections from American life,
but rather *constitutive elements of*
that life.

—Cornell West, *Race Matters*

Breaking In

Race and Intertextuality

As he concludes his introduction to *Nation and Narration,*
Homi Bhaba, alert to the rhetorical shiftiness of his pronouns, asks:
"When did we become 'a people'? When did we stop being one? Or
are we in the process of becoming one?" (7). We might ask in our turn,
"Who are we to ask such questions?" Bhaba puts these questions to us
ensconced in quotation marks, proffering them as questions persistently asked by those, such as black South Africans and Palestinians,
"who have not yet found their nation," representing these questions
of the unrepresented as interrogatives that "remind us, in some form
or measure, of what must be true for the rest of us too." What is

true of "the rest of us," as it is represented to be true of the unrepresented, is that we are ours for the asking; in forming ourselves to ask such questions we become the people of the question. American readers, educated under the state sign of oneness out of multiplicity, the sign given currency on our great seal, shape themselves into a people on state occasions represented by a Latin motto that few of us can parse. The very sign of our unity is spoken over our heads in a language not our own. Yet we have made that sign coin of our realm, and we identify ourselves in the spending of it. We, the people, know what we mean when we say "we," or at any rate we think we know what is meant when, in the political celebrations of our peoplehood, our leaders say "we" in our place. Yet one has only to look at photographs of such events, the dedication of the Lincoln Memorial for one example, to see how difficult it has been for us to become a people. In aerial photographs of the crowd that turned out to honor the Great Emancipator and the savior of our nation's wholeness, one sees a dark line of demarcation drawn through the crowd marking the place where America divided itself against itself, where one America bordered upon becoming another.

America is a postcolonial body rent by racial difference. The many peoples of the African continent, peoples of diverse languages, cultures, and physiognomies, began to become *a* people under the enterprising gaze of slave drivers, who became white people in the act of differentiating themselves from those they would own and sell. In the view of Kwame Anthony Appiah, "[T]he reality is that the very category of the Negro is at root a European product: for the 'whites' invented the Negroes in order to dominate them" (62). Race was constructed in America on just such purely instrumental grounds, as is immediately evident upon inspection of our currently defined legal categories of race and ethnicity. The one thing that unites these categories is the absence of any consistently applied defining principle in their creation. The invention of races did not occur overnight, nor has it yet ended. As Evan Watkins has noted:

> "Race" as a *changing* social construct doesn't just name "whites" or "blacks" or "orientals" in an epistemological vacuum. Race is an organization of social relationships which, among other things, helps define and is defined by the exclusion of specific groups from

economic and intellectual authority, from the possession of capital or of human capital resources. A great many ethnic groups in the United States were typically first designated as "races," and early studies on intelligence testing such as those carried out by C. C. Bigham, H. H. Laughlin, and Lewis Terman in the 1920's were cited as scientific evidence for the intellectual inferiority of the Southern European "races," who were the major target of the immigration quotas imposed by Congress in 1924. (210)

"Black" and "White" do not designate discrete territories of clearly definable, essential racial being in America, or even essential cultural histories and traits. They often serve as terms to obscure the operations of a deeper racist signifying practice, a practice that produces race and difference in a constantly fluctuating mechanism of oppression. But they also have a historical existence as strategic terms of resistance. Race serves simultaneously as the means by which hegemonic discourse organizes its policing functions, erecting boundaries that define and oppress an other, *and* as the ever-shifting strategic locus from which others assault and reterritorialize American identity. Clearly "races" are textbook examples of discursive formations, and in their discursive evolution it has been possible, say, for the "race" of Italians in America to become merely one people, one ethnicity, among many. Equally clear, however, is the law of racial discourse in the United States by which all African Americans constitute an immutable race, never returning in the eyes of the native speakers of American racial discourse to the discrete African ethnicities from which they came, and never becoming as a group simply one ethnicity in anyone's celebrated mosaic. And while few today would hold any putatively white people from different regions of the globe to belong to different "races," most Americans would unite them in a whiteness defined against the black race. The daily workings of these delineations are everywhere in evidence. White people belong to ethnic groups in the 1990s and may choose at will to assert or deny their ethnicity; black people are simply and irrefutably black. Our news reporters tell us of "ethnic strife" in Eastern Europe; they tell us of "tribal conflicts" in Africa. In our media "black on black violence" is a problem within a race; "white on white violence" is a meaningless signifier. Such modes of discourse reveal simultaneously the instability of race as a concept and the persistence of race as an oppressive defining trope in American culture.

That defining begins in the barracoons of Africa and is reified on the Middle Passage; once in the American state, it becomes the process by which Americans hold themselves apart from one another. The English-only movement has its precursor in the slave pens of the American colonies, for, unlike any other immigrant group in American history, the Africans who endured a forced migration to the New World were required at once to abandon their first languages and to speak the English of their oppressors, and thus the same language that divided them each from the natal tongue of African conversation became their point of contact with the other Africans with whom they were now to form a race. In *12 Million Black Voices,* Richard Wright describes this paradoxical, multidirectional, forced language acquisition:

> When we were first brought here from our innumerable African tribes, each of us spoke the language of his tribe. But the Lords of the Land decreed that we must be distributed upon the plantations so that no two of us who spoke a common tongue would be thrown together. So they shackled one slave to another slave of an alien tribe. Our eyes would look wistfully into the face of a fellow-victim of slavery, but we could say no word to him. Though we could hear, we were deaf; though we could speak, we were dumb!
>
> We stole words from the grudging lips of the Lords of the Land, who did not want us to know too many of them or their meaning. And we charged this meager horde of stolen sounds with all the emotions and longings we had; we proceeded to build our language in inflections of voice, through tonal variety, by hurried speech, in honeyed drawls, by rolling our eyes, by flourishing our hands, by assigning to common, simple words new meanings, meanings which enabled us to speak of revolt in the actual presence of the Lords of the Land without their being aware! Our secret language extended our understanding of what slavery meant and gave us the freedom to speak to our brothers in captivity; we polished our new words, caressed them, gave them new shape and color, a new order and tempo, until, though they were the words of the Lords of the Land, they became *our* words, *our* language. (40)

In writing these words Richard Wright has enacted a theory of race and intertextuality in American signifying practices, citing the language as a place of perpetual resistance and transversal. Those whites who claimed to own Africans, and who sought to extend their ideology of race and chattel slavery by embedding their assumptions in the very speech of their fellow Americans, desired power over the bodies of Africans, and hence power over the speech of Africans. In their practical necessity of instructing Africans in an instrumental language, whites began a centuries-long tradition of attempts to control the meanings of black lives. The slave owners and their white factotums attempted to extend their power to limit the motions of Africans in this land to a power to limit the vocabularies, and hence the thoughts, of Africans. While with their own discourse they may have tried to convince themselves that slaves were not human, or at least not human in the same sense as themselves, white speakers of English in America could not stop themselves from speaking with their human chattel, in ways they certainly did not speak with their livestock, and made no attempt to stop themselves. Indeed, one seldom acknowledged aspect of the oppressions of slavery has been that for hundreds of years African Americans have had to endure the unceasing discourse of whites, who would never stop talking to them. To the contrary, one form of the linguistic colonizing of African minds in America was the unremitting effort to transmit the presuppositions of racist ideology into those minds, to convince them that they weren't really minds at all. But if English was the means by which the African's higher consciousness, which was held not to exist, was to be colonized, it also became a first site of African resistance, the birthplace of African-American meaning and culture.

Deleuze and Guattari define as the first characteristic of any minor, or minority, literature the fact "that in it language is affected with a high coefficient of deterritorialization" (*Kafka* 16). Richard Wright, in his reflections upon the history of African-American language acquisition, effectively erases whites as language instructors and portrays the slaves as having taken the territory of English from its white owners in a sort of guerilla countermove. Whites, who attempted to fence in entire areas of discourse in English, were superseded as Lords of Language by a new class of signifying masters. In taking the words out of the mouths of the masters, the Africans remastered the semantic values of English, and became African Americans, using their newly reformulated English to create hitherto unavailable meanings and to confound the masters themselves on the site of their own speaking. Vèvè Clark, following Houston Baker's examinations of the mastery of form and the deformation of mastery, has termed this deterritorializing motion *"the reformation of form,* a reduplicative narrative posture which assumes and revises Du Bois's double consciousness. In the wider fields of contemporary literary criticism, this reformative strategy approximates the deconstruction of mastery" (42). This deconstruction of mastery manifests itself in a metaleptic troping within the common body of American English, and that language has become an oscillating register of resistance, contestation, and renewal as terms are put into play, reformed, and rejected in the continuing interactions of race and language. Houston Baker, meditating upon that moment of linguistic rupture and renewal described by Richard Wright, observes that "Africans uprooted from ancestral soil, stripped of material culture, and victimized by brutal contact with various European nations were compelled not only to maintain their cultural heritage at a *meta* (as opposed to a material) level but also to apprehend the operative metaphysics of various alien cultures. Primary to their survival was the work of *consciousness,* of nonmaterial counterintelligence" (*Workings* 38). The vehicle of that counterintelligence is the same language with which the white masters sought to colonize the disputed territory of African intelligence, the same language made different as it passed back and forth between the races by constant signification. In the estimation of Henry Louis Gates, Jr., "Repetition, with a signal difference, is fundamental to the nature of Signifying(g) [*sic*]" (*Signifying* 51).

Inevitably this deterritorializing signification effects a sort of linguistic blowback in the mouths of the masters as they overhear, repeat, and misconstrue the signified figures of the Africans they have brought into their midst. As in the present repetition by many white critics of Gates's repetition of the critical gesture of African-American signifying, there is a constant redoubling of linguistic direction in the American conversation. American English, like American music, beats with a black heart. Even as Anglophile a poet as T. S. Eliot will attempt to insert ragtime among his shoring fragments, evidence supporting Homi Bhaba's belief that "America leads to Africa; . . .

the peoples of the periphery return to rewrite the history and fiction of the metropolis" (*Nation* 6). But, in the same way that classic jazz recordings remastered for stereo often feel denatured and stiffened, when African-American signifying tropes are adopted, adapted, and remastered in white speech, they undergo a sea change. The rag-time of T. S. Eliot is assuredly not that of Scott Joplin, and the jazz poems of Hart Crane are not the jazz poetics of Louis Armstrong. But neither are they uninflected English, which is one reason Eliot re-mained a Missourian even in his most monarchist Anglophile phase. Where would one draw a line between the return to white speech and white mythology of blackened signifiers, Africanized Englishes and their varied musics, and the resignifying minstrelsy in which whites dress up their language in blackface to represent their own represen-tations of blackness to themselves? Just how different are the projects of T. S. Eliot and Al Jolson? Does Gertrude Stein's *Melanctha,* as Charles Bernstein suggests, to some extent produce a set of "counter-racist currents that flow through the linguistic explorations of *Three Lives*" (50), or does Stein's reinscription of white imaginings of black speech, her orthographic display of racial difference, simply fall back upon itself, "othering" itself while at the same time further immuring black speaking subjectivities in the tar baby of white discourse?

Racial signifiers, like all other signifiers, point away from them-selves and slide over one another in their rush to an elsewhere. There is no localizable, essential point of origin in either blackness or white-ness for any single racial signification for the reason that there is no locatable, essential race in America. The races, and their signifiers, exist only in relation to all other points in our systems of racial sig-nifying. Just as the terms *black* and *white* serve, not, as observation will always confirm, to denote clearly demarcated differences in skin pigmentation, but to organize the meanings of human lives beneath constructed racial rubrics, so do language practices recognizable as racially motivated among native speakers serve to carve up territo-ries of racial connotation rather than to reflect preexistent cultural facts. Further, each attempt to draw borders within the language of race and to establish ownership of a territory encounters and is coun-tered by the already-in-place deterritorializing language of the other. America's mulatto past, though nearly invisible in the political dis-course of the late twentieth century, is continually disseminated within its language. Each speaking subject speaks a language of racial difference and amalgamation. Each child who comes to an American language is filled with a linguistic miscegenation and will never succeed in separating the imbricated genealogies of the English in his or her mind. For the American conversation race has always been, as Hortense Spillers describes it, "the storm center of the US culture text—'race' as that awful moment of incestuous possibility *and* praxis, yearning *and* denial, refusal *and* accomplishment, wild desire *and* repression, that cannot be uttered and that cannot *but* be uttered" (14). As white writers set out to classify races and their attendant attributes and abilities, they were not, we must remember, describing even an observed actuality but were, in fact, creating a reality by means of their inscriptions, bringing racial difference into being. Yet, even as this writing was under way, African writers in America, newly become Negroes, were altering the emergent system of racial differentiation by seizing upon its markers and radically redeploying them. Thus a system of racial signifying came into being in America whose multitudinous marks were unstable and polysemous because each writing of them, each speaking of the code, was a writing and a speaking in motion against itself, pointing simultaneously to differing mythic originary sites, which unseated the code itself. *None* of the letters was delivered as addressed.

Among the first markers of American writing's difference within itself is the black line drawn by pens in white hands around the constituted field of the literary in an attempt to bring into being an inside and an outside, to create an aesthetic space determined by race. The residue of that first marking is evident in the continued reassertion of racially determined limits to the category of literature and to literary value. As recently as 1973, Cleanth Brooks, R. W. B. Lewis, and Robert Penn Warren, in the editing of their *American Literature: The Makers and the Making,* consigned the writings of Frederick Douglass to a section labeled "Literature of the Nonliterary World," a most peculiar oxymoron indeed, though one that eloquently replicates the contradictions America refused to face through its history as it continued to converse with those it had begun by defining as incapable of holding up their end of the conversation. In *American Literature: The Makers and the Making,* John Woolman's *Some Considerations on the Keeping of Negroes* appears, along with Franklin's autobiography, in a chapter titled "An Emergent National Literature." Frederick Douglass, the only African-American writer in volume 1 of the anthology, is represented by a selection from his second autobiography, *My Bondage and My Freedom*, which is labeled by Brooks, Lewis, and Warren as "Political Writing." It isn't until volume 2 that these editors recognize a category of "Black Literature" in the American corpus. Similarly, and more recently, when Charles Johnson's novel *Middle Passage* received the 1990 National Book Award in fiction, conservative reviewer Carol Iannone, who had not bestirred herself the previous year when an unknown white author won the prize, complained that the National Book Award was following some sort of ethnic agenda that would lead to a "democratic dictatorship of mediocrity." Echoing Thomas Jefferson's dismissal of Phillis Wheatley, Iannone intoned that Johnson's *Middle Passage* was hard to take "seriously as literature" (qtd. in Hale 24). Henry Louis Gates, Jr., who has considered at length the literary responses of African Americans to their presumed inhuman lack of a literature, argues that "unlike almost every other literary tradition, the Afro-American literary tradition was generated as a response to eighteenth- and nineteenth-century allegations that persons of African descent did not, and could not, create literature" (*Figures* 25). Thomas Jefferson's *Notes on the State of Virginia* strikes the characteristic note in this regard with its assertion that "the compositions published under [Phillis Wheatley's] name are below the dignity of criticism" (135). But Wheatley was already writing within the boundaries that Jefferson and others sought to score around the American text. In a move that would prove prophetic, Phillis Wheatley wrote that Africa was already inside the corpus Jefferson tried to whiten, that in fact Africans had a hand in the writing of his canonical texts before he came to them. Outlining one strategy black writers have adopted, Gates holds that "reacting to the questionable allegations made against their capacity to be original, black writers have often assumed a position of extreme negation, in which they claim for themselves no black literary antecedents whatsoever, or else claim for themselves an anonymity of origins as Topsy did when she said she 'jes' grew" (*Figures* 114). But, as we find in Wheatley's poems, another response to whites' assertions of literary primacy is to take the territory from beneath their feet. In her poem "To Maecenas" Wheatley writes:

> The happier *Terence* all the choir inspired,
> His soul replenished, and his bosom fir'd;
> But say, ye *Muses*, why this partial grace,
> To one alone of *Afric's* sable race;
> From age to age transmitting thus his name
> With the first glory in the rolls of fame?
>
> (11)

The very canon to which Jefferson would bar African access is already populated by Africans, who attain first glory. It is to that already Africanized honor roll that Wheatley makes her appeal for approval. It is those Jefferson himself might honor who will, despite his and others' protestations, encourage the literary acts of Phillis Wheatley. "I'll snatch a laurel from thine honour'd head," she tells Maecenas, the literary patron of antiquity, "While you indulgent smile upon the deed" (12). The less indulgent eye of Jefferson, establishing a literary practice that would persist into the present, cannot read the Africanity of his canon. If Africans cannot be literary, then literature cannot be African. Because it would lower the dignity of criticism to read Wheatley's compositions as literature, Jeffersonian criticism refuses to read them. But black writing goes on, takes place, disseminates itself throughout the American textual body, and makes it impossible for the American body politic to speak unproblematically the purely white mythology of its own genesis, despite its continued refusals to read. The Jeffersonian moment of refusing to read black texts as texts, refusing to admit blacks access to the category of the literary, is mirrored in a concomitant refusal to read the blackness of the American text, an unwillingness to undertake the fuller reading of American writing that would take into account and perhaps account for the seemingly undeniable black presence in white writing. Speaking of this dual refusal among white American readers in *Playing in the Dark,* Toni Morrison comments that "what is surprising is that their refusal to read black texts—a refusal that makes no disturbance in their intellectual life—repeats itself when they reread the traditional, established works of literature worthy of their attention" (13).

In the midst of the multiplying overdeterminations of American texts must be figured the oscillations of racial difference and its signifying shiftiness. Within each ironic reading of American signifiers is secreted the overironized displacement of race and its multitudinous tropes, race as an intertext of American reading and American rejections of reading. The history of our writings is a nomadic affair of constant "othering," in which the white writers describe the black as radically other, and the black writers describe themselves as radically other than what the "others" have defined as their ontological reality. We are, then, simultaneously audience and actors in a perpetual, racially marked, radical redoubling of rhetorics and writings. The African-American speaker or writer produces an English that, in the estimation of Nathaniel Mackey, "isn't so much broken as broken into" ("Other" 57), deterritorializing it, refiguring it as the site of struggle against the colonizing effects of the very language broken into. At the same time, black writers open the canons of that language and find black writing already inscribed there among its founding tropes. Those who would speak white power must speak it in an already African accent, and black writers breaking into print in America find themselves already there behind the white textual veils of signifying blindness, those veils persistently reerected by white discourse in its redoubled efforts not to read the Africanity of its own texts, not to hear the blackness of its own tongue.

Did any of those white authors of our past understand that in writing themselves into history *as* white writers they were founding their essential subjectivity upon, depended for their very being upon, the existence of black people, that the fundament of this newly essential being was predicated upon the black bodies of African slaves? Was this always an unsounded dependency effect of the dependency upon slavery? What depends from these facts? How do we, now, as a people, take up the refused readings and visit this scene of division and deprivation, this site wherein we have spoken that which does not become us? How do we now reread ourselves within that space where, in the view of Gilles Deleuze, "the double is never a project of the interior; on the contrary, it is an interiorization of the outside. It is not a doubling of the One, but a redoubling of the Other. It is not a reproduction of the Same, but a repetition of the Different. It is not the emanation of an 'I,' but something that places in immanence an always Other or a Non-Self" (*Foucault* 97–98).

If Americans have proved themselves consistently unwilling to engage this doubled reading, it may be because they have, without remarking it, always understood the cost to themselves of undoing racism. American writing may have long harbored within itself a last refusal, the refusal to recognize, as Étienne Balibar has recognized, that "the destruction of the racist complex presupposes . . . the transformation of the racists themselves and, consequently, the internal decomposition of the community created by racism" (Balibar and Wallerstein 18). In the political unconscious of American writing there may rest a displaced fear, a fear that an American community that does not rest upon the racist construction of a white self may no longer be America.

How can ethnicity be produced? And how can it be produced in such a way that it does not appear as fiction, but as the most natural of origins? History shows us that there are two great competing routes to this: language and race. (Balibar in Balibar and Wallerstein, *Race* 96)

"White" and "black" were terms invented to absorb anything said about them, to contain all possibilities. (Simone, *About Face* 213)

In America there has been little competition between the route of language and the route of race in producing the ethnic fiction that ideologies of race are not ideologies at all but simply objective descriptions of material facts. Our language is the body that carries the virus of racism. As Judith Stein has defined it, "The word race has been the principal ideological construct which Americans, black and white, have used to confront the numerous questions stemming from the existence of slavery. But the persistence of the term is not equivalent to biological or historical continuity" (103–4). Ideologies of race are transmitted in a language that seeks, by speaking the same words to us over and over again, to prevent our reaching other answers to those questions stemming from the history of slavery. The naturalizing discourse of racism, having divided us against ourselves, tells us that we really were always already so divided, that we are innocent of divisiveness, that calling attention to our history of division is in itself divisive, that "prejudice" isn't racism, and that "prejudice" is the given of human interactions. Individuals who choose to think of themselves as white give up the need to think further about an array of other troublesome questions. So long as they are "not black," they feel little need, in the latter part of the twentieth century, to produce a justifying positive assessment of just what being "white" might entail culturally. The brute fact of their assumption of whiteness assigns them a place within an ideology they need seldom articulate, one that performs at the same time the task of dominating African Americans and the task of denying that ideological domination still takes place. In the words of Timothy Maliqalim Simone, "[O]nce a system of mechanisms has been constituted capable of objectively ensuring the reproduction of the established order by its own motion, the dominant class has only to let the system they dominate take its own course in order to exercise domination" (71).

In America, the language of race allows white people to evade responsibility for the assumptions by which they live. It allows them to cling to an American innocence of primal oppressions. Because of the language of race, white people can believe that so long as they aren't individually and directly engaged in the physical suppression of black people, they are free of the signifying effects of racism. With the language of race, white people tell each other that the terms of their discourse are descriptions of essential cultural traits, that cultural traits are freely assumed, but that they essentially coincide with skin color. Thus, if black people fail as a class to flourish within the freedoms American society provides to them, it must be because individual blacks fail to make appropriate choices in managing their life resources. The problem with this logic is visible in the way that I have here formulated it, in that blacks are *already* considered as a class in the premise of the argument. If what popular discourse addressed truly confined itself to a consideration of individual choices and determinations, there would be no need to speak of black people as a class at all, or of white people for that matter.

Toni Morrison, adopting and adapting the methodologies of discourse analysis pioneered by Michel Foucault and put to such good use in Edward Said's studies of Orientalism and Christopher Miller's works on Africanist discourse, describes an American Africanist discourse (*Playing* 6) that constructs American subjectivities and assigns them on the basis of skin color. American Africanism posits that individuals make their choices in life in their capacity *as* black people and that black culture, at least as it is currently construed in public discussion, fosters the making of poor choices within a free market of ideas, opportunities, and behaviors. Thus, to be black is to be, by popular attribution, a member of a culture predisposed to the making of inappropriate selections for a successful American life. To be white is to be seen as not to be black, and thus to be culturally inclined toward the making of proper moral and economic choices. Such a formulation, by displacing attention from the consequences of history to a presumed repertoire of freely assumed cultural traits, permits white people to think of themselves as untainted by racism at the same moment in which they think of black people as a class that is morally and socially inferior. "Talk of race," according to Kwame Anthony Appiah, "works as an attempt at metonym for culture, and it does so only at the price of biologizing what *is* culture, ideology" (45). The irrationality of conceptions linking biological race, however that is described, to the social constructions of culture is immediately evident. Europeans knew little of depth regarding the cultures of Africa before deciding what modes of being were defined by black skin, and the later acquisition of increased knowledge of African cultures has done precious little to alter racialist assumptions. As Appiah so plainly puts the matter, "If, without evidence about his or her impulses, we can say who is a Negro, then it cannot be part of what it is to be a Negro that he or she has them; rather it must be an a posteriori claim that people of a common race, defined by descent and biology, have impulses, for whatever reason, in common" (33). Still, racism has not receded from its role in history simply because white and black people have learned more about one another. Nor have racists suddenly grasped the fallacy of their root premises and gone about the business of dismantling the social effects of racist thought.

This has not happened precisely because the discourse of American Africanism exists so that white people may retain both power and innocence. The mistake in the thought of many abolitionists of the past, and of some liberal humanists of the present, has been to believe that racism was a special case of prejudice that would eventually yield to empirical experience; that if white people really got to know black people, racism would vanish. Africanist discourse exists so that white people will not have to get to know black people. Africanist discourse tells white Americans that they already know black people and black culture. It exists so that white people may be white.

"What is in play here," in Étienne Balibar's analysis, "—whether in academic theories, institutional or popular racism—is the categorization of humanity into artificially isolated types, [and thus] there must be a violently conflictual split at the level of social relations themselves. We are not therefore dealing with a mere 'prejudice'" (Balibar and Wallerstein 9). Racial discourse, as an apparatus for the production and replication of all-encompassing explanations justifying this violent conflictual split, cannot make itself vulnerable to the more empirical and rational arguments of traditional humanism. Traditional Western humanism generated the identification between the idea of the human and the idea of cultural whiteness. The post-Enlightenment reason of humanism articulated the explanations that identify culture with skin color. This is not to say that all the lessons of the Enlightenment are to be rejected, but to observe that they have not been sufficient in themselves to destroy the racism that Western reason elaborated. Racism in the West has produced what Appiah terms a "cognitive incapacity," which names itself as objective truth. Appiah reasons that "most real-live contemporary racists exhibit a systematically distorted rationality that we often recognize in ideology. And it is a distortion that is especially striking in the cognitive domain: extrinsic racists, however intelligent or otherwise well informed, often fail to treat evidence against the theoretical propositions of extrinsic racism dispassionately" (15). Equally damning is the tendency of ideological racism to brand efforts to examine its cognitive incapacities, efforts to read the operations of Africanist discourse in the American historical text, as overtly political and swayed by passion, in contrast with its own assumed posture of dispassionate, nonideological objectivity.

Ideological racism acts, through the constant circulation of its propositions, to render American language amnesiac. In identifying race with culture, in describing the cultural repertoire as both freely chosen and heritable, Africanist discourse encourages Americans to forget that "the 'culture' of an ethnic group is precisely the set of rules to which parents belonging to that ethnic group are pressured to socialize their children" (Wallerstein in Balibar and Wallerstein 83). These discourses of race further encourage Americans to forget the historical particulars that bring such pressures into being. In the end, the words *black* and *white* absorb everything. They are asked to do the work of social organization and explanation. When our understanding of culture is determined by skin color, it becomes clear that our language of cultural explication has been reduced to the most severely minimal signifier. Race is a paradigmatic instance of reification. Race can offer no satisfactory answers to our nation's most vexing of self-inflicted problems because it is that problem. Yet the endlessly circulating tokens of racial signifying are as palpable to us as money, and just as real. In his study of race in postmodern America, Timothy Maliqalim Simone argues:

> It is in race that the postmodern world today finds its most exemplary vanishing point. Race appears as if it is something fixed and permanent, immune to being altered by the ideas or expressions used to address or comprehend it. Yet, what does it really mean? To what extent does it have anything to say about specifiable differences between peoples, cultures and histories? The point here is that when we talk about race we are never sure what we are referring to: a dilemma which posits many contradictory futures and opportunities. (11)

In effect, this means that race has nothing to say to us in postmodern America and that it won't stop saying it.

If this is true, then reading race in American texts must always appear as simultaneously excessive and unfinished, as a nomadic enterprise unwelcome in some disciplinary homes, as an oppositional practice continually seeking its own dissolution. The fact that race is a consummately empty signifier, that it is constituted out of a people's desire for power over others, out of their desire to name themselves as not-other, that it is a reification with no material ground, does not mean that it no longer has material consequences. The fact that race is a reification, that it names something that really doesn't exist, does not mean that we can speak as if "race" didn't exist. In our time, one of the ways that racist discourse perpetuates itself while refusing to accept its name is by asserting that it is black people who, by constantly reminding whites of race, bring about racial division; it is people society identifies as culturally black who can be counted on to make a problem of themselves by calling attention back to the work race has done, thus disrupting the placid conformity of racism's white noise. Paradoxically, we can hope to reach an end to speaking of race only once we have read the languages of race in all of our texts, and only after we have read our complicity in the racial determinations of power. We will have to go on reading as white people and as black people until we are able to produce readings that hasten a day when white people will be willing to destroy the community they bring into being by conceiving of themselves as people who are not black. This may be the most important task before us as Americans. In the words of Kwame Anthony Appiah, words that eerily and unerringly prefigured the words spoken by Rodney King to a world watching over television as Los Angeles burned around him: "[S]ince it is too late for us to escape each other, we might instead seek to turn to our advantage the mutual interdependencies history has thrust upon us" (72).

Such a task requires the reading of difference and race, but the task is only delayed and exacerbated by readings that ground themselves in a pluralist politics of identity and essentialism. White readers must now learn what African-American texts have known for so long, that doubling of consciousness described by W. E. B. Du Bois that finds a historical echo in Jacques Derrida's advice to a Europe now trying to come to terms with itself anew: *"What is proper to a culture is not to be identical to itself"* (*Heading* 9). Race is excessive and unruly. To re-read the racial significations of America's literary texts is to engage in a double reading, to differ with texts and to differ from ourselves. Toni Morrison proposes that "the contemplation of . . . black presence is central to an understanding of our national literature and should not be permitted to hover at the margins of the literary imagination" (*Playing* 5). Her statement does not mean simply that the works of black authors should be read in ways that they have not been read in the past, though we most assuredly should undertake such readings; she also calls for an exacting rereading of those texts at the supposed center of American experience. Morrison's call is for a reading that will account for the ways that black presence ignites "critical moments of discovery or change or emphasis in literature not written by [blacks]" (*Playing* viii).

It has often been remarked that the politics of readings that seek an essentialized identity in the racial and ethnic margins may quickly become a way by which racialist domination can be reasserted. Guattari and Negri note in another context how "all too often these experiences have been described in terms of marginality. Marginality was quickly drawn toward the center . . ." (41). The challenge to more traditional reading practices represented by efforts to read in the margins of the American imagination of itself has often been recuperated by pluralist readings that have the effect of recoloniz- ing those very margins. In presenting a pluralist politics of ethnic identity as a social ideal, dominant modes of reading reassert racial- ist modes of discourse at the same time that they contain the more excessive and nomadic strategies of "minority" writers and thinkers, all in the guise of celebrating racial and ethnic difference. When the academy embraces a pluralism of ethnicity and identity, it makes of it a strategy much like liberal industry's modes of "managing diversity," and within this pluralist form of diversity, some remain more equal than others. Pluralism posits, once again, that writers express stable and preexisting identities that they have by virtue of belonging to a particular race or ethnicity. As Appiah has pointed out, though, if a reader already can identify the race of an author prior to discovering the author's identity in the text, then that author's possession of the traits of identity assigned to that race by the reader cannot truly be said to be racially determined.

In the process of describing a potentially more useful mode of cultural critique, Abdul JanMohamed and David Lloyd remark that "one of the primary objects of such a cultural criticism will accord- ingly be the mendacious cultural 'pluralism' which is the great white hope of conservatives and liberals alike. The semblance of plural- ism disguises the perpetuation of exclusion . . ." (9). So normative have the assumptions of pluralism become in American discussions of race and ethnicity (my own university, San Jose State, requires that all students meet a cultural pluralism requirement as part of their general education package) that the mendacious history of plural- ism is largely forgotten. Yet cultural pluralism, from its beginnings in the early part of the twentieth century in the works of such theo- rists as Horace Kallen, has always advanced an essentialist argument. In articles such as "Democracy versus the Melting Pot: A Study of American Nationality," which appeared in the *Nation*, Kallen pro- duced a liberal argument that continued to produce racialist effects even as it opposed itself to racism, and Kallen's commitment to essen- tialist positions remained a hallmark of his pluralism throughout his career. Philip Gleason, in "American Identity and Americanization," describes Kallen's indebtedness to earlier racialists:

Because cultural pluralism came to be understood as liberal, anti-Anglo-Saxon and anti-racialist, it comes as some surprise to discover that Kallen shared the kind of romantic racialism represented by Anglo-Saxonism before it was absorbed into biological racialism. Kallen's racialism was romantic in that he valued diversity as such and did not attempt to rank any human groups as superior or inferior according to any absolute scale of racial merit. But he also resembles the romantics in attributing the distinctive characteristics of peoples to inborn racial qualities whose origin and nature were obscure. (99–100)

It is this essentialist reasoning that forms a constant in Kallen's development of the ideal of cultural pluralism. Four decades after first formulating his version of a pluralist approach to ethnicity, Kallen called for the development of a new study of "cultural totalities" that he termed "culturology." Here, Kallen describes the larger sense of cultural totality in a seemingly innocuous vocabulary: "The group culture will seem to have a nature independent of them all; to be wholly different from its parts, with ways and works evincing its own different laws of persistence, struggle and growth, and capable of determination without reference to the dynamic specificity of its parts" (45). This culturology, however, immediately falls into the logical fallacy that Appiah has noted so often in racialist thought. Kallen always presupposes the unifying structures of the cultural totality he analyzes, thus smuggling an essentialist premise into an argument that attempts to theorize the changing nature of cultures. Edward Said has recently offered a cogent formulation of this fallacy: "If you know in advance that the African or Iranian or Chinese or Jewish or German experience is fundamentally integral, coherent, separate . . . , you first of all posit as essential something which, I believe, is both historically created and the result of interpretation—namely the existence of Africanness, Jewishness, or Germanness, or for that matter Orientalism and Occidentalism" (*Culture* 31–32). This is precisely why critics such as E. San Juan, Jr., wish to "challenge pluralism as the discourse and practice of atomistic liberalism" (115). The normative pluralism that has become the pedagogical standard in American academies is mendacious to the extent that it reinscribes hierarchy even as it attempts to ensure equality and understanding of diversity.

An emphasis upon a cultural politics of identity and identification produces an ideology in which, as Dana Nelson outlines the phenomenon, "the 'prejudice of equality'—identifying the racial Other with one's own 'ego-ideal'—while in many ways more *humane*, is finally no more effective in creating real understanding *between* the Subject and Other than the 'prejudice of superiority'" (88). Attempting to foster (and manage) diversity, a humanist cultural pluralism forgets again and again that "race is . . . the organizing principle of social relations; it is not a fixed essence" (San Juan, Jr. 52), and, as E. San Juan, Jr., so astutely recognizes, "what results is a normative pluralism that effectively eliminates those cultural and political differences which it claims to be respecting in the first place" (140). In the end, "Cultural Pluralism and the American Idea" may not prove to be "that orchestration of the cultures of mankind which alone can be worked and fought for with least injustice, and with least suppression or frustration of any culture" that Horace Kallen and other champions of his culturology had hoped for (Kallen 100), for it remains clear who is in charge of the orchestration and whose diversity is being managed. Cultural pluralism, rather than deconstruct the oppressive histories of American races, provides us with a second reconstruction of those histories, a reconstruction that, not for the first time in American history, presents itself as a renewed humanism.

Pluralism repeats the hegemonic assumption that white people already know who black people are, and it rewards black writers who speak for that expected identity and in the requisite voice, while escorting to a true margin of oblivion those black writers who self-consciously bring racial difference into being by writing. African-American writers who assist a self-constituting white readership in "discovering" again the blackness it already knows may be more likely to be anthologized, to the extent that their writing also assists that readership in maintaining itself as a white community. Those writers likely to be truly and permanently marginalized are those whose writing foregrounds the dynamic of intertextual movements of difference that disrupts existing ideals of power, agency, and subjectivity. In speaking of the fashion in which the language of empire continues to structure the production and reception of African literature, both outside and inside Africa, Kwame Anthony Appiah offers a firm rejection of liberal pluralisms: "[T]alk about the production of marginality by the culture of the center is wholly inadequate by itself. For it ignores the reciprocal nature of power relations; it neglects the multiform varieties of individual and collective agency available to the African subject, and it diminishes both the achievements and the possibilities of African writing" (72).

We are not born as white or black subjects. We must be taught to act as white or black agents. Pluralism, by its reinscription of racialist ideologies of the continuity of cultural inheritance, greets us with an apparatus of expectations. Pluralism in our time, like slavery in the nineteenth century, is one of those pressures that guides us to adopt the cultures we are supposed to inherit. Pluralism wears the benign aspect of tolerance for difference while measuring that difference from a still central norm. It also presents a malign aspect as it seeks to hold in check the free play of difference by telling us that we are born to certain modes of subjectivity. Even though the ideologies of race exercise hegemonic power within American conversation, they have not produced a monolithic response among the dominated. If it were true that the hegemony of race completely constrained what it is possible for Americans to think, then American writing really would be as boring as the model put forward in most contemporary multicultural college anthologies, which all too often, in their public-spirited celebration of cultural identities, present readers with writings that are nearly identical in their constant rediscovery of the same "voice" and subjectivity, a literary version of "managing diversity." Such anthologies engage in a process of what William Spanos has called accommodation, a process of literary recolonization of imaginative space. "This process is epitomized by the example of the most recent Norton anthologies," in Spanos's view, "which have broadened the scope of selections for the purpose of 'enriching' rather than interrogating the tradition" (*End* 218). A more radical writing and reading attempts to rethink the palimpsestic and unstable history of American writing positions. Such a more radical approach is called for by Lisa Lowe in her essay "Rereadings in Orientalism":

The view that a dominant discourse produces and manages Others, universally appropriating and containing all dissenting positions within it, underestimates the tensions and contradictions within a discourse, the continual play of resistance, dissent, and accom-

modation by different positions. By beginning to account for resistance, yet continuing to recognize the functioning category of
"otherness" in discourse, I believe we must consider instead the
heterogeneity of acts of representation. . . . Discourses are what
I call "heterotopical"; discourses are heterogeneously and irregu-
larly composed of statements and restatements, contestations and
accommodations, generated by a plurality of writing positions at
any given moment. (142–43)

A "heterotopical" reading of American literature, a reading that
would begin to chart the critical moments of discovery attendant upon
black presence in American writing, must be a reading that follows
the radical mobility of subjectivities and agencies in American cultures. It must be a reading willing to take writing wherever it can go,
rather than a reading that always and only finds itself already written
into the text as a single and self-possessing subjectivity.

Concepts of intertextuality offer most powerful models for such rereadings of American race and American texts. If past readings have
appealed to positivist racial presence, to an extrasystemic point of
reference in a stable racial subjectivity, whether of author or reader,
an intertextual reading would discover racial meaning in the play
of difference and would read the production of racial difference as
constitutive of, rather than reflecting, social identities. Intertextual
readings would pursue the diffusion of racial significations across
the textual mapping of American consciousness. Such a reading requires that we find meaning in texts in their relations with other texts.
Rather than segregating our readings of African-American literary
creations, we must, as the very name African-American literature
implies, read black texts in their fulsome implication in all English
writing. This is never a matter of once more subsuming the particularities of experiences written as black beneath an occupying force of
white determinations. It is a matter of recognizing the permeability of
the walls racism has erected in language, of reading the significations
in the explosive passages back and forth between the meaning system
brought into being as white writing and the systematic disruptions of
black writing.

In its most basic sense, intertextuality describes, not just the direct
textual sources exercising an influence upon a subsequent text, but

the transposition of sign systems. This understanding of intertextuality, which will be the point of departure for much of the writing in this book, results always in the alteration of writing subjectivity because, in Julia Kristeva's formulation, "it specifies that the passage from one signifying system to another demands a new articulation of the thetic—of enunciative and denotative positionality" (60). The historical segregation of American signifying practices has left us with disjunctive systems of racial meaning, but disjunction is also a characteristic formal principle of New World writing: from Equiano's narrative to Whitman, from Dickinson to Douglass, from Jean Toomer to Maxine Hong Kingston, from Amiri Baraka to John Ashbery, from Nathaniel Mackey to Susan Howe. While black and white writers can and often do mean differently when using the "same" words and forms, it is also the case that our languages could never be wholly pulled apart and that the radical passage of significations back and forth within language has characterized the most inventive American writings. The works of Melville, Faulkner, and Toni Morrison offer ample examples. To read this passage work demands a willingness to reterritorialize oneself, to resite ourselves within a transfigured language. As Kristeva describes such transpositions:

> This process comes about through a combination of displacement and condensation, but this does not account for its total operation. It also involves an altering of the thetic *position*—the destruction of the old position and the formation of a new one. The new signifying system may be produced with the same signifying material; in language, for example, the passage may be made from narrative to text. Or it may be borrowed from different signifying materials. . . . If one grants that every signifying practice is a field of transpositions of various signifying systems (an inter-textuality), one then understands that its "place" of enunciation and its denoted "object" are never single, complete, and identical to themselves, but always plural, shattered, capable of being tabulated. (59–60)

White resistance to such modes of reading the racial texts of American imagining represents a fear of just such a shattering of enunciative position. The thetic position many white readers have refused to let go of is that they are white. Their language may be transforming them despite their continued resistance.

From the moment Africans were forced to adopt English as their primary tongue in America, the sort of intertextuality described by Kristeva in her *Revolution in Poetic Language* was inevitable. It was impossible for numbers of African peoples to begin speaking and writing as black people in America without radically altering their subjectivity. What slave owners were reluctant to admit was that their newly prized whiteness was just as alterable. A historicized reading today must take account of the innumerable ways in which America differs from itself. Critics such as Stephen Henderson, Hazel Carby, Houston Baker, Hortense Spillers, and Henry Louis Gates, Jr., have begun the work of theorizing and tabulating the polysemous signifying forms elaborated by black Americans. Such work must be carried forward along with equally insistent readings of the blackness of white writing. We read Melville within the text of Ralph Ellison's *Invisible Man,* but we must also read Melville differently because of Ellison's text. We must read the transcendence of Ralph Waldo Emerson alongside our reading of the blackness of Huck Finn. We must attempt to understand what the Middle Passage means in black consciousness, and how it means differently in the texts of Harriet Beecher Stowe, and how her texts figure differently when read by black writers. We must read the texts that black writers inscribed between the lines of America's master texts, and we must read the echoes of those palimpsestic black texts in the writings of white readers.

As should be apparent in Kristeva's formulation, intertextuality also offers a radically material model for human consciousness. In rejecting the givenness of inherited white or black identities we are accepting a constructivist view of the self. An unspoken premise of the essays offered in this volume is that intertextuality describes the palimpsestic and self-differing construction of the writing subject. We are not wholly given to ourselves at birth, but neither are we the wholly owned psychic subsidiaries of the hegemonic system of racial identification. Our construal of ourselves, even as contemporary racial subjects, is an identity formation in transit. Nancy Grey Osterud, in *Bonds of Community,* describes a dynamic view of the relationships between self and significance:

People's sense of self and interpretation of the world are based on their social experience, and social meaning resides in the ways various perspectives are integrated or counterposed in the culture. People are active participants in rather than passive objects of this process. Too often, social scientists treat subjectivity separately from causality, as if people's lives were determined by external forces beyond their comprehension or control and the meanings they make of their experience have nothing to do with the factors that shape their situation. While this approach may reflect the alienation and sense of powerlessness that pervades modern social life, it replicates rather than penetrates the mystification and reification of social relations. Just as there is a dialectical relationship between social experience and social structure, so there is a dialectical relationship between meaning and causation. (10)

In reifying race, American Africanist discourse naturalizes and mystifies social relationships in the guise of objective description of inherent and stable human nature. An intertextual view of human consciousness sees the self as continually resiting itself and as reconstituting consciousness elsewhere as it accrues experience and transposes meanings across its layerings of inscription. In such a materialist view of the self, the mystic writing pad is never erased, but it is always overwritten. Because each subject is differently sited in human culture, each individual really is unique, just as we'd always dreamed. But the self moving through space and time is also always in the process of differing from itself, of assuming new thetic positions. The totalizing impulse of American Africanist discourse is to freeze difference in place and to impose a sycophantic white coherence upon reality. Writing, however, even the writing of racists, undoes that imposed coherence. The banal observation that all language is social reveals to us that all writing presents the text of an other to another. Even that writing that seeks to immure black experience within a silence beneath the imposed significations of white discourse cannot attain complete closure. It must be read, and thus it must open itself to rewriting by the other in whose place it would speak. Writing opens itself to what Homi Bhaba, rereading Lévi-Strauss, calls "the *uncanny* structure of cultural difference" (*Nation* 313), that structure that, rather than revealing the stability of our innermost self, allows us "to coincide with forms of activity which are both *at once ours and other*."

Our language is at once ours and other. This excessiveness of language shows to us the excessiveness of race. Africans were forced to come to America as human supplements. Africans *were* that which white people, who held themselves to be wholly self-present and self-sufficient, required to undertake their project as white people in America. African Americans rapidly became a writing supplement, producing texts that were at first denied as writing and that were then accepted, but only as a quasi-literary extra, an appendix to the main business of American culture. American culture, still, is predicated upon the existence of that black presence, that African excess, and if this supplementary writing were removed, the thetic position of America itself would be fundamentally altered in ways that whites themselves would probably now find unacceptable. Hence black writing always exists as a sign the masters refuse to read because it is always a sign that they have not mastered their subject. In his essay "DissemiNation," Homi Bhaba explains why black writing is simultaneously too much for white readers, always extra, and too much with white reading for its disruptive powers to be ignored: "The minority does not simply confront the pedagogical or powerful master-discourse with a contradictory or negating referent. It does not turn contradictions into a dialectical process. It interrogates its object by initially withholding its objective. Insinuating itself into the terms of reference of the dominant discourse, the supplementary antagonizes the implicit power to generalize, to produce the sociological solidity" (*Nation* 306). Racial discourse is a generalizing engine that brings into being the agents of its own destruction. Racism will not survive the cultural difference it describes. We have always been a house divided, because we have always been the site of a redoubled national text. Black writing, even black separatist writing, is a pure product of America because, as Amiri Baraka once reminded his readers, paraphrasing William Carlos Williams, the African American is "a pure product of America" (*Home* 111). If America is to survive itself, it must learn to differ in, from, and with itself. Black Americans accused of being divisive by being black might well ask their accusers Homi Bhaba's initial question, "When did we become 'a people'?" White Americans may not be prepared to answer that question. The space between question and answer is the kind of intertextual interstice from which a productive reading of race and difference might emerge. America is a postcolonial space that has called into being its own metropolitan center and set its own boundaries. The cultural boundaries of America are another matter. Intertextual readings will follow the continual recession and reimposition of those boundaries through our literature and will find, as Bhaba has found, that we are always rewriting a "boundary of cultural difference that never quite adds up, always less than one nation and double" (*Nation* 318).

The chapters that follow are not meant as an exhaustive tabulation of the intertextual possibilities of reading race in American culture. They are essays beyond a boundary, into a deterritorialized America in which the races make themselves up, and unmake themselves, as they go along. These chapters are tentative chartings of a refigured America that has always been here. They are neither first nor last steps; they are the lost steps of an inter-American dance that we have all been doing all along.

> Style, my man,
> undoes the grandest among us.
> (Jay Wright, *Boleros* 87)

"Omen? omen?—the dictionary! If the gods think to speak outright to man, they will honorably speak outright; not shake their heads, and give an old wives' darkling hint."

—Ahab, in Melville, *Moby Dick*

The Sense of Unending

A Postscript to C. L. R. James's *Mariners,*

Renegades, and Castaways: The Story of Herman

Melville and the World We Live In

End we all must. Frank Kermode's volume *The Sense of an Ending* ends, as did the series of lectures upon which it is based, though it clearly ends elsewhere and otherwise. Kermode maintains his ends always in sight, *before us,* in his title, as this is what it means, for him, to make a sense, in a word or in the world. But even if his ends are variant, which is not to say deviant, where do we who come after, who read afterwards, end up? If his ends are always in sight inside the book, if they are horizons rather than conclusions, then they may differ less than we'd thought from the beginning or middling.

This is perhaps less of a departure from Kermode's line of reasoning than it might seem. The text encompasses fictive ends and therefore brooks no conclusion, and Kermode appears to take this textual property into account when he compares life to the life of narrative. "Men," he says, "like poets rush 'into the middest,' *in medias res,* when they are born; they also die *in medias rebus,* and to make sense of their span they need fictive concords with origins, and ends, such as give meaning to lives and poems" (7). In this formulation, life exceeds its fictive ends, as indeed all referents exceed signification, but what is easily overlooked is that narrative too exceeds its own boundaries. The telling of an end marks the fictiveness of that end. Kermode achieves his ends by arraying narrations between the mythic poles of apocalypse and cyclical rebeginning, but in his telling he transgresses these ends. The surest conclusion we might draw from either story, apocalypse now or later, or the eternal return to origins, is that neither has yet taken place. If, as Ishmael and Job, "I only am escaped alone to tell thee" (qtd. in Melville, *Moby Dick* 573), then I am always and only epilogue, and that more than anything else gives form to my inconclusive prophecy.

Kermode looks for "the form that an end implies" (123), because he expects the anticipated end to give final form to that which it concludes. "And of course we have it now," he asserts, "the sense of an ending. It has not diminished, and is as endemic to what we call modernism as apocalyptic utopianism is to political revolution" (98). His example, though, is more telling than he in his talk seems to know. It is true that the projected ends of revolutionary movement give form to it, but the continual recession of these ends brings about an ongoing fluctuation of form. The Marxist withering away of the state is not yet a historical end, an apocalyptic wall against which we throw ourselves, but, in its continued nonoccurrence, a creamy pool in which Marxism's shifting shapes float. As the narrative of political history advances, the modern imagination engages in the altering of form that a dialectical movement past posited endings implies. Not final form, but the sense of unending derives from *epilogos,* the textual drive to say more.

This runs counter to the epinastic common sense of our everyday experience of plot. We can, after all, see the end, and many of us look ahead to it to decide whether it is worth the bother of reading through to. This seems only natural. Kermode claims we want conclusion. Early on in his study *Reading for the Plot*, Peter Brooks notes that "children quickly become virtual Aristotelians, insisting upon any storyteller's observation of the 'rules,' upon proper beginnings, middles, and particularly ends" (3). Antony Lamont vociferously insists, "[W]hether a yarn is tall or small I like to hear it well told. I like to meet a man that can take in hand to tell a story and not make a balls of it while he is at it. I like to know where I am, do you know? Everything has a beginning and an end" (in O'Brien 89). This sounds much like the sentiments expressed by the carpenter on board Melville's *Pequod:* "I like to take to hand none but clean, virgin, fair-and-square mathematical jobs, something that regularly begins at the beginning, and is at the middle when midway, and comes to an end at the conclusion; not a cobbler's job, that's at an end in the middle, and at the beginning at the end" (525). And when C. L. R. James arrives for the first time at the end of his study of Melville, *Mariners, Renegades, and Castaways*, he titles it "A Natural but Necessary Conclusion" (132), implying, as might Kermode, that this ending is so of a piece with what has gone before that it is virtually a foregone conclusion.

But the very naturalness of these asseverations should give pause to any right-thinking postantediluvian. Brooks's assertion about children sounds so correct that readers may fail to note its lack of support within the text. A similarly formulated assertion might as easily argue that anybody who has ever told stories to children has probably had the disconcerting experience of hearing the child greet the tale's climactic, satisfying, and natural conclusion with the demand "What happened after that?" Children's literature, we might also note, is rife with moralizing epilogues and nonendings of the "all lived happily ever after" variety. Mr. Antony Lamont, for his part, has abundant reason to yearn for neat textual boundaries. He makes his complaint as a character hired on by Dermot Trellis, a bad author who is himself a character in the novel *At Swim-Two-Birds*, by Flann O'Brien, and who impregnates Lamont's sister Sheila in a particularly interesting instance of giving birth to characters. Lamont is also a bad author, troubled by vague end zones as well as by Trellis, who has by this time become his brother-in-law, in Gilbert Sorrentino's novel *Mulligan Stew*. The *Pequod*'s carpenter, as so often occurs in Melville, undercuts his plea for workmanlike endings that coincide with their conclusions by his own actions. Even as he makes his case for the clear-cut job of work, he is working to transform Queequeg's coffin into the life buoy that will shoot out of the maelstrom to save his narrator at novel's end so that he can communicate the carpenter's case, that same coffin life buoy that bears upon it not only the signs of the carpenter's labor but the mysterious inscriptions of Queequeg's body.

The history of C. L. R. James's "'Natural but Necessary Conclusion'" continues the problematics of last words. The chapter's title appears in quotation marks, punctuation that could easily cast doubt upon both the necessity and the naturalness of these last words. But the title is in fact a quotation, repeating James's own words in his introduction to the volume, where he announces that the experiences he will recount in his conclusion "profoundly influenced the form the book has taken" (3d ed. 7), a note in keeping with Kermode's theories regarding the formative powers of conclusions. James's "'Natural but Necessary Conclusion'" seems to have lost some of that power by 1978, however, for it disappears from the edition published in that year, along with the introduction that promises the conclusion. That has been replaced with a biographical introduction authored by George P. Rawick. In this version, *Mariners, Renegades, and Castaways* ends at chapter 6 and ends again with a new afterword by James in which he notes matter-of-factly that "the world in 1978 cannot be what it was in 1953" (3d ed. 174), the year of publication of the first edition. It doesn't end there, though. In 1953 James dedicated his project to his son. The inscription reads: "For my son Nob, who will be 21 years old in 1970 by which time I hope he and his generation will have left behind them forever all the problems of nationality" (1st ed. vii). By 1978 only one of those hopes had been met, and since the study purports to be the story of Melville and the world we live in, the form of that story had to change. The second edition, the necessary conclusion having been ejected, is dedicated simply, "For my son Nob" (2d ed. viii). By 1984 the story has changed further, the ending still having not fully arrived, and the dedication has become a matter of three paragraphs, concluding with the now elderly James's hope to have left the errors and ignorance of public miseducation "behind for the future" (3d ed. 6). The promissory introduction has returned along with a new preface, and the "'Natural but Necessary Conclusion'" of chapter 7 has been returned to its place. It doesn't end there either, though. In its current form, chapter 7 appears in a truncated version, missing the final three pages of the original. The book's conclusion now trails off in ellipses, leading to the afterword of 1978.

This is more than a mere matter of bibliographic eccentricity; it gets to the heart of what I have to say about how we look at the end of what anyone might say. Bibliography is a bookish matter, and what I think the history of James's reflections on Melville helps us to see is that the book cannot contain the text's conclusions. In the present instance this has both textual and political ramifications.

Derrida has said that "that which is beyond the closure of the book is neither to be awaited nor refound. It is *there*, but *out-there*-beyond-within repetition but eluding us there. It is there like the *shadow* of the book" (qtd. in Harvey 243–44). Here he appears to be advancing a dialectical explanation of textual excess that is akin to James's comment about leaving things behind for the future and that James takes in his turn from his reading of Hegel. Hegel's play of assertion and negation gives us a text that is endlessly productive, one that brings forward a sense of thrown-ness. Each thesis comes to us bearing the traces of its genealogy and carrying within it the trace of the not-yet. Hence we find Hegel looking always to "the future in the present," a phrase that James takes as the title for his first volume of selected writings. Dialectic stripped of psychologism and transcendence leaves us with the excessive thesis of supplementarity. "Thus writing is what Derrida calls the 'supplement *par excellence*,' in the sense that it is never full, yet always too full and overflowing its own boundaries" (Harvey 150). The text of *Mariners, Renegades, and Castaways* is not a book, not even a critical edition containing all three versions along with the complete manuscript of *Moby Dick*. In the characterization of Irene Harvey, "[T]he text is not a book, for Derrida, but rather exceeds this totalization. The book is surely a text, but the reverse is not and cannot be the case. What this means for thought is that the 'text,' as inscription, leaves spaces, indeed constitutes spaces within itself which exceed itself" (Harvey 145). It is this opening out of itself of the text that produces the inconclusive nature of narrative as well as an intertextualizing that, as we shall see, in its turn eludes the cloture of canon formation. Despite the all too evident physical boundaries of the book, and seemingly to spite the calculated confines of curricula, the text in the West is more like a relational database system than an eternal, unchanging form; it is ever inviting our entrance and always offering nodes by which other texts might attach themselves.

Further, there is a quite practical feature of narrative, whether of traditional fiction or of the fiction of tradition in which the West constitutes itself as history, that operates against our commonsensical desire for closure. As E. S. Burt observes in his essay "Developments in Character," there is a sense in which narrative offers a special instance of the hermeneutic circle:

> [W]hile we follow the development of the protagonist's character over the narrative in our naive first reading, in fact the end toward which the development leads is in sight from the very beginning, in the figure of the narrator the hero has become. . . . [*The Confessions*] take as their horizon the final revelation of the original fold in the narrative: the end, the self developed, has become the beginning, the self being exposed. That fold had to occur for the narrative to be possible, and the narrative itself is the unfolding of the fold as interpretation. (197)

The story of Jonah requires the regurgitation of its protagonist so that Jonah's prophecy may be unfolded as it had been foretold. But the survival of Jonah is always the foregone conclusion, and his prophecy is inconclusive precisely in that it can never be finally and forever interpreted or unfolded, because, as prediction, it is unending. Likewise, when we read Poe's *Narrative of Arthur Gordon Pym of Nantucket*, the one thing that is evident to us as we follow that character toward that surpassingly strange polar vortex into which his narrative leads is that A. Gordon Pym does not end quite at book's end. The existence of the narrative itself argues against such a conclusion and demands explanation. What we are left with is the most convoluted of foldings, a note in another hand that seeks to interpret the endlessly uninterpretable inscriptions in the text's chasms, "the Ethiopian characters so mysteriously written in their windings" (736). An analogous fold, which might be more accurately classified as a Mobius band, exists in the epilogue to *Moby Dick*. The whale has sounded, withdrawing from our sight the text of his own hoary history etched in his skin, taking with him into the soundless vortex all those who with Ahab had sought his end. Ishmael is left clutching the similarly inscribed coffin life buoy, floating with us in the creamy pool of his own narration. It is this end that has been before us from the time we were first instructed to call him.

In her lecture "'Postmodernism,' 'Poststructuralism,' 'PostMarxism,' 'Postanalytical Philosophy,' 'Postpedagogy': Where Is the 'Post' Coming From?" Gayatri Spivak undertakes an analysis of some of the political features of the recent post. Pointing to the fashion in which, since at least the post-Enlightenment, the West has constituted its narrative as history-as-such, she identifies in both radical and conservative thought a tendency visible in Kermode's *Sense of an Ending.* She holds that

> the autobiography of the West imposed itself upon the theater of Imperialism as history-as-such. . . . At a certain point . . . the West began to lay claim to the place of the only sometimes prospective end of history. All utopian discourse of brotherhood or sisterhood participates in this. . . . Now what we have is a situation where even the end of history is not enough. We have to claim that there is something after the end of history to which the West can lay claim. . . . This post is not simply the desire to go on, but a claim to survivorship.

This, I think, is why some Melville criticism looks upon *Moby Dick* primarily as a survivor's narrative rather than as a salvage operation. If the West stakes a claim to a post in the future, it is largely because it cannot constitute a narrative of itself that ends itself. The West as narrator must continually throw itself forward as a speaking voice of the foreseeable future. The problem is that Western historical foresight is constantly excluding others from its narrative and maintaining its privileged position as emitter and former of the discourse of power. What disturbs Spivak, and C. L. R. James, is that the Western text is always one in which "I only am escaped alone." The rest of the world is sounded like the wounded whale, and the West takes its place of precedence, offering its interpretations and prophecies as gospel. There is no one outside Ishmael's narrative to dispute his presentation, but where the text of Western power and Melville's text differ is in the extent of their openness to the texts of the rest of the world. Melville's narrative is, as James rediscovers, a realm of meanest mariners, renegades, and castaways representing what the West represents to itself as realms of darkness and savagery, but nonetheless representing them as announcing their own discourse in ways that are not offered in other quintessentially Western works of survival such as *Heart of Darkness*. Even as Ishmael declares himself the sole survivor, his position as narrator is secured upon an empty, floating signifier that refigures beyond his end the savage mysteries of Queequeg, Queequeg who was to have been Ishmael's legatee. The West's narrative impulse is often as Spivak has described it. The narrative of our history looks to a postmodernism, a postmaelstrom discourse in which each can say, as Ishmael does upon concluding his will, "I survived myself; my death and burial were locked up in my chest. I looked around me tranquilly and contentedly, like a quiet ghost with a clean conscience sitting inside the bars of a snug family vault" (228). But when Ishmael does become the survivor of his own text, it is upon Queequeg's last testament that he rests, Queequeg, who was to have been Ishmael's "lawyer, executor, and legatee" (227). It is the story of those mariners, renegades, and castaways that Ishmael lies upon.

—————

The West's desire for a posthistorical clean conscience is a conclusion to be foregone, which we leave behind for the future in order to begin the unending rereading that Melville's novel calls for in its epilogue. For if we eschew the snug, smug loneliness of the family vault of the West's imagined postcivilization, we can read Melville as C. L. R. James, Charles Olson, and others who at midcentury prefigured our postculture did, as a great opening of textual space into which the world as text and imagination may enter. We may then see the *Pequod,* not as the democratic ship of state subsuming national difference under the sign of the survival of the imperial self, but as a floating signifier, as an island whose isolatoes are at home anywhere on the face of the earth.

Early and late, Melville's texts are marked with this sense of unending and opening outward. *Mardi*'s concluding sentence reads: "And thus, pursuers and pursued, fled on, over an endless sea" (543). *Moby Dick*'s narrator signals to the reader near the outset that the text at hand is far from a neatly bounded artifact frozen in final form. "God keep me from ever completing anything," Ishmael writes at the end of a paragraph that begins with a one-word sentence reading "Finally." "This whole book," he goes on, "is but a draught—nay, but the draught of a draught. Oh, Time, Strength, Cash, and Patience!" (145). The cash, of course, never came, at least not in appreciable quantities for this book, and *Moby Dick* was some time in achieving the canonical status it now enjoys, a fact that may be due in no small part to this very draftsmanlike quality of the text. But Melville's narrator displays a fine understanding throughout of the status of his own text and of the properties of textuality generally. As James notes, "Melville . . . begins with the accepted practices, beliefs and even literary methods of his time, and then consciously and with the utmost sureness leaves them behind or rather takes them over into the world he saw ahead. He saw the future so confidently only because he saw so clearly all that was going on around him" (3d ed. 46). There are occasions when Ishmael, simply looking at what is before him, finds examples of what we now term poststructural textuality and flags them for our attention. One of the clearest of these is the matter of the hieroglyphic markings on Queequeg and upon his coffin. It is a departed prophet who has written in the cannibal's flesh these markings that are illegible to Ishmael but that he interprets as complete theories of heaven and earth and a treatise on the art of attaining truth. It is the art of attaining truth, not the truth itself, that Queequeg bears upon his person, and as if to underscore the unending quality of that art of attainment, Queequeg transcribes this hermetic treatise onto his coffin, and it is this same treatise that eventually bears the weight of Ishmael's survival in much the same way that those Ethiopian markings drive forward the narrative of Gordon Pym.

There is a later bit of sympathetic magic when Ishmael composes a further text on textuality, describing the similar scorings in the flesh of Moby Dick himself. "But what I am driving at here is this. That same infinitely thin, isinglass substance, which, I admit, invests the entire body of the whale, is not so much to be regarded as the skin of the creature, as the skin of the skin . . ." (306). What better definition of the relationship between form and substance might we find than this remark upon the slate surface of Moby Dick's body? The form and structure of this novel are not the outer containment of experi-

ence. The skein of this draftsman's plot is not the skin of its content,
but the skin of the skin. It is a permeable surface, inseparable from
its depths, into which experience marks itself. "In some instances, to
the quick, observant eye, those linear marks, as in a veritable engrav-
ing, but afford the ground for far other delineations," Ishmael finds,
noting the existence of a kind of underwriting or subtext that serves
as the base for further writing. "These are hieroglyphical. That is,
if you call those mysterious cyphers on the walls of pyramids hiero-
glyphics, then that is the proper word to use in the present connection" (306). Absent some extratextual Rosetta stone, these markings
are as indecipherable to Ishmael as are the cicatrices on Queequeg's
skin and their replications in the workings of the coffin life buoy. "The
mystic-marked whale remains undecipherable" (306), writes Ishmael.
Though etched in a real surface, these hieroglyphs are, as signifiers,
virtually unbound and thus subject to infinite interpretation, recalling the hermeneutic activities of the *Pequod*'s crew when staring into
the scene figured upon Ahab's doubloon. Ishmael, like the present
reader, can only activate the significations of these signs and wonders
in relationship to his experience of the world in which they are situated. No divine author shall step forward to fix their meanings for
him, and he makes no effort to fix them permanently for his own
auditors.

This, then, is the predicament of Ishmael at book's end. "The
drama's done. Why then does anyone step forth?—Because one did
survive the wreck" (573). Melville may seem plainly to propound the
narrative instinct for postepisodic survival here, but it is a survival of
a plainly problematic sort. To begin with, the imperial self has been
marginalized by its own narrative: "[F]loating on the margin of the
ensuing scene . . . I was then, but slowly, drawn towards the closing
vortex" (573). Additionally, the closing vortex turns out to be a decidedly decentering influence upon the self: "When I reached it, it had
subsided to a creamy pool" (573). Lastly, what is centered at the end is
not the narrative self, the postapocalyptic survivor, but the markings
in the skin of the skin: "Gaining that vital centre, the black bubble
upward burst; and now, liberated by reason of its cunning spring, . . .
rising with great force, the coffin life-buoy shot lengthwise from the
sea, fell over, and floated by my side" (573). The novel culminates
in epilogue with the mysterious signs of the whale's skin sounding

and the similar signs of savage mystery and the art of attaining truth thrusting themselves in the opposite direction, shooting upward to serve as salvation for the orphaned survivor. This is a curious sort of Bakhtinian heteroglossia in which one speaker within the dialogism repeats the untranslated tongue of the other. The surviving self must cling for life to the baffling signs of the other, and if Melville does give Ishmael the last word, it is, as I have pointed out, a word that floats upon the eternally interpretable subtext of the castaway.

There are few better examples of intertextual influence than this sense of unending in the creamy pool of Melville's epilogue. It appears to work its way infectiously upon the texts of post-Melvillean writers who approach its vital center. This is seen easily enough in the works of that most Melvillean of New England poets, Charles Olson, whose own study of *Moby Dick, Call Me Ishmael,* precedes C. L. R. James's book by just a few years. The last lines of Olson's *Maximus* poems published in his lifetime read: "I set out now / in a box upon the sea" (203), lines that have obvious resonance in this context. These lines too are epilogue and new beginning. They did not appear in the earlier version of the volume read publicly by Olson, and their exact date of appendage to the volume remains unknown (*Maximus* 501–2). As Melville's epilogue seems to cry out for further inscription and interpretation, Olson's lines drew him forward, and a full volume of additional *Maximus* poems were written before his death. Likewise, the Caribbean-born C. L. R. James, quintessentially non-canonical outsider and castaway within North American letters, saw in Melville the real opening of the West, the opening of itself of Western narrative that shows its future in itself, the unending future in the present.

To be alone and poor is, in a sense, everybody's fate; but some people have been alone and poor in a very literal sense, as most of us have not; and in solitary confinement some of them have tested the gaiety of language as a means of projecting their humanity on a hostile environment. And it is by speaking for a few moments about the book of one such man that I can best begin to say what I have to say in this final talk. (Kermode, *Sense of an Ending* 156)

With these words Kermode begins to end his series of talks on the sense of an ending. It is interesting that he takes as his point of departure a representative of the noncanonical, Christopher Burney's book *Solitary Confinement*, which I think appears on few English department reading lists. In a very important sense Kermode's opening gesture is premonitory of Western academia's growing interest in the discourse of marginalia in the intervening decades. In retrospect, William Spanos has said of the imperial discourse of the center that "especially at times of cultural and socio-political crisis—when, that is, its empire is threatened by a knowledge explosion that precipitates the emergence (or deterritorialization) of the hitherto repressed 'other'—[it] fictionalizes itself as marginal—a disinherited remnant, but one chosen to fulfill the cultural mission of a 'higher cause'" ("Uses" 8). This is one more maneuver by which Western narrative lays claim to power over the beyond, by exercising its power to define the realm of the marginal and appropriating the territory beyond its borders. Again, both radical and conservative elements practice this to some extent. Conservative narrative posits the survival in an imperial ever-afterward of its "higher cause," the Work with a capital *W*. More radical elements seek their survival in a postcivilization by staking out the territory outside the borders set by the centers of discursive power, by representing the margins to themselves, and by representing the marginal as existing within themselves. Both tendencies leave little doubt, however, about who shall do the representing. In addition, as Barbara Johnson has remarked: "[B]ecause deconstruction has focused on the ways in which the western, white male, philosophical-literary tradition subverts itself *from within,* it has often tended to remain within the confines of the established literary canon. If it has questioned the boundary lines of literature, it has done so not with respect to the noncanonical but with respect to the line between literature and philosophy, or between literature and criticism" (75). The Western critique in its most radical, deconstructive garb continues to marginalize the non-Western and the noncanonical, even as it on occasion represents the noncanonical to itself.

I too begin to conclude my observations by turning to the discourse of the poor and the confined, by examining another who has projected his humanity onto a hostile environment by testing the gaiety of language. However, rather than enact a fictionalized marginalization of myself, I hope to follow the appropriation of the opening from within of Western narrative by the "marginal" discourse of the Third World. In *Mariners, Renegades, and Castaways*, C. L. R. James, an African-American scholar born in Trinidad, one who was to be ejected beyond the boundaries of the American legal canon specifically because of his critique of imperial discourse, seizes upon the epilogical ending of Melville's *Moby Dick* as a means of inserting the critique from the other "into the middest" of the narrative of the West. The American critical establishment eventually lifted *Moby Dick* from its earlier position of benign neglect, but in canonizing that text it has secured its survival upon the floating coffin life buoy of the text of the other. James, as castaway and isolato, offers to aid us in the further opening of that hieroglyphic text of the unsounded world.

The affinities between Melville and C. L. R. James extend beyond the text of *Moby Dick*. At one point in his life Melville was imprisoned on an island among renegades and castaways, perhaps unjustly. Had he not found means of escape and later signed on a Nantucket whaler, we might never have read of the great white whale. In 1952 C. L. R. James was also imprisoned on an island among the castaways and isolatoes of myriad nations. We honor our narrative of Ellis Island as a story of access to the spirit of American democracy, but in so doing we often forget that on Ellis Island the traffic moved in two directions. In 1952 C. L. R. James was incarcerated there awaiting deportation after nearly fourteen years in this country, largely on the basis of his public speaking and his published books. It was there that James wrote his study of Melville, and his jailers, carefully reviewing his manuscript for dangerous content, were to be his first readers. The resulting work is equal parts literary criticism, political critique, and brief against deportation. It is offered as evidence in all three areas of discourse simultaneously.

"*Moby Dick* will either be universally burnt or be universally known in every language as the first comprehensive statement in literature of the conditions and perspectives for the survival of Western civilization" (3d ed. 96), announces James in terms that indicate he too saw the fold at the close of Melville's novel as the site wherein the West would either bind itself to the text of the other for survival in the world of the post or continue its deadly misconstrual of that text. A reading of that fold that emphasizes the survival of the self as subject is a reading more closely aligned to the spirit of Ahab than to that of Ishmael. James would be more likely to agree with the reading of Charles Olson, who finds in the epilogue the "END of individual responsible only to himself. Ahab is full stop [*sic*]" (*Ishmael* 119). In James's understanding, Melville's genius is located in his ability to read the future in the present, to recognize the crises portended by the monomaniacal self-interestedness of the subject as represented in the character of Ahab, and to delineate an internationalist, prophetic position beyond the boundaries of the West and its manifest destiny. For C. L. R. James:

> It seems that at very great crises in human history, and they must be very great, an author appears who becomes aware that one great age is passing and another beginning. But he becomes aware of this primarily in terms of new types of human character, with new desires, new needs, new passions. The great writer . . . conceives a situation in which this character is brought right up against things that symbolize the old and oppose the new. The scene is set outside the confines of civilization. (3d ed. 124)

That scene is set beyond land's end, on the *Pequod*, where, as on Huck Finn's raft, the established order is undone: "The *Pequod* is taking a voyage that humanity has periodically to take into the open sea, into the unknown, because of the problems posed to it by life on the safe sheltered land" (3d ed. 59). In the course of this voyage the process of social stratification organized to support the triumph of the imperial self is laid bare and tested. Nearly all the men in this enterprise are, like James, islanders, and many, most notably Ahab's harpooners, are representatives of races declared savage and primitive by the defining discourse of Western destiny. But when placed in crisis, Melville suggests, the mad incantations of the primitive and the abominated produce a saving response to Ahab. Melville creates a world in which, as James outlines, "the most abased shall lift himself to the most exalted positions. The most abased of the crew on board is Pip, a little Negro from Alabama, the lowest of the low in America in 1851. It is Pip who in the end will be hailed as the greatest hero of all" (3d ed. 25; James has failed to notice that Melville's text gives two birthplaces for Pip, one in Alabama and one in Connecticut). This again is a dialectical motion that levers us out of the current social thesis on into the region of the text in the epilogue:

> What Melville did was to place within the covers of one book a presentation of a whole civilization so that any ordinary human being can read it in a few days and grasp the essentials of the world he lived in. To do this a man must contain within his single self, at one and the same time, the whole history of the past, the most significant experiences of the world around him, and a clear vision of the future. (James 3d ed. 122)

We can say of Melville, and James would probably want this to be said of him as well, that his writing bears within it that archetrace of both future and past that forms the text's excess. When we read *Moby Dick* in this sense we participate in what Peter Brooks terms the strange logic of narrative: "If the past is to be read as present, it is a curious present that we know to be past in relation to a future we know to be already in place, already in wait for us to reach it" (23). This is not to say that origin and end are synonymous. James illuminates the distinction by pointing to one of Ishmael's subnarratives, the tale of Steelkilt's revolt. In rebellion against an Ahab-like mate and a weak captain, Steelkilt and some of the crew mutiny and escape to their homes. But, James declares: "That's all. Everything goes back to just where it was before. That is exactly what would have happened in 1851 if there had been a revolt on the *Pequod*. We would have been left in the end exactly where we had been at the beginning" (3d ed. 60). The future Melville's narrative encrypts for us is not one in which a simple, albeit bloody, change of rulers leaves the structure of rule itself intact. What will become Ishmael's unending sense is bodied forth in Queequeg's flesh at the beginning, it is traced in the wood of the coffin life buoy, and it rises from its position of abasement and submersion, from the swirling wreckage of Ahab's past, as the basis of all that has gone before, Ishmael's survival as reader of the untranslatable art of attaining truth.

Mariners, Renegades, and Castaways operates similarly at the boundaries of Western discourse, making its case for *Moby Dick* as exemplary of America's narrative future, and for itself as gloss upon the opportunity afforded by the epilogic of Melville's text. James takes a cue from one of his fellow prisoners, a man he identifies only by his initial. "On Ellis Island it was M who stood for what vast millions of Americans still cherish as the principles of what America has stood for since its foundation" (3d ed. 139). James finds on Ellis Island the reassertion of an American tradition that he sees as the antithesis to the monomaniacal self-interest of those who would preserve their own political power by erasing the text of the other. "Here was I," he writes, "just about to write, suddenly projected onto an island isolated from the rest of society, where American administrators and officials and American security officers controlled the destinies of perhaps a thousand men, sailors, '*isolatos*,' renegades and castaways from all parts of the world" (3d ed. 132–33).

What he does on Ellis Island is in effect to repeat the crime that brought him here. In arguing against James's appeal of his deportation orders in 1950, a government attorney had advised the court that C. L. R. James was the author of *World Revolution, Black Jacobins,* and *A History of Negro Revolt,* reminding the judge that the founders of revolutionary movements had often been writers (3d ed. 163). From this experience James retains one fertile image. "I cannot get the picture out of my mind," he recalls. "I see [the attorney] always standing on tip toe, hand outstretched, delivering to the judge the final, the undefeatable argument—a book I had written in 1937" (3d ed. 166–67). James still sees the book as the undefeatable argument, hence his case is continually reopened, and this is always a reopening of the text. So it is no wonder that James advances text and testament as a means of maintaining his open and never shut case. In the last chapter of the first and third editions he tells the stories of his studies of Melville and of his struggle to remain in the United States, because he believes his "total experience should be told" (3d ed. 152). Appropriately enough, this last chapter follows his last chapter on Melville, which is titled "The Work, the Author, and the Times," where he attempts to give an indication of the total experience of that earlier author. James's thesis has been that Melville was able to perceive in the crises and characters of his own time the future directions of the Western project, or the projection of the West, and so his concluding portrait of the author of *Moby Dick* has formed the critical narrative that leads up to it, the *Story of Herman Melville and the World We Live In.* In so doing, James has composed a narrative of his own in which he attempts to read the text of his own time and crises under the light of Melville's text, and this intertextual play takes its form from the end that is before us. But that end is another fold, strikingly like the epilogue to *Moby Dick,* because at the time of composition James does not yet know how his story is to end. As Ishmael is left on his floating island, an orphaned signifier to be gleaned by the searching *Rachel,* James sits on Ellis Island looking to the postimprisonment future and waiting. This has obvious consequences for the form of his narrative, the skin of the skin. To tell his total experience is to tell a tale of incompletion. He seems aware of this fact. Reflecting, for instance, upon that portion of his plot that concerns an illness and his treatment on the island, he says: "I have told the illness as a connected story. But it was not connected. . . . To a man in my condition, there was added not only the sense of unwarranted inhuman persecution, but a never-ceasing battle to put an end to it" (3d ed. 145). Because the battle is not only against pain but also against political persecution and monomania, the book cannot seem to conclude itself in any of its various editions. The conclusions James does arrive at are all forward looking, imbricating the not-yet over the then, as when he writes: "In the end I finally came to the conclusion that my experiences [on Ellis Island] have not only shaped this book but are the most realistic commentary I could give on the validity of Melville's ideas today" (3d ed. 132). I think this is true even of the 1978 edition, which jettisons this same conclusion. James's offering of Melville as valid textual evidence for the conclusions we must draw today is so thoroughly shaped by his own experience of America that the absent chapter is again a foregone conclusion, an absent cause of the text at hand. James's predicament is visible in Melville's. The present conclusion to *Mariners, Renegades, and Castaways* remains an open question. James simply lays his study before the reader as his prosecutor had laid his earlier texts before the courts: "With all due respect I have to say that I believe I have given sufficient evidence here to show the grave injustices which are being perpetrated in the name of the law, and that it is inconceivable to me, and, I am positive, to the great majority of American citizens, that the laws of the United States prevent the judiciary from putting an end to them . . ." (3d ed. 173). His plea trails off in expectant ellipses, as *Moby Dick* empties out into the italics of its epilogue, because no matter how positive James may feel about his predictions, he cannot yet know their absolute outcome. We must, however, return to the original edition to read the full opening out of James's first ending. Where we now read ellipses, in 1953 James recommences with what is for him an increasingly characteristic claim: "I have only a few more things to say" (1st ed. 201), he says, and then proceeds to a description of the book's publication. It is a moment akin to Gilbert Sorrentino's introduction into the opening of *Mulligan Stew* of all the letters of rejection, real and imagined, that met his manuscript on its way to print. C. L. R. James, who is after all a Marxist, includes in his last words a description of the material conditions of his work's appearance. This is not mere postmodern posturing; James is also, in these last pages, asking that money be sent to his defense fund, and he is at pains to assure his readers that their contributions are not to be used to defray the cost of his book's publication. This is the most open and sincere invitation to reader response criticism I have yet to encounter in a work of literary analysis.

Further, though, we find in these back pages a literal fold of the sort described by E. S. Burt in his "Developments in Character." Having earlier explained that he concludes with an account of his own crisis because it has given form to the writing that precedes its narration, James now shows that the writing has simultaneously shaped that same experience: "I publish the protest with the book on Melville because, as I have shown, the book as written is a part of my experience. It is also a claim before the American people, the best claim I can put forward, that my desire to be a citizen is not a selfish nor a frivolous one" (1st ed. 202). If the end of a personal narrative is always in sight, as were the markings of Queequeg, in the person that the author has become, it is also true, as we find in this statement of James's, that the writing of that narrative has played a role in the production of that person. The end of the work permeates the text at all points, and the text is perpetually going about the business of constituting its own ends, producing its own subjects.

James's first, unreprinted end is the perfect example of this. In that text on Melville, James appears as the alien laying his claim as best he can for the right to be declared that which he has already demonstrated he is, the most integral member of the American body politic. We cannot later separate his ends from his origins, no more than we could separate the skin of the skin from that which it encompasses.

James's work will not suffer cloture; at its end it opens itself to the reader, asks that the reader enter into its project, that we read the "alien" text our survival floats upon and imbricate it with our own, and that we defend the text of the other. C. L. R. James's *Mariners, Renegades, and Castaways: The Story of Herman Melville and the World We Live In* looks forward from an immediately altering present and literally calls to the reader to join in the construction of the postcrisis narrative structure. The choice in readings seems to be between the self-echoing, neatly closed-off voice of the family vault, or the voice of the coffin life buoy savagely inscribed and then reworked by meanest mariners and isolatoes. James's voice at the point where his own narrative trails off could well be a partial translation of that hieroglyphic scene of signing read out by some inquisitive Ishmael who had bothered to study its spectral figurations.

AFTERWORD

"I have only a few more things to say." That is how C. L. R. James began the last half hour or so of every talk I ever heard him give. While I was typing the draft of this chapter, word was relayed to me that Cyril Lionel Robert James had died in London, eighty-eight years after his birth in Tunapuna, Trinidad, on January 4, 1901. It was difficult to believe that this life, so closely identified with the liberation struggles of this century, had ended before the work was finished. A mark of James's continued engagement in the critical debates of his era is the letter posthumously published that he wrote to Professor Frank Kermode one day in 1982 after listening to Kermode's BBC talk on *King Lear* the previous evening. In characteristic spirit, James ends his letter by suggesting that Vanessa Redgrave is the one contemporary actor suited to the "colossal task" of playing the role of Edgar (*Reader* 242).

I knew C. L. R. James first as the author of *Black Jacobins*, later as a teacher, and always as the model of what a committed intellectual work should be. I would like to dedicate this study to his memory.

Dr. James ended the third volume of his selected writings, *At the Rendezvous of Victory*, with a speech he gave in 1981 in which he applied the lessons of Poland's great Solidarity movement to other struggles around the world, a speech I read over to myself often while thinking about the enormous changes that have come to Europe and the former Soviet Union. He concluded that day with these words about the liberating movement that arises from among the people themselves, words that I heard him repeating in my mind as I received word of his passing: *"And I want to end by telling you: I don't know that I will see that. I have been in the world a long time. But I expect to see it in South Africa before I go and when it comes in the United States I may be away but you can be certain that if I am away I will do my best to come back. I will have plenty to tell you but you will have plenty more to tell me about American Solidarity. Thank you"* (272–73).

When my mistress left me in charge
of the house, I had a grand time: I got
Master Tommy's copy books and a pen
and ink, and, in the ample spaces
between the lines, I wrote other lines, as
nearly like his as possible. The process
was a tedious one, and I ran the risk of
getting a flogging for marring the highly
prized copy books of the oldest son.
—Frederick Douglass,
  My Bondage and My Freedom

You are
Black Lazarus risen from the White
Man's grave
—Melvin B. Tolson, *Libretto*

Melvin B. Tolson and the Deterritorialization of Modernism

"In 1932 I was a Negro poet writing Anglo-Saxon sonnets as a graduate student in an Eastern University" ("Odyssey of a Ms." 8). These are the words that Melvin B. Tolson chose to describe himself as he had been at the outset of his odyssey as an artist, a description that, while recalling the formal beginnings of other modernist poets such as William Carlos Williams, resonates yet more profoundly with Frederick Douglass's recollections of his first interlinear strides toward freedom and a style of his own. But the interlinear tracings of both Douglass and Tolson soon began to diverge radically from their models. Not merely glosses or even really copying, the writing between the lines of Frederick Douglass and Melvin B. Tolson is a repetition elsewhere of the model that eventually displaces the model; it is a *rewriting* that comes to read itself as prior to the lines of the master. Both Douglass and Tolson run the risk of being flogged for marring the highly prized lines of Master Thomas, and yet each in the end has succeeded in writing "other lines" that challenge the territorial claims of the master text of Western hegemony. Each sought an opening within the dominant text of his time and placed into that space radical representations of African-American aesthetics whose eventual effect is to assert their own primacy over the stylings of the master class. Tolson's later style, far from being a mask adopted simply to gain entry to the master's house, is a means by which Anglo-American claims to the ground of modernism are set aside.

Certainly Tolson has been flogged for his later style. The terms of the critical argument over his corpus seem to have been set by the authors of the prefaces to his two last books, Allen Tate and Karl Shapiro. Just as Shapiro's preface was a response as much to Tate's as to Tolson's verses, critics who have come at Tolson afterward, black and white alike, have raged and ranged between the Scylla and Charybdis of Shapiro's two most provocative praises of Tolson's poems: that they were "outpounding Pound" (12) and that in them "Tolson writes and thinks in Negro" (13). Indeed, many of Tolson's earliest reviewers and critics seem to have been as exercised, either favorably or negatively, by Shapiro as by Tolson. This is certainly the case in Sarah Webster Fabio's 1966 essay "Who Speaks Negro?" and Josephine Jacobsen, reviewing *Harlem Gallery* for the *Baltimore Evening Sun*, spends roughly half of her print space arguing with Shapiro. Just as it has proved nearly impossible to speak of Tolson's late books without speaking of their prefaces, few have found it possible to speak of the development of Tolson's style without expressing suspicion, sometimes severe, about its origins and its racial politics. In characterizing the reactions of Langston Hughes to Tolson's belated public attention, Arnold Rampersad writes that "*suddenly*, having overhauled his craft according to the most complex tenets of high modernism, and having renounced the militant pro-Marxism of his first volume, *Rendezvous with America*, Tolson was now sporting laurels of a quality never before conceded by white critics to a black writer" (234, emphasis added). The "suddenness" of Tolson's stylistic transformation is of course belied by those poems published between the appearance of *Rendezvous with America* and *Libretto for the Republic of Liberia,* as well as by the documentary evidence in the hundreds of drafts collected among Tolson's papers at the Library of Congress. But Hughes's feelings, at least as they are reported by Rampersad, also unfairly associate Tolson's alterations of poetic mode with a betrayal of his earlier politics. This conclusion requires a belief that radical politics require a certain form of poetics, a belief that, according to Rampersad, Hughes held. Hughes wrote to his friend Arna Bontemps at the time of the publication of Tolson's *Libretto* recalling that Tolson had said he would "write so many foreign words and footnotes that they would *have* to pay him some mind!" (qtd. in Rampersad 235), attributing, as others have, the most mundane of motivations to Tolson and failing to consider Tolson's ironic humor about his public reception. Further, though, as Rampersad represents the shape of this betrayal, "the poet laureate of an African country [Tolson] had written the most hyper-European, unpopulist poem ever penned by a black writer. Did it not matter that very few of the American Friends of Liberia, and even fewer Liberians themselves, could understand the poem . . . ?" (193). (For the remainder of this discussion I will follow Rampersad's usage of "populist" in its popular, contemporary sense, not in its historical sense.) Elsewhere Rampersad has referred to Tolson's poetic transformation as "gentrification" (193).

It is the confluence of racial, political, and aesthetic questions, perhaps inevitable in America, that underscores the peculiarity of these charges against Tolson. No one seems to take Tolson to task in this fashion for his use of white models in his earlier verse. Though the influences of Sandburg and Masters are readily apparent in those early poems, few would accuse Tolson of having deliberately adopted those models to curry favor with the white literary establishment; fewer still would see in his use of Masters as a model a betrayal of potential black audiences. And yet one might argue that Tolson sounds *more* like his white models in the early than in the late poems. While the *Libretto* and *Harlem Gallery* are clearly indebted to Pound, Eliot, and Tate, they *sound* like none of those poets, and Tolson's late poems differ substantially in form and tone from the one white poet they most resemble in diction, Hart Crane. Still, the suspicion of Tolson's poetics persists.

The charge that Tolson has severed himself from black readers is made still more strange when it is made by white critics. In an early review of *Harlem Gallery* Laurence Lieberman reported this experiment:

> It may well be that my problem in reading this book is that I am not Negro. Well, I have just spent a year teaching at the college in St. Thomas. The student body here is about ninety percent Negro, and nearly every Negro land I can think of is represented, including Africa and the States. Though English is the mother tongue for nearly all of the students, there is so much variety of accent and dialect, I have to struggle to understand what they are saying in class (as indeed they must struggle to understand each other). Africa is the land of *their* racial heritage, quite as much as it is Tolson's. I have tried to get the students—and some of them are promising poets—to become interested in reading Tolson's book. They do not understand him. He simply does not speak their language. (456)

The tortured progress of Lieberman's logic in this passage will be familiar to inveterate readers of white criticism of black writings. The reviewer begins by momentarily conceding to a racialist argument, that perhaps the fact of whiteness is in and of itself a block against his understanding of a black poem. But then, by producing evidence of uninterested or confused black readers he dismisses both the racialist argument *and* Tolson's poem. Despite the opening concession, the white teacher retains a position of primacy over both the poem and the students. "Hey, I tried, but you just weren't black enough" seems to be an apt paraphrase. One could easily imagine a black professor undertaking a similar experiment, attempting to interest a class of white students in the verse of Wallace Stevens, Hart Crane, or Gertrude Stein. Perhaps such a professor would, faced with failure, assert that these poets simply do not speak the students' language. But would our imaginary professor be likely to accuse the poets in question of being less authentic, less white, or less in touch with their traditions than the students? This is exactly what Lieberman, despite a few complimentary things he has to say about Tolson's poem, goes on to do:

The Trinidadians and British Guianese I have met in St. Thomas have a more seminal dispute with Western Culture than any American Negro I have ever read, including Tolson and Baldwin. The Negroes of Trinidad and British Guiana have had Western Culture shoveled down their throats by the United Kingdom at closer range than the American Negroes. Some of the more outspoken among them dismiss the entire civilization arising from the Greeks as barbaric, and favor an Egypt-oriented definition of our cultural heritage. However absurd their claim, they at least offer a possibility for a new major direction and tradition for the modern world. Tolson does not offer this, so far as I can see. (457)

Lieberman is playing a game here that no black writer can possibly win. He simultaneously berates Tolson for failing to find a black readership in his classroom and sets himself up to judge who among black writers does most to break with the traditions of Western culture, traditions about which they make "absurd claims."

That some African-American critics played similar games with his work was something that pained Melvin Tolson. Among his papers is a telling note in which he speaks of himself in the third person, remarking that the Poet Laureate of Liberia "was warned to stop using complex words that did nothing but give delirium tremens to poetry readers of the *Black Gazette* or *Ebony* and *The Negro World*." On the reverse side of this note Tolson has written starkly: "Negro critics beat poets of color / Keep step in the coffle" (cont. 4). And in a letter to Allen Tate, Tolson observes that "if the vanguard White poet is isolated, his Negro fellow is annihilated between the walls of biracialism" (Tate Papers). It is a mark of Tolson's determination that he refused to keep step in the coffle; it is a disservice to this poet to claim that he effected his successes by cozying up to the masters.

It is understandable, however, that Tolson's readers feel that he wished to be recognized for having brought modernist techniques to African-American verse. On June 1, 1949, pretending an oversight, Tolson appends this postscript to a letter to Tate: "I forgot to mention, Mr. Tate, that I believe the LIBRETTO marks a 'fork in the road,' a change in direction, for what is called Negro Poetry. Between me and you, it's long overdue!" (Tate Papers). It is this sort of remark that has earned for Tolson some animosity from later readers. And when, in a letter dated March 15 of the following year, Tolson refers to Tate's preface to the *Libretto* as the Negro's "Literary emancipation proclamation" (Tate Papers), most readers will share a level of exasperation. Who, we must ask, is being freed from whom, by what means, and for what future literary sharecropping? But a reading of Tolson that sees him only as a literary chameleon trying to assimilate with all deliberate speed is achieved at the price of ignoring the full complexity of Tolson's own, often playful remarks, and at the greater cost of not sufficiently reading what Tolson has in fact written.

In the unpublished novel "All Aboard!" one of Tolson's characters makes a comment to a mother that might easily have been directed later to Tate and Shapiro: "'Mrs. Graves,' he said mockingly, 'after you've spent your hard-earned bucks on your only son, how d'you expect him to talk?' He shook his forefinger at her. 'Didn't Toussaint L'Overture Graves study the same books white boys study?'" (364). The advent of someone like Tolson should come as no surprise to American readers. But as the name of Tolson's earnest scholar, Toussaint L'Overture Graves, indicates, while he studied the same books as the white boys, he studied them differently and to different ends. The outcome of his studies portends something rather different from what many of his critics have imagined. What Tolson came to attempt was a decolonizing of American letters, a task that he saw as linking him to Whitman. "In attempting to decolonize American [literature]," Tolson notes, "Whitman was compelled to emphasize and glorify the Americanism of his art" (cont. 4). Tolson is a decolonizer after Whitman and Toussaint L'Ouverture; he will emphasize and glorify the *African* Americanism of his art, and he does it on the plain of the master's colony, on the site of the colonized master text of modernism. Tolson even goes so far as to suggest a modern revision of Whitman, a poet of whom Tolson says in one note, "There was no other with his ethnic empathy" (cont. 4). Tolson offers an amendment toward the updating of his precursor: "The bronze god was Paul Robeson, the All-American of all time. Yes, if old Walt Whitman, America's greatest poet, had seen that, he would have included Paul Robeson in America's greatest epic, *Leaves of Grass*" (*Caviar* 32).

Melvin Tolson's *Libretto for the Republic of Liberia* and *Harlem Gallery* are poems that, like the longer works of Pound and Eliot, have designs upon their audience. But they are works that constitute a considerably different audience from that addressed by those white modernists, and that constitute that audience on a different ground. Efforts to portray Tolson as a poet who betrayed his populist instincts to achieve the elite readership of academic modernism require that we ignore the nature of his poetry and the breadth of Tolson's own remarks. While it is true that Tolson took some comfort from John Ciardi's new critical distinction between the "vertical" and the "horizontal" audiences (Farnsworth 111–12), looking to possible future readers for fuller vindication, and while he was able to make jokes out of his understanding of the primary book-buying public, writing in one note, "My poetry is of the proletariat, by the proletariat, and for the bourgeoisie" (cont. 10), it is also true that Tolson's works, far from being addressed only to experts, question the territory of modernist expertise and present knowledge as a link between poet and populace, a link that the populace should strive after as strongly as the poet:

> Is it too much to ask
> of homo sapiens the sweat of Hellas
> in order to enjoy Sophocles and Aristophanes
>
> .   .   .   .
>
> Even Elvis Presley and Bojangles and Patanjali
> require of their devotees the rigor
> of four dimensions.
>
> (cont. 4)

If the words of the modernist bard do not occupy quite the same relationship to the public as do the proverbs of folk wisdom, they might still fill a similar function:

> The value of a proverb
> the elite never know:
> it is the people
> who reap and sow
> as the words list or blow.
>
> (cont. 8)

Marked in his notes as a "thing to remember" is the assertion that "Negro artists [are not] alienated in Aframerica like white artists" (cont. 4); rather, "the pessimism of the white man throws into new relief the new Demiurge in Negro life and Africa." To Tolson's view the African-American writer had no choice but to be a race man: "Racial bias forced him into race consciousness" (cont. 4). Though he thinks of the poet as being in a cultural vanguard, he argues against the Eliotic position on culture: "If Mr. Eliot had read Dr. Oliver Cox's Race, Caste and perhaps Class, he would not have written his 'Class and the Elite'" (cont. 4). In fact Tolson saw his work as offering a way out of what he saw as Eliot's dead end, placing himself in a more heterogeneous modernism with writers such as Williams, Hughes, and Crane, *contra* Eliot: "'The Bridge' is a way out of the pessimism of 'The Waste Land.' The 'Libretto' is a vista out of the mysticism of the 'Four Quartets'" (cont. 10).

Far from being an elitist, Tolson was a tireless propagandist among the people for his brand of modernism, as a teacher, a popular public speaker, a columnist, and a poet. Michael Bérubé has recently provided an apt appraisal of the type of populist aesthetic found in *Harlem Gallery*:

> On this count the poem is unambiguous: to do anything less than disseminate modernism to the masses is to give in to cultural forces which would patronize and condescend to "the people" by giving them the kind of art which, in Clement Greenberg's words, "predigests art for the spectator and spares him effort, provides him with a shortcut to the pleasure of art that detours what is necessarily difficult in genuine art." (127–28)

In his regular columns in the *Washington Tribune*, which ran from 1937 through 1944, Tolson constantly suggested readings to his audience, generally couching these suggestions in the most contemporary terms: "If you want to get the lowdown on the ancient Greeks, read Sappho, the Minnie-the-Moocher of her day" (*Caviar* 55). He plugged Margaret Anderson's magazine, *Common Ground*, giving the address for potential subscribers, and, in the tradition of Walt Whitman and Ezra Pound, he plugged his own poems as well: "Of course, I want you to read 'Rendezvous with America.' . . . I just received word that the *Atlantic Monthly* is bringing out my poem, 'Babylon.' Some of you read 'Dark Symphony.' Well, I hope you like this last piece. It has an interesting history" (*Caviar* 270). It is true that Tolson quite consciously wrote more simply in his journalism than in his verse, but it is also true that he genuinely hoped that many of the people in his *Washington Tribune* audience would also be among the readers of his verse. If some white writers and their works were alienated from their people, "The mouths of white books choke with dust," Tolson notes (cont. 8), Tolson sees himself much in the role of an organic intellectual, as Antonio Gramsci has defined that term.

Odd as it may at first seem, this is in part an explanation for some of the esoterism in Tolson's works. In his effort to rearticulate modernism as a populist American aesthetic with African roots, Melvin Tolson reconfigured the audience for modern art, revising and reappropriating Eliot's objective correlative. It is this movement that explains an otherwise perverse-sounding note among Tolson's papers. He writes: "I have hidden my identity as a Negro poet in words . . . / thus am I more militantly a Negro" (cont. 4). The eye is drawn so strongly to the word *hidden* in this remark that its sense seems hopelessly contradictory. How can it be possible that one might be more militantly Negro by in any way hiding an identity as a Negro poet? What Tolson's possibly unrescuable comment appears in the fuller context of his works to portend is a militant alignment with a history of African and African-American signifying practices, what Tolson sometimes refers to as "Deepi-talki" (cont. 4; *Libretto* 24). Michael Bérubé describes Tolson's approach as the "adoption of modernist technique as a guerilla strategy, a means of letting revolutionary discourse sound in the ears of conservative whites by masking that discourse in a no longer revolutionary poetics" (145). The poet did see his work as a guerilla strategy, but, as Bérubé later points out, Tolson "did not consider himself to be writing for solely white audiences" (168). Neither did Tolson view whites as necessarily his primary audience, nor did he see modernist poetics as no longer revolutionary. To the contrary, he came to see modernist poetics as having been already arrived at by African aesthetics, thus rendering the African-American tradition primary rather than merely imitative.

At one point in his development Tolson separated himself from Eliot, Tate, and other Anglo-American modernists on the grounds of content. In a speech at Kentucky State College, Tolson told his listeners:

Imitation must be in technique *only*. We have a rich heritage of folk lore and history. We are part of America. We are part of the world. Our native symbols must be lifted into the universal. Yes, we must study the techniques of Robert Lowell, Dylan Thomas, Carlos Williams, Ezra Pound, Karl Shapiro, W. H. Auden. The great revolution has not been in science but in poetry. (cont. 9)

Yet Tolson's rearticulation of modernism led him eventually to assert African progenitors in the realm of technique. Tolson could claim that his esoteric modernism made him more militantly Negro because he claimed that the aesthetic had roots in African and African-American poetics. His audience was not composed entirely of conservative whites. He writes in one place, "*I talk with old slaves* / (Deepi-Talki)" (cont. 4). Melvin Tolson was an inveterate collector of African proverbs and African talk. Among his papers are page after page upon which he has patiently copied out proverbs unearthed in his reading. He notes of these proverbs and poems, "Sometimes the Africans go esoteric on us" (cont. 4), and he traces that tradition of African esoterism into African-American song and speech. "Esoterica," he notes; "meanings of spirituals like symbolism today in poetry. / Exs: 'Go Down Moses' / 'Steal away to Jesus' / *I talk with old slaves*" (cont. 4). It is this rearticulation of modernism as African that surfaces in remarks Tolson made to his audience at the Library of Congress when he was invited to read there late in his life:

> You know, poets like to do a great amount of double talking. We think very often that the modernists gave us that concept of poetry, which is untrue. Because I can go back into the Negro work songs, the spirituals and jazz, and show you that double talk of poetry. And I can even [clicking his fingers for emphasis] *go to Africa, as I shall do tonight, and show you that double talk of poetry.* Especially in metaphors and symbols. So I'm doing some double talk here.

Having found in the African proverbs a source he could cite to justify the seemingly esoteric diction of his rearticulated modernism, a source that antedates *and*, in his view, influences his more immediate modernist models, Tolson goes on to elaborate a theory of rhythmic signifying rooted in African-American tradition, a theory related to

Frost's ideas about sentence sound, and a theory whose source Tolson suggests in an aside may already have found its roundabout way into the American canon:

> Now it is said that you have to watch these poets, because with their beat they're always trying to make you suspend your intellect. And then he's got you in charge. You know how Edgar Allan Poe could do that; [clicking his fingers for emphasis] *sometimes saying nothing, but that beat would get you.* And of course, I don't know; he might have got it from the old Negro preacher.
>
> My students often come to me and say: "Well, I went to hear old Reverend So-and-so when I went home during the holidays. And you know the man didn't say *anything*, and everybody was just rocking, . . . rocking."
>
> I said, "You need a course that you haven't got in college yet." [Steps away from the podium and stamps out a rhythm with his feet to demonstrate.] What did that old preacher do? He set up a rhythmic pattern, just like the poet. (Library of Congress reading)

Those who would oppose Tolson's variety of modernism to an oral, vernacular tradition, clearly favoring the latter, make at least two mistakes. First, they neglect to consider fully the implications of the fact that the oral tradition is represented by poets *in writing*. Second, they often present a grossly reduced vernacular for our consideration. Tolson's turning to the heritage of African proverb and the traditions of pulpit performance is part of an aesthetic that celebrates and continues the richness of verbal signifying practice among the people. In *Blues People,* his seminal study of African-American vernacular music, Amiri Baraka claims for black language practice an aesthetic much like Emily Dickinson's, supporting his assessments with a passage from Ernest Borneman's "The Roots of Jazz": "In language, the African tradition aims at circumlocution rather than at exact definition. The direct statement is considered crude and unimaginative; the veiling of all contents in ever-changing paraphrase is considered the criterion of intelligence and personality. In music, the same tendency towards obliquity and ellipsis is noticeable" (qtd. in *Blues People* 31). Similarly, Tolson had written in his notes that "the direction of a poet is indirection. To speak in military terms, the prosifier says 'Forward! March!' but the poet says, 'Oblique! March!'" (cont. 10).

In *Understanding the New Black Poetry,* Stephen Henderson identifies among the features of a black aesthetic in language virtuoso naming and enumerating, metaphysical imagery, compressed and cryptic imagery, and hyperbolic imagery (33). (Coincidentally, Tolson once began to make notes for a talk entitled "Hyperbole in Negro Poetry" [cont. 4].) These are but a few of the "innumerable forms" of black linguistic elegance Henderson posits in opposition to those who would reduce "black" linguistic style to a very narrow register. For Henderson, as for Tolson and Baraka, "there is this tradition of beautiful talk," and that tradition will not be confined within any critic's closed notions of a "street" language. "Don Lee, for example, can use the word 'neoteric' without batting an eye and send us scurrying to our dictionaries. The word is not 'Black' but the casual, virtuoso way that he drops it on us—like 'Deal with that'—*is an elegant Black linguistic gesture*" (Henderson 33). Melvin B. Tolson finds in the vernacular of the African-American preacher *and* his flock the same thing he finds in the language arts of Africa, a highly allusive, hyperbolic, compressed metaphoricity, and what Houston Baker has termed virtuoso "mastery of form" (*Modernism* 15). In *Harlem Gallery* Tolson presents this as a sustaining feature of black life: "Metaphors and symbols in Spirituals and Blues / have been the Negro's manna in the Great White World" (91). Speaking to his newspaper readers in Washington, D.C., Tolson said, "There is majesty in old John Milton's *Paradise Lost.* But no greater majesty than you'll find in one of God's old trombones. At his best, the old preacher had the poetry of word and motion— if you get what I mean" (*Caviar* 53). Having schooled himself in the techniques of Anglo-American modernism, Tolson proceeded in the last years of his life to reverse the roles of master and student. Having inscribed his lines, as it were, between the lines of modernism's master text, he was now suggesting that the master text had in fact copied itself out of the text of African traditions. The sea turtle had eaten his way out of the great white shark, had eaten "*his* way to freedom / beyond the vomiting dark" (*Gallery* 141). It comes as no surprise that such audacious signifying has provoked consternation in some readers:

> We chewed this quid a second time,
>   for Black Boy often adds

the dimension of ethnic irony
to Empson's classic seven.
(*Gallery* 122)

━━━━━━━━━

Thus, thus, the Negro scholar in our day
Is born to be a genealogist.
(Tolson, "Negro Scholar" 80)

When in 1965 interviewer M. W. King asked Melvin Tolson about his having "out-pounded Pound," Tolson immediately responded, "Well, I did go to the Africans instead of the Chinese" (87). Pound too had gone to the Africans, but he had gone with Frobenius as his guide, thus replicating some of the errors of that source, and his own biases prevented his pursuing fuller studies of the development of African civilizations. By the time of this interview with King, Tolson had been going to the Africans for decades, partly at least to fulfill the role of genealogist, to fill in the ahistorical nothingness to which European art, philosophy, and history had consigned Africa, and to reveal the fuller genealogy of modernism, which includes African sources. In the 1965 interview he remarks that "Gertrude Stein's judgement that the Negro suffers from Nothingness revealed her profound ignorance of African cultures" (87) and then reads into the record just a few of the hundreds of African proverbs he had collected when preparing to write the *Libretto for the Republic of Liberia*. Having read some of the same proverbs to his audience at the Library of Congress, he challenges them: "Now you ask the modern poets to make metaphors as good, proverbs as good." Bringing his genealogy around to America, he introduces his poem to old Satchmo, Louis Armstrong, repeating Stein's notorious remark and admonishing his listeners, "Now you listen to this and see if there's any truth to that; and you've *heard* the African proverbs." Coming back to Stein in *Harlem Gallery*, Tolson provides a literal genealogy:

The Toothpick, Funky Five, and Tippling Tom!
Ma Rainey, Countess Willie V., and Aunt Harriet!
Speckled Red, Skinny Head Pete, and Stormy Weather!
Listen, Black Boy.

Did the High Priestess at 27 rue de Fleurus
assert, "The Negro suffers from nothingness"?

(74)

This artful list Tolson terms the "real *ancients* of the jazz world" (cont. 7), and it is meant as self-evident refutation for an audience that recognizes any of these names.

Throughout his career Tolson collected information about African culture, particularly information that belied the myth of an Africa without a history or that unsettled the myths of European primacy. From Mommsen he collected the observation that "it was through Africa that [Christianity] became a world religion," and on the same sheet of paper, while reading Du Bois, Tolson is reminded that Moses married a black woman (cont. 4). From Franz Boas he copied out the assertion, "Any one who is familiar with the history of Africa before its subjugation by the Europeans knows the industrial skill, the artistic genius, the political ability of the Negro. In every region from West Africa through the Sudan to South Africa we have proof of it" (cont. 4). On draft pages of the *Libretto* he notes: "Culture of 14th Century Africa equal to Europe's" (cont. 9), and in the final version of the poem he transforms his historical researches into lyric genealogy:

> Solomon in all his glory had no Oxford.
> Alfred the Great no University of Sankore:
> Footloose professors, chimney sweeps of the skull,
> From Europe and Asia; youths, souls in one skin,
> Under white scholars like El-Akit, under
> Black humanists like Bagayogo.

(17)

Of Bagayogo he had also written in "The Negro Scholar": "When Anglo-Saxons laud the Venerable Bede, / Let Africans remember Bagayogo" (81). Of special interest to Tolson was the Kingdom of Benin. In the margin of his working drafts of the *Libretto* he notes that "Professor Van Luschan considered the craftsmanship of Benin workers equal to the best ever produced by Cellini" (cont. 9). Beyond seeing the arts of Benin as having equaled European accomplishments, he sees them as having been the source of much that is modernism: "The listening ear can hear / among the moderns, blue /

tomtoms of Benin" (*Harlem Gallery* 59). In his working draft for the *Libretto* he had already claimed for Benin an influence upon the most revolutionary reconceptualizing of space by modernist artists such as Braque and Picasso: "Benin, whose ivory and / bronze statues gave lyricism and / Space reality to modernistic art . . ." (cont. 8). By the time he completed the *Libretto,* he had upped the ante, contemporizing the claim in one direction while giving it greater specificity in another:

> The Bula Matadi, diesel-engined, fourfold-decked,
> swan sleek, glides like an ice-
> ballet skater out of the Bight of
> Benin, the lily lyricism of whose
> ivory and gold figurines larked
> space oneness on the shelf ice
> of avant-garde Art . . .
>
> (51)

Thus Africa is "No waste land yet" (*Libretto* 15), neither the dark continent portrayed by Eliot, Conrad, Stein, and Crane nor the waste land that Eliot's Europe had become, but out of Africa had come much of the most provocative aesthetics of the modern. Tolson finds:

> The ground the Negro Scholar stands upon
> Is fecund with the challenge and tradition
>
> That Ghana knew, and Melle, and Ethiopia,
> And Songhai: civilizations black men built
> Before the Cambridge wits, the Oxford dons
> Gave to the Renaissance a diadem.
>
> ("Negro Scholar" 81)

Robert M. Farnsworth in his biography of Melvin B. Tolson argues that "Tolson clearly saw himself in the vanguard of an army of black cultural soldiers who would make the African past a centerpiece of the world's future . . ." (168). This could only be accomplished, however, by displacing white hegemony not only over modernist aesthetics but also over the idea of America and its history. In adapting African musical traditions to the Western scale and tempered instruments, African Americans forever altered both the music of Africa and the

music of the West. In his plans to create a Harlem anthology that
would serve a function similar to that of the *Greek Anthology,* Tolson
had to look at both Harlem and the Western classical traditions differently (Tolson Papers, cont. 7). In writing *Libretto for the Republic
of Liberia,* which is organized in sections following the Western musical scale, Tolson, who had already begun to rearticulate modernism
as virtuoso African-American form, undertook a confrontation with
American history on a transformed ground, displacing white experience from its position of centrality and refiguring both the Middle
Passage and the Pilgrim story.

His earlier poem "Rendezvous with America" had begun this process by placing the experiences of the Middle Passage on an equal
level with the mythic progenitors of white America: "Time unhinged
the gates / Of Plymouth Rock and Jamestown and Ellis Island"
(cont. 9). "Rendezvous with America," having unhinged accepted historical primacies, adopts a questioning rhetorical strategy:

> America?
> America is the Black Man's country,
> The Red Man's, the Yellow Man's,
> The Brown Man's, the White Man's.

In this enumeration the white man's claim to proprietorship comes
last, and thus "Rendezvous with America" sets the pattern for the
Libretto in both form and rhetorical stance. The *Libretto* does not stop
at its allusion to the fact that Africans preceded the Pilgrims in the
New World ("'the Negroes have been in this country longer, on the
average, than their white neighbors; they first came to this country
on a ship called the Jesus one year before the Mayflower'" [62n]);
it portrays the founding of Liberia as an altered return to a site of
civilization that precedes the American:

> Before Liberia was Songhai was: before
> America set the raw foundling on Africa's
> Doorstep, before the Genoese diced west,
> Burnt warriors and watermen of Songhai
> Tore into *bizarreries* the uniforms of Portugal
> And sewed an imperial quilt of tribes.
>
> (16)

At the opening of his *Libretto* Tolson recalls the form of his own earlier poem while simultaneously seeming to offer answers to Countee Cullen's questioning refrain in "Heritage," "What is Africa to me?" (250), *and* distancing himself again from Eliot's "Waste Land":

> *Liberia?*
> No micro-footnote in a bunioned book
> Homed by a pedant
> With a gelded look:
> You are
> The ladder of survival dawn men saw
> (13)

Liberia is not the ahistorical blank of Eliot's Africa; neither is it the impotent tribal dirge of the Eliotic modern. It is rather the fecund soil upon which African and American histories rerendezvous, the territory upon which both histories are to be reconstituted. Middle Passage and colonizing pilgrimage cross here in a reconstruction that undoes canonical versions of American heritage. Where his earlier poem had claimed for African Americans a rendezvous with America at Plymouth Rock, in the *Libretto* Tolson figures forth a black pilgrimage, one that retraces the Middle Passage to rewrite a redemptive history on the territory of a new, African-Americanized Africa. Tolson, writing to an unidentified correspondent, said this of his intentions:

> In the fifth section, I picture the brig *Elizabeth* taking Elizah Johnson and his Black Pilgrim Fathers to West Africa. The dilemma again: the White Pilgrims sail west, but the Black Pilgrims sail east! Using a new stanzaic form—
>
> > This is the Middle Passage: here
> > Gehenna hatchways vomit up
> > The living and the dead.
> >
> > This is the Middle Passage: here
> > The sharks grow fattest and the stench
> > Goads God to hold his nose!
>
> I tried to pack into these lines the tragedies of thousands of blacks lost on their [way] to America. Later, I picture the Black Pilgrims

landing on Providence Island. I hope I've captured the heroism of it! At least nobody has tried to do it before in verse. (cont. 8)

One cannot help but think here again of Tolson's story in *Harlem Gallery* of the sea turtle eating its way through the devouring shark to freedom. The same waves that wash over the bones of many thousands gone during the Middle Passage now reverse the myth of English pilgrimage and carry African Americans to their Providence Island, where they will build an Africa made different by the American sojourn. The Black Pilgrim Fathers will establish Liberia as a city on a hill, as "A moment of the conscience of mankind!" (15). Reversing the colonial expropriation of African resources, Liberia is to make possible the defense of freedom on African soil against racist, European adventures that threaten all the world:

> *The rubber from Liberia shall arm*
>
> *Free peoples and her airport hinterlands*
> *Let loose the winging grapes of wrath upon*
> *The Desert Fox's cocained nietzcheans*
> *A goose-step from the Gateway of the East!*
>
> (20)

A New World music is to sound for a "Futurafrique" in which the "Parliament of African Peoples signets forever the *Recessional of Europe*" (55). The ethos of this new New World is summed up in Tolson's citation of the words of Jehudi Ashmun, the white pilgrim who overturned the founding mythos of America by sailing to a lost colony of freed slaves in West Africa:

> "My Negro Kinsmen,
> America is my mother,
> Liberia is my wife,
> And Africa is my brother."
>
> (29)

No elitist betrayal of populist poetics, the *Libretto* draws upon many of the most ready-to-hand mythic figurations to point the way to the Futurafrique's realization of the American democratic promise in African lives on African soil:

> The Parliament of African Peoples plants the winged
> *lex scripta* of its New Order on
> Roberts Avenue, in Bunker Hill,
> Liberia . . .
>
>   (52)

Here will be realized the Whitmanian democratic vistas "with leaves
of grass and great audiences . . ." (53). If the Parliament of African
Peoples also "trumpets the abolition of itself" (55), it is more a sign
of Tolson's lingering Marxism, his hope for an eventual withering
away of oppressive state apparatus, than of any doubt about his, or
Africa's, project. The Parliament will abolish itself eventually because,
as American mythology claimed for its institutions, the "Parliament
of African Peoples decrees the Zu'lhijyah of Everyman," and in eter-
nizing "*Afrika sikelel' iAfrika* . . ." (53) the *Libretto* simply sounds the
notes of self-saving determination that are today a rallying cry for the
liberation movements in South Africa: "Africa save Africa."

Tolson's *Libretto for the Republic of Liberia,* in the process of redirecting America's founding myths and redeploying the sources of
modernist influences, also displaces the hegemonic view of African-
American intellectual development as secondary and imitative by
erecting as its own framework the trope of African-American pilgrimage to literacy and educational independence. Following in the
tradition of Frederick Douglass, W. E. B. Du Bois, Mary McLeod
Bethune, and other writers, Tolson was, in the *Libretto,* memorializing
the liberatory impetus of black educational institutions. In addition
to placing in his poem allusions to the legendary centers of African
learning such as Timbuktoo, which rival and precede many Anglo-
American centers for the dissemination of white intellectual hegemony, Tolson has created a poem in the *Libretto* whose very being is a
commemorative to Tolson's African-American alma mater, as well as
to African learning and philosophy generally.

Tolson's status as the only American artist to have been named Poet
Laureate of another nation, Liberia, is more often noted with surprise and credited to Tolson's own cleverness than reckoned for what
it most immediately is, tribute to the institutions that have contrib-
uted most to the ongoing cultural cross-fertilization of African and
African-American life. Few white American intellectuals are at all

familiar with the histories of what we have come to call historically black colleges and universities, fewer still know that two of the most important African-American poets, Melvin B. Tolson and Langston Hughes, both studied at Lincoln University, fewer yet are aware of Lincoln's place of primacy as the oldest such institution in North America, and I doubt that any of Tolson's earliest white critics knew of Lincoln's connection with the history of Liberia before learning about it from Tolson. Writing to Dr. Horace Mann Bond, a classmate of his at Lincoln who had later been named to the presidency of the university, Tolson promises: "In my *Notes* to the poem (it requires them) I am seeing that Lincoln University shall come to the attention of the superintellectuals of the English-speaking worlds" (qtd. in Farnsworth 146). I believe we are justified in reading more than a little irony in Tolson's reference to Anglo-American superintellects. Little of the history he was contending with in his *Libretto* was known to these superintellectuals, many of whom blithely assumed that Africa and its diaspora had no history to speak of. The *Libretto*'s notes were required at least in part to alert readers to the documentary evidence of this history; it was then up to the readers themselves to contend with the implicit ironies.

Tolson's notes inform us that "Lincoln University, the oldest Negro institution of its kind in the world, was founded as Ashmun Institute. The memory of the white pilgrim survives in old Ashmun Hall and in the Greek and Latin inscriptions cut in stones sacred to Lincoln men. The annual Lincoln-Liberian dinner is traditional, and two of the graduates have been ministers to Liberia" (64n). The annual dinner and the contributions of Lincoln alumni to American-Liberian diplomacy both mark originary links between the school and the African nation. The American Colonization Society, formed in 1816, was not, as its name might imply, a society for the furtherance of American imperial desire but a society organized to work for the repatriation of Africans to their native continent. As such, it was simultaneously a colonizing and decolonizing undertaking. It was their lost colony that Jehudi Ashmun and his wife sailed to join, along with a number of freed African Americans, in 1822. Ashmun Institute was established by that same American Colonization Society for the purpose of training future leadership for Liberia. Ashmun Institute was subsequently rechristened Lincoln University. (As it happens, Tolson had been a student at Lincoln High School in Kansas City and had published juvenilia in the *Lincolnian* in 1917 and 1918.) What Tolson found in all this was a powerfully fecund metaphorical site on which the boundaries between colonizer and colonized, between primary and secondary, original and imitation, were so fluid as to become less than boundaries, undoing the traditional typology of the story of America's progress. For Tolson, Middle Passage and pilgrimage are terrible mirror images of each other reflecting historical horrors and redemptive human possibility. There is a city on a hill in Africa that is both precedent and descendant to the New Canaan in America. The Atlantic becomes a profoundly signifying divider, like the "*paseq*" that Tolson inscribes in his *Libretto,* drawn from his copy of Holy Scripture, and that he calls the "most mysterious sign in the literature" (66n). It is an unsounded textual sign floating an oral and oracular tradition. It is an interruption that denies the boundary lines we would draw between Scripture and speech, between *écriture* and lecture, an unspeakable parting of the scriptural seas. Tolson places these powerful signs in play, displacing the priority of the master text between whose lines he inscribes. This was not a symptom of arcane obfuscation but an opening of textual possibilities that others might follow. Tolson teased his students often by telling them that the white man put everything he didn't want black people to know in the library. Like William Carlos Williams's, Tolson's texts broke through the library walls, releasing knowledge and language from their prison house. They are an assault upon Anglo-American modernism's territorial designs, and they have not been read much.

> Behind the curtain, aeon after aeon,
> he who doubts the white book's colophon
> is truth's, if not Laodicean, wears
> the black flower T of doomed Laocoon.
>
> (*Libretto* 34)

These lines, looking back to Hawthorne's "black flower of civilized society, a prison" (*Libretto* 66n), though they indicate Tolson's cognizance of the difficulties his text would encounter in the Great White World, are not where he chose to end. He ends instead at the point where the scale completes its ascent to the originary note, where pilgrimage and Middle Passage join, where:

The Parliament of African Peoples pinnacles *Novus*
    Homo in the Ashmun Interna-
    tional House, where, free and
    joyful again, all mankind unites,
    without heralds of earth and water . . .

                                  (52)

He ends: *"Honi soit qui mal y pense!"* (55). He ends, as he will end
Harlem Gallery, chronicling "a people's New World odyssey" (*Gallery*
173). The texts of Melvin B. Tolson have not been read much, but
they have been read to great effect. They have worked their influence
on both sides of that permeable but impassable *paseq* of American
culture, the endlessly reinscribed line descried by W. E. B. Du Bois
as the problem of the twentieth century, the color bar. The white
poet William Carlos Williams, reading a section of Tolson's *Libretto*
in *Poetry* magazine, immediately replicated Tolson's audacious act by
writing Tolson's poem into book 4 of *Paterson* and by inscribing his
own reading between the lines of Tolson's text (*Paterson* 183–84). And
the works of Melvin B. Tolson have had incalculable effects among
African and African-American thinkers, both aesthetically and politically. There is at least one thing that two West African writers and
activists had in common with Lyndon Baines Johnson. Johnson signed
a note to Tolson thanking him for the autographed copy of his book
that Tolson had presented to the White House library during a visit to
the executive mansion. Years earlier, at the request of Horace Mann
Bond, Tolson had inscribed special copies of *Libretto for the Republic of
Liberia* for two African populists whose interest in reading his work
may have been more immediate. One of these was Nnamdi Azikiwe, a
former Lincoln student who went on to serve as president of Nigeria
and who authored the book *Renascent Africa*. The other, also a Lincoln University graduate, was the first postcolonial leader of Ghana,
Kwame Nkrumah. In the years 1943–45, while he was a student at
Lincoln, this young, radical African scholar held a number of important meetings with an African-Caribbean scholar, a dedicated reader
of poetry, who was in the United States doing the difficult work of cultural and political organizing against capitalist hegemony, meetings
for the discussion of a topic Tolson would certainly find interesting,
"the value and techniques of illegal work" in decolonizing Africa and

securing a modern African territory (Buhle 136–37). This African-Caribbean revolutionary scholar with whom the African revolutionary scholar met on the grounds of this oldest of African-American intellectual institutions was C. L. R. James. Thus was the intellectual triangle trade that Tolson tropes in his poetry embodied and enacted. It remains to be seen how the world shall construe its reading.

Then Peter say, "You must

   Be crazy, I vow,

Wherein hell dja think Hell *was*,

   Anyhow?"

—Sterling Brown, "Slim in Hell"

   It is not Dante,

nor Yeats. But the loud and drunken

pilgrim, I knew so well

in my youth. And grew to stone

waiting for the change.

—Amiri Baraka, *The Dead Lecturer*

Amiri Baraka and the Harrowing of Hell

If Amiri Baraka has not been castigated in quite the same way that Melvin B. Tolson often is for having modeled his poetic revolution at least in part on the breakthroughs of some of the white poets he read and learned from, it is no doubt due to the public vehemence with which he distanced himself from white influences in the period during which his works explored a philosophy of cultural nationalism. Early in his career he was sometimes dismissed by white academics because of his similarities to Allen Ginsberg, Jack Kerouac, Robert Creeley, Charles Olson, and Frank O'Hara and because of some white critics' racist inability to discern the differences in his developing work from those other writers. More recently, some reviewers dismiss him precisely for not writing enough like those earlier models, while other critics point to the continuities that exist in his early and later styles. But where Tolson has been attacked for deliberately transforming his work under the influence of high modernism, Baraka publicly and deliberately worked his way apart from those postmodernist artists with whom he had earlier linked his projects. Baraka's efforts to separate himself further from the white poets he worked with and learned from in the early fifties and sixties were not, however, an abandonment of the postmodern critique of contemporary forms; rather, they were an intensification of that critique. While much of Baraka's writing from the late sixties and early seventies champions the metanarratives of cultural nationalism and its attendant myths, and while his work since that time rests upon the metanarrative of Marxist historicizing totality, his greatest contribution as a writer may be his creation of an African-American postmodernist mode of poetics, one that subjected its early white influence to a scathing interrogation and emerged as one of the most powerful developments in recent American verse. He went to jail and through hell to accomplish this.

On numerous occasions Baraka has spoken of his only published novel, *The System of Dante's Hell,* as the locus of his struggle to extricate himself from what he had come to view as the confining influence of his early models. Because of his later period of nationalism, this has inevitably raised profound questions about his having turned to the *Inferno.* As Jerry Ward has formulated the seeming paradox: "How does so thoroughly European a work, canonized by histories of taste and intentions, function for a twentieth century Black American writer in quest for alternatives to the Western literary tradition?" (58). But what Baraka, perhaps intuitively, had come to realize as he moved toward a confrontation with his own influences over the ground of style was that, as Ward goes on to assert, "for the black writer immersed in European literature, the gesture of liberation is not retreat (which is largely impossible) but frontal assault. The gesture may or may not be conscious" (59). At some level Baraka understood that as a writer attempting a revolution in a Western language, there was no eliding the force of that language's literary history. One could not simply step aside and write in a different language, nor could one leave the weight of learned Western tradition behind to rejoin, uninflected, an African language tradition. What was required was a deliberate contestation for power within an American language, a struggle to achieve the rightful place of power for African-American language and form, a confrontation with the writing of the West on the ground of its farthest outpost. Homi Bhaba has described Fanon's realization of that same necessity: "I take the language and make of it, and I use it, and I use the advantages of it and I expel what is not advantageous in it, and that is the sign of my freedom—that I can use that language, that I can question. I'm not a fixed entity in time and space, I'm an evolving cultural agent" (Interview 67). *The System of Dante's Hell* is the sign of Baraka's freedom. In subjecting postmodern modes of poetic creation to a descent into the hell that late twentieth-century Western civilization had prepared for its citizenry, in using the canonical form of Dante's *Inferno* as a structuring guide for his surreal meditations upon the infernal forces brought to bear by the West upon African peoples, Baraka was harrowing his own language. Expelling what he has so often referred to as the uselessly literary, he was making clean in a trial by fire that which he found to be the usefully literary. Refusing to be celebrated as a prodigious, though fixed, literary entity, Baraka hoped upon entering this hell to be an evolving cultural agent, one "who is loud / on the birth / of his ways," one who would not be satisfied to remain within the identity he had constructed in his early work and who could proclaim as he does in *The Dead Lecturer*, "When they say 'It is Roi / who is dead?' I wonder / who will they mean?" (79).

Over the years since, Amiri Baraka has often attested to the value of those early literary relationships with the poets of the Black Mountain, Beat, and New York schools. In a personal interview some years ago he reiterated his belief that "they were, and certainly still are, very important poets who *must* be learned from." The poets he had joined forces with in one mode or another, many of whom he published in the magazine *Yugen* and the newsletter the *Floating Bear*, and among whom he appears as the only African-American poet in Donald Allen's essential *New American Poetry* anthology, formed a sort of united popular, and populist, front against the deathly forms of midcentury verse that had caused the young Leroy Jones to despair of his ever being a writer with a public to address. In *The Autobiography of LeRoi Jones* Baraka remembers vividly his feelings upon looking into an issue of the *New Yorker:*

> I had been reading one of the carefully put together exercises *The New Yorker* publishes constantly as high poetic art, and gradually I could feel my eyes fill up with tears, and my cheeks were wet and I was crying, quietly softly but like it was the end of the world. . . . I was crying because I realized that I could never write like that writer. Not that I had any real desire to, but I knew even if I had the desire I could not do it. I realized there was something in me so *out,* so unconnected with what this writer was and what that magazine was that what was in me that wanted to come out as poetry would never come out like that and be *my* poetry. (118)

It was not, however, the end of that twenty-two-year-old poet's world, and by the time he had begun to publish as LeRoi Jones, he had found a way to make a public place for that within him that was so "*out,*" and he had begun to make common cause with other writers unlikely to find a welcome at the *New Yorker.*

"I tended to be kind of at the cross-roads of all those schools," Baraka reminisced during our discussion of that period. Already an activist, he had come to understand the politics of publication in the genteel, late New Critical era of the early fifties and had begun working to create places where the new, postmodern aesthetic could emerge, places like his magazine *Yugen,* the newsletter the *Floating Bear,* and his living room. As much an instigator, proselytizer, and teacher as a student, Baraka did indeed become a sort of nexus for the forces of the new, antiestablishment, democratic front of young poets in the Pound-Williams line of descent. "I think Ginsberg and Olson really opened up my eyes about form," he recalls, but he "learned from all those guys." Even at that early stage Baraka was a highly politicized artist, and his subsequent differentiations among those early influences are often marked along lines of political interest: "The thing that brought Olson and me together was his enormous intelligence and the great deal of information he had, about poetry in particular. . . . I think Olson and I were closer politically than Robert Creeley and I were. Olson is aiming at a materialist kind of line."

These years in which he entered into relationships with white writers as diverse and "out" as Ed Dorn, Diane di Prima, Fielding Dawson, Olson, Creeley, Ginsberg, Paul Blackburn, and others are also the years in which he was meeting other young black writers, such as A. B. Spellman, Tom Weatherly, Askia Toure, poets who remain largely invisible to the critical establishment to this day; all these writers, white and black, were drawn together for similar reasons. Introducing his anthology *The Moderns,* in which portions of *The System of Dante's Hell* appear, Baraka placed his fellow authors in a determinedly postcolonial context: "Let me just say that the work in this collection does exist out of a continuing tradition of populist modernism that has characterized the best of twentieth-century American writing. [Its] common stance, if one can be honestly found (and I obviously believe one can) is perhaps one of *self-reliance,* Puddin'head Wilson style" (xvi). Further, he identified this writing as being in a more adamantly American mode than that which "had been cut off from that tradition by the Anglo-Eliotic domination of the academies" (x–xi), and he declared that the characters presented in the fictions found in this volume, after the fashion of Melville, were renegades and castaways:

> Selby's hoodlums, Rechy's homosexuals, Burroughs's addicts, Kerouac's mobile young voyeurs, my own Negroes, are literally not included in the mainstream of American life. These characters are people whom Spengler called *Fallaheen,* people living on the ruins of a civilization. They are Americans no character in a John Updike novel would be happy to meet, but they are nonetheless Americans, formed out of the conspicuously tragic evolution of modern American life. The last romantics of our age. (xiv)

Out of this rich mix of romanticism, politics, and aesthetic "outness," Baraka composed poems in the fifties and sixties that, while they are unmistakably *his,* equally unmistakably bear a family resemblance to those of his mentors and friends. In fact, it may be those poems that are most clearly the product of Baraka's brilliant meshing of sociopolitical exploration with fast, harsh, lyric prosody that also most clearly recall the styles of Olson and Creeley. These lines from the closing canto of "A Poem for Willie Best" illustrate the resemblance:

His head is
at the window. The only
part
   that sings

(The word he used
     (we are passing St. Marks place
     and those crazy jews who fuck)

                                    to provoke

in neon, still useful
in the rain,
   .To provoke
some meaning, where before
there was only hell.

                                       (*Lecturer* 26)

In 1947, Charles Olson had written these lines in the poem "Move Over," finally published in 1951, which make use of similar diction and prosody to make an equally political statement:

Merchants.   of the sea and of finance

(Smash the plate glass window)

The dead is the true face
of Washington, New York, a misery, but north and east
the carpenter obeyed
topography

                                       (*Collected* 66)

In the years 1956–58, Robert Creeley composed a poem titled "Goodbye" that underscores the accuracy of Baraka's observations about the relative political distance between Olson, Creeley, and himself. Creeley's poem enacts the same sort of syntactic compression using similar diction to a more immediately interior purpose:

          She stood at the window. There was
          a sound, a light.
          She stood at the window. A face.

          Was it that she was looking for,

he thought, was it that
she was looking for. He said,

turn from it, turn
from it. The pain is
not unpainful. Turn from it.
                    (*Collected* 159)

In retrospect what is remarkable is the diversity among these poets,
how each of them, moving toward his own necessities, could take from
each of his friends just so much as was needed at a time when their
isolation from the literary mainstream in America must have seemed
unbreachable, at a time when their own support of one another was
the only type of support forthcoming.

But for Baraka it became a constricting relationship. Increasingly
as his work developed through the early sixties, Baraka felt that the
forms he had arrived at with the models of his white friends and
earlier white poets before him were inadequate to the expression that
proceeds from African-American experiences, and that the language
of the New American Poetries as they were then constituted brought
with it the weight of political views and historical conditions that were
no longer his. The interior resistance he felt as he struggled to find
a place in his poetry for his more strongly politicized and national-
ist views is evident in "Notes for a Speech," the poem that concludes
Preface to a Twenty Volume Suicide Note and presages the tone of *The
Dead Lecturer:*

                    Black

words throw up sand
to eyes, fingers of
their private dead. Whose
soul, eyes, in sand. My color
is not theirs. Lighter, white man
talk. They shy away. My own dead souls, my, so called
people. Africa
is a foreign place. You are
as any other sad man here
american.

                                        (47)

As the first-person narrator of the tale "Heroes Are Gang Leaders" puts it, Baraka could not rest with the feeling that he was "merely writing poems for Joel Oppenheimer and Paul Blackburn," but wanted to address himself to "everything alive" (*Tales* 65) and to help his "own dead souls" in the fight for self-determining life. More and more he found himself arguing against the bohemian political quietism of many of his friends and against the tendency among the more politically oriented of his white associates to subsume the distinct historical situatedness of black Americans under some, to their view, larger sensibility. "That whole book, *The Dead Lecturer*," Baraka told me in our 1979 interview, "actually is about that—trying to see my way out of this kind of morass of connections with things I wasn't totally in favor of." Setting out to free himself from that morass, to get away from the feeling he was beset by that he was falling back upon riffs laid down by Creeley, Olson, and others (*Autobiography* 167), he began a series of directed prose improvisations, surreal cantos based upon his own memory impressions, which he later linked to Aimé Césaire's project in *Return to My Native Land* (*Autobiography* 166). Offering an explanation that he has repeated frequently in other interviews and in his memoirs, Baraka told me:

> In terms of trying to get away from that whole form and content that I thought was boxing me in, I wrote this thing called *Dante*. . . . I just wrote . . . I abandoned any attempt to make sense. I just wanted to find out what I really wanted to say somewhere, instinctively, automatically, without any prethought about it. Although, I developed a method of doing that where I would focus on an image that I wanted to talk about, and I would write all the things that that image conjured up in my mind. And I found I could get away from all those old, ready-made forms . . . and that's the way I broke out of it.

The experiment Baraka embarked upon was simultaneously an exploration of the history that had brought him to this moment, a confrontation with the infernal oppression of black people in this land, and a cleansing in the cauldron of experience for his literary language, searing off the "useless" and revealing the "useful." We should not be surprised, then, to find that Baraka's language after this experience is not radically different from the forms and diction of his earlier works. He still scores his page directed by his own take on Olson's ideas of projective verse; his poetry is still measured by the breath and body guided by theories he'd felt out in black music and found replicated in the practice of the Beat and Black Mountain schools. His subsequent works often make a greater stretch in time, like the jazz soloists who so strongly affected his aesthetics. They are also often more direct and make even greater use of scripted black syntax. But they continue to appear in the staccato, imagistic, and at least somewhat abstract forms of *The Dead Lecturer* as recently as the poems of his epic sequence in progress, *Wise / Why's:*

> dirt growing in his mind
> songs black land came in to
> curl your poetry blind.
> Banjo
> waves and sinking bones
> play eyes on sky
> blood music
>   (*Reader* 491–92)

The superficial differences in Baraka's verse after the mid-sixties are matters of degree, placing stronger emphasis upon elements that had been present all along. What has happened is that in writing *The System of Dante's Hell,* in progressing from the short, surreal bursts of the early sections to the "fast narrative" of the later sections and reaching a form he felt to be "genuinely" his own, in which he could "begin to stretch out, to innovate in ways [he] hadn't thought of before" (*Autobiography* 167), Baraka was refracting a blacker form for the postmodern. By the time he had reascended from his journey through the given, he had made these modes his own and had established the poetic practices that would serve as the proving ground for a theory of the Black Aesthetic.

The choice of Dante as the site for such a confrontation is not at all contingent. In Dante Baraka saw not only the founder of a form and a tradition in epic verse but a poet who was deeply implicated in and suffering from the political battles of his day. Dante was the fomenter of a revolution in poetic diction, offering his scathing cantos in the vulgate of the people of his time, a populist strike that would have held obvious appeal for Baraka. In his *Inferno,* Dante had composed an effective lyric protest at man's departure from the divine telos, from the spiritual necessities of the race. In the words of Archibald T. MacAllister, whose introduction to the *Inferno* appeared during the period of Baraka's earliest publications, Dante's work was "the realm—or condition—of the 'dead people,' those who have rejected spiritual values by yielding to bestial appetites or violence, or by perverting their human intellect to fraud or malice against their fellow men" (xxv). This description could as easily be applied to the denunciations of Moloch by Allen Ginsberg and clearly coincides with Baraka's estimation of contemporary America. Dante's schemata provided a structure within which Baraka could carry out his destruction of the bohemian logos and his descent into the history of his own self, and Dante represented for Baraka his originary contact with the love of literature. Baraka recalls in his *Autobiography* that Nathan Scott, a professor at Howard University in Washington, D.C., had been the instigator of his first studies of Alighieri. "Nathan Scott's preaching about Dante," he reports, "conveyed an *intellectual* love for literature that I hadn't seen. It was like some minister pushing us toward Christ, but Scott was pushing us toward Dante Alighieri. And it was directly due to this that I later went back to read Dante when I was able" (75).

Just as Baraka had used rather than imitated the models he discovered in the poems of his white friends, he set out to use the *Inferno*. Theodore Hudson, remembering that in *Black Music* Baraka had defined such use as the employment of some idea or system to illuminate some other, possibly quite dissimilar system, argues that this is the sense in which Baraka "has 'used' in his system Dante's thematic concepts" (112). Thus, in breaking from Eurocentric practice for the telos of a black aesthetic, Baraka uses the form of invention derived from Dante and the postmodern languages of the New American Poetries to reach a parallel but different system of aesthetics and thought, to produce a difference within the American logos, to make American writing differ from itself, and to make black writing. William J. Harris notes the paradox this involves: "[R]ejecting the white avant-garde artists was also to be true to them; turning their weapons against them was still to use the weapons they gave him" (*The Poetry* 30). What Baraka understood about this paradox was twofold: First, the weapons he held were all that he was to have; second, those weapons would be altered *by* his use of them. In writing his name across the page of American literature he was making a black mark against it and making it a black art. It is a deliciously Dantesque paradox. Dante, following Virgil, finds that he must climb *down* Satan's haunches to reach *up* toward Purgatory and Paradise. Even in recent works such as *Wise / Why's*, Baraka presents this paradoxical other-directedness as being an aspect of black consciousness in North America, a postindustrial variant of Du Bois's double consciousness:

> heaven people
> say see heaven
> they seeing
> up side down
> (*Reader* 492)

The white man's heaven is the black man's Hell. (Traditional)

We had been in jail scarcely twenty minutes, when a swarm of slave traders, and agents for slave traders, flocked into jail to look at us, and to ascertain if we were for sale. Such a set of beings I never saw before! I felt myself surrounded by so many fiends from perdition. A band of pirates never looked more like their father, the devil. They laughed and grinned over us, saying, "Ah, my boys! We have got you, haven't we?" . . . Then they would curse and swear at us, telling us that they could take the devil out of us in a very little while, if we were only in their hands. (Douglass, *Narrative* 310)

> (devil dropped a book on my head)
> (Baraka, *Selected Poetry* 48)

In his article "*The System of Dante's Hell:* Underworlds of Art and Liberation," Jerry Ward characterizes *The System* as "a novel of purest iconoclasm, the godterms of Euro-American culture being exposed for the empty shells of meaning that they are. The telos of the American system of hell (existence) is death" (62). In Baraka's novel the telos of Western civilization is withdrawn from the beyond of either afterlife or posthistory and is shown to have been empty all along. What Baraka gives his readers is a divine comedy devoid of divinity, of either God or Satan, in which all the most oppressive demons are human, in which all sin is against others or self. It is not the Sartrean hell composed of all "other people" but one that some other people have prepared for the rest of us. Where Milton wrote to justify the ways of God to man, Baraka writes to show that "justification" is an empty signifier, that the progress of the West is no more really than a bridge to Newark, that "God is simply a white man, a white 'idea' in this society, unless we have made some other image which is stronger and can deliver us from the salvation of our enemies" (*System* 153). *The System of Dante's Hell* sounds the empty depths of Western justification. It does not yet offer that other, stronger image, but it blasts clear a space within the signifying systems of postmodernity that Baraka has spent much of his subsequent career attempting to fill, first with the mythos of cultural and racial essentialism and then with the progressive dialectic of Marxist teleology.

But it is first of all as a process of transforming the status of language that this novel must be viewed. Little attention has been paid so far to the columns Baraka wrote around this time for the newsletter he edited with Diane di Prima, the *Floating Bear,* but many of them bear directly upon an understanding of what Baraka was trying to accomplish in his prose. Writing in 1962 under the pseudonym "Johannes Koenig," Baraka proposed in a series of notes entitled "Names and Bodies" a number of tenets, reminiscent of Gertrude Stein in some ways, that are adamantly antihumanist even as they attempt to turn our attention to a more "human" view of art and thought. In these notes Baraka denounces the artifactualism of the humanist tradition in its post–World War II guise and quickly dispenses with a humanist heaven:

> HEAVEN
> (a repository of nouns? Names
> Artifacts again?) God I hope not. And equally HELL, I
> really believe is the place only where what surface of
> your being comes closest to being irremediably *lost* (to
> you, i.e., is Named . . . thruout all eternity.
>
> HELL again a simple receptacle for
> a process. Verb surfaces, articulations. A place
> of *naming.*
>
> (272)

This description of an odd sort of inverse Adamic moment, a hellish naming, easily applies to the style of *The System of Dante's Hell*, quickly named surfaces bristling past on the dark streets of the damned and the lost, where they have been driven together by the deific Super Makers as products of a system. But hell too, in Baraka's view, is a nominative nowhere: "HELL any positivist can tell you 'does not exist.' There is no such *place*. But I feel there is an area of act that is hell. A process of hellishness. Of being Hell. Hell-ing" (*Bear* 272). *The System of Dante's Hell* is that area of act, and it is a dedication to poetry *as* act that marked one of the points of congruence between Baraka and the other writers of the New American Poetries. In such a no-place as Baraka describes there can be no place for the a priori knowledge that once held the West afloat in a sea of belief, nor for that tightly knit web of reason as given us by the Enlightenment. Baraka's inferno is lodged in the gap into which Reason collapsed in the modern era. Baraka's knowledge of that gap and of its inhabitants is firsthand; he knows that this is where he lives. He places himself in opposition to the kind of academics who overlook the gap in fixing their gaze upon the artifactual past. In his guise as Johannes Koenig, Baraka argues:

> The Structure of the Academy is:
>
> > Against, the street, or, versus.
>
> Knowledge, THERE, for the taking. What is around, us,
> all. The Radio.
>
> You can pick up things, I say! Look Here. Or wherever
> YOU work.
>
> But they go against the casual, for what? What is
> beneath their fingers and eaten earlier. Not
> necessarily Giotto, unless there is someone ate him, as
> I sd, Earlier.
> > > They, those walking groves of trees,
> Refuse mana. They refuse
> all light. Or, finally, feeling.
>
> > > > > > > (*Bear* 467)

(The mention of Giotto is intriguing here. The name of Giotto, painter of the only surviving contemporary portrait of Dante, refers

in a sort of deep etymology both to a foundry, the hellish place of fab-
rication, and to a ghetto [Mesher 402–3].) Though Baraka's persona
does follow a guide into "The Bottom" near the end of his narrative,
Theodore Hudson is right to point out that, unlike Dante, Baraka
is "a participant, a citizen" (112) in the hell of his writing. His is a
firsthand experience of the process of helling, one that will not seek
solace in the intervention of the incontrovertible deific:

> The purely expressive is First Principle. Where it proceeds from.
> Out of what (bag)) If art is, as I say, something that can make it
> seem extremely important to be a human being, then that must
> rule out so many things. (And I will put down here something
> like P's Progress because it harps too much on The Form this im-
> portance will take. Not because it is a closed ethical cycle . . . La
> Commedia is too . . . but because Bunyan got his ethics, his binding
> formulae, from dead gossip. The Italian, I think, was religious. He
> had been hit by the single rightness of his laws. (As Milton, assur-
> edly, wasn't. As no goddamned secular type protestant has EVER
> been. And Wont. And why? Because they wd always backtrack into
> Reason. To Explain it (in terms of Science, Economics, Physics).
> Mostly, of course, for the entrepreneur. So he cd get in . . . and sell
> peanuts during the recessional.)
>
> Milton comes almost purely out of hearsay too. I doubt if he had
> any real Visions. Bunyan was a deadbeat.
>
> .   .   .   .
>
> Nowledge never is seen as contemporarily available. It must come
> from some incontrovertible source. (Of course, we know there's
> not anything by that name in our modern world. In Dante's world
> there was.)
>
> (*Bear* 467–68)

Baraka is thus using the most canonical of Western poets, Dante, to
contest the rest of the canon, taking from Dante both form and example. Like Dante, Baraka writes of hell in the vulgate and peoples
it with the persons and texts of his own time, that which he knows
firsthand. Baraka knows what Dante knows, that there is to be no
direct deliverance from the bestiality he witnessed in hell, that he
would have to work his way through the horrors that faced him in

the postmodern Western world before he could "begin to put history back in our menu, and forget the propaganda of devils that they are not devils" (*System* 154). At the end of the prose piece "New Sense," Baraka speaks of "we black people caught up in Western values. So deeply. Having understood the most noble attempts of white men to make admirable sense of the world, now, reject them, along with any of them. And the Mozarts are as childish as the hitlers" (*Tales* 96). Baraka's vacating of Dante's form, Dante's scheme for making sense of the world, was the means by which Baraka sought to make sense of his world, now. Having gone so deeply into Western values, he found them empty shapes reflecting the inferno that had been constructed in their name. Salvation, if it was to be had at all, would come to those who passed through those gates, with their damning inscription, in order to dismantle them, the form of a process of helling.

The text produced by this means is not as random as it may appear, or as Baraka's own remarks about his mode of composition might lead us to expect. There are innumerable internal connections. For example, in portraying his earliest life, the protagonist remembers days when he "stayed at school and loved a girl named Peaches" (*System* 57). Near the end of the novel, in the climactic scenes in which the narrator finds his history in the Bottom, where his "history" ends and his white-talking persona dies "in the arms of some sentry of Africa" (129–30), it is a woman named Peaches (what fated fruit is this?) who brings him to himself as "no one the white world wanted or would look at" (130). Similarly, in the "Hypocrite(s)" chapter the character Otis addresses the narrator from the hellish perpetual future, telling him, "I still know Whatley and he still thinks you're a punk" (67). This is a ghastly prophecy from the future. Two chapters later, in "The Eighth Ditch (Is Drama," that same Otis, and then "Wattley," interrupt a scene in which one representation of the narrator's character is raped by another. There are, in addition, a number of connections to other works by Baraka, most particularly to the plays that he was just beginning to write. Ora Matthews, Ray, Foots, James Karolis, all figures familiar from plays such as *The Toilet*, appear, fixed forever in the hell of their youthful sin. In another instance, someone among "The Diviners" says, "You're going crazy . . . in here with dark glasses and the light off," to which the narrator adds, "It was a yellow bulb tho, and it sat well on my shoulders" (50). The leader in Baraka's short tale "The Alternative" is found in the same circumstances: "That cat's nuts. He was sittin' up in that room last night with dark glasses on . . . with a yellow bulb . . . pretendin' to read some abstract shit" (*Tales* 9). References to Dante abound, and they are far from superficial. Baraka's invocation of the *Vita Nuova* at the opening of his sixth chapter is apropos in a semiautobiographical work written in the vernacular, and written, at least in part, as an imaginative history of the author's polis and as an explanation of the author's own mode of writing. (Did Baraka learn from Nathan Scott, or later, that Dante had been a moderate "White" in the political and military clashes between the "Blacks" and "Whites" in Florence?) The novel is organized around the Bolgias of Dante's model, descending to the most evil ditches of the Malebolge, and the narrator is not merely the traveler within this course but the epic poet of its discourse, like Dante. As the youthful protagonist was found reading through dark glasses under a yellow light, so Dante is portrayed, "Lovely Dante at night under his flame taking heaven. A place, a system, where all is dealt with . . . as is proper" (99). In "THE JOINT," among the heretics, the identification is made complete as the narrator is guided toward the death of white history and the culmination in collapse of national epic: "He pointed, like Odysseus wd. Like Virgil, the weary shade, at some circle. For Dante, me, the yng wild virgin of the universe to look. To see what terror. What illusion. What sudden shame, the world is made" (126). The punishments rendered to the inhabitants of Baraka's hell are straight out of Dante. Among "Thieves," "(snakes writhe in the ditch, binding our arms. Our minds are strong. Our minds)" (76), and "The Diviners" suffer "Heads twisted backwards" (49). For an explanation of the confusing coextensiveness of times, Baraka cites the *Purgatorio* directly: "The portions of the Mountain under light and shade at noon day. Cf. *Purg*. IV. 'When it is 3 P.M. in Italy, it is 6 P.M. at Jerusalem and 6 A.M. in Purgatory'" (47), a portion of the *Purgatorio* in which Dante, pausing in midascent of the mountain, receives an explanation to relieve his confusion at finding the sun to his left. Beatrice appears among Baraka's cast, though she appears here in hell as a whore, and Baraka has a decidedly fifties American view of that forest we get lost in halfway through life: "Can you plunge into the woods? Lying by the stoop. Sell those gas heaters. Cook that food. Clean that building. Go to church" (43).

Hell is, throughout Baraka's novel, a discursive phenomenon. In a postscript titled "Sound and Image," which echoes the author's notes on hell and nomination in the *Floating Bear,* Baraka answers his own rhetorical question: "What is hell? Your definitions" (153). The line sustains an ambiguity Baraka renders across the course of this descent in his floating use of pronouns. "Your," the reader's, definitions supply hell with its rhetorical force and with the names that fill its evil ditches. At the same time, hell is a spiritual state configured for black people by white definition: "Hell in the head. . . . The flame of social dichotomy. Split open down the center, which is the early legacy of the black man unfocussed on blackness" (153). This explanation of his use of Dante's figures to form the hell that whites define for blacks in America again figures Du Bois's double consciousness behind the veil of racial definition. Baraka has come here to a stage in which he needs more "Bolgia academic brown leaves" (49) like he needs another hell in the head. What he needs, he feels, is to get back to where he was, as "Ishmael back, up through the thin winter smells" (11), moving toward a unified, unveiled consciousness. He does not dream of a return to undivided innocence, of an Edenic blackness with no memory of the oppressive sojourn in the West, but of a new spiritual state in which he has expunged the devils from his own heart. But at the opening of *The System of Dante's Hell* he *is* the betwixt and between Du Bois describes. Baraka writes: "Deep Blue Sea. I, myself, am the debil" (53).

All Baraka's literary past is present in this hell. A list of the authorial shades encountered in these ditches includes Thomas Hardy, Dylan Thomas, Baudelaire, Dante himself, John Wieners, Proust, Joyce, Eliot, Yeats, Olson, Ginsberg, Pound, Cummings, Apollinaire, Odysseus, Virgil, Beckett, Fielding Dawson, Bertran de Born, Thomas Jefferson, and a grouping that brings together "Shakespeare rattled drunkenly in the fog, folksingers, a thin Negro lying to his white girlfriend" (103). While the litany of African-American musicians in the novel is equally lengthy, black writers other than Baraka himself aren't significantly named in hell, partly owing to Baraka's doubts during these years about the viability of earlier "Negro" literature. "Were there really a Negro literature, now it could flower," he writes in "The Myth of a Negro Literature." "If there is ever a Negro literature, it must disengage itself from the weak, heinous elements of the culture that spawned it, and use its very existence as evidence of a more profound America" (*Home* 114–15). The narrator of Baraka's novel is attempting just such a prolonged disengagement. But, like Baraka's character Clay in *Dutchman*, this narrator who has read so deeply among the West's literary arts does have another profound tradition to draw upon, present by implication in the appearance of Baraka's grandfather in his hell. In his poem "Why Didn't He Tell Me the Whole Truth," Baraka remembers how his grandfather promised him a silver dollar if he'd learn James Weldon Johnson's classic "The Creation" by heart, an offer that seems to counter his mother's having him "saying the Gettysburg Address / in a boyscout suit" (*Selected Poetry* 174). Baraka never memorized Johnson's poem, but he found his grandfather Russ's copy of *One Hundred Amazing Facts about the Negro, with Complete Proof,* by J. A. Rogers, while plundering his grandfather's room, and in later life his grandfather increasingly served Baraka as an image of heroic pride. That same grandfather Russ, the image of a man who had his African-American literary tradition by heart, who carried African-American verse with him where he walked, is memorialized in *The System*. This "Race Man" is, appropriately, a trustee in the church, smiling and important, looked upon with awe by his grandson in the balcony (61).

But, as his presence here indicates, the church will not save him from *The System*, any more than the writers named can save themselves by their arts. As in the opening pages of the *Inferno*, the writers named by Baraka as he catalogs the inhabitants of hell occupy a status as virtuous, or not so virtuous, pagans. They seem to be arrayed at least partly according to Baraka's construal of their errors, and in part according to their value to him. Thus, while the narrator "loved Eliot for his tears" (58), Eliot's revision of the tradition is itself in need of revision because "Africans lived there and czechs" (58), and because in a consciousness that includes "A belly rub, a christmas tree, a negro. Autumn is correct always. In the dark instinct" (33–34). Eliot, who had little time for things African, recast a Waste Land that had still its Tiresias. For Baraka, having Eliot in his head was a sign of the prodigal's darkness he wrestled with. The companions of his childhood, for all their suffering, "still sprawl in light." "The prodigal lives in darkness," having "lost those clear days" (31). The light of the Western Enlightenment and its modernist fragmenting led to the sort of "blind adventure" Baraka's wandering prodigal finds his way through, the obscurity of that great forest in which "Eliot, Pound, Cummings, Apollinaire were living across from Kresges," and he "was erudite and talked to light-skinned women" (31). A double effect is achieved by Baraka by writing into his canticles these canonical and contemporary names. On the one hand, Baraka smashes the Euro-centric hold on Western art by "colorizing" the canon, by putting the Western tone scale of art through the signifying changes of African-American expressive transformation. (Things are indeed changed on the blue guitar, as Wallace Stevens told us.) Hence, in hell "Bach was colored and lived in the church with Handel. Beckett was funeral director with brown folding chairs. On W. Market St. in winter the white stripe ran down the center of my thots on the tar street" (11). At the same time, however, there is a process by which Baraka takes the canonical under his signifying control while becoming a part of it. In the fourth canto of Dante's *Inferno* at a similar moment, when the Italian bard has encountered the great patriarchs of Western verse, we read:

> They turned towards me with signs of recognition;
> And my master smiled to see them do so.
>
> And then, they did me a still greater honour;
> They took me as a member of their company,
> So that I was a sixth among those great intellects.
>
> So we went in the direction of the light,
> Talking of things of which it is well to say nothing,
> Although it was well to talk of them at the time.
>
> (63)

At this point in his journey Baraka is unguided, without a master, and as he writes *from* his hell, he does not feel the reticence Dante shows here with regard to explicitly detailing the conversations of the damned. Clearly, Baraka is a member of this company, and this is partly the cause of his own damnation. The white writers he names are "Hung in words, lying saints. The martyrs lose completely light" (*System* 29). The words of the saints, even the Beat saints, fail to illumine, fail to point the way to some concrete way out. But it is difficult for Baraka to put these devils behind him. "YOU LOVE THESE DEMONS

AND WILL NOT LEAVE THEM" (59), reads a legend in the eighth circle. One of Baraka's self-described sins was that in moving to bohemia he had distanced himself from the realities on the pavements of Newark, he "had forgotten all their blackness" (55), but he cannot leave entirely behind any of those he has encountered on his life's path. Even while moving back toward the grace of the remembrance of blackness, he looks back fatally to the songs that follow him from his friends: "I am myself after all. The dead are what move me. The various dead" (59).

This motion into and away from the canon was carried further in a curious way beyond the pages, but over the text, of *The System of Dante's Hell*. The dramatic section titled "The Eighth Ditch (Is Drama," one of the first portions of the book composed, was first published in issue number 9 of the *Floating Bear,* the newsletter Baraka co-edited with Diane di Prima. (In Baraka's account of this episode in his *Autobiography* he inexplicably identifies di Prima as "Lucia DiBella," though he uses her correct name in a different context.) The newsletter was sent free to a list of artists and writers, among whom was the young poet Harold Carrington, then completing a prison sentence in New Jersey. One of the first readers of Baraka's new work, in which he sought to write himself out from under the influence of white writers, was that most representative functionary of the established order, Carrington's prison censor. In October 1961, first Baraka and then di Prima were arrested by United States postal authorities and the FBI on charges of sending obscenity through the mails. Under Attorney Stanley Faulkner's advice, the *Floating Bear* editors requested a hearing before a grand jury. It is di Prima's recollection that Baraka provided the testimony at the hearing because only one of the editors was allowed to make a statement before the panel. In two days of testimony Baraka proved, to the satisfaction of this critical assembly at least, that he was part of the canonical company. Baraka's and di Prima's memories coincide on the manner of the presentation. "He brought in a ton of stuff that at one time or another had been labeled 'obscene': everything from *Ulysses* to Catullus. He read for hours to the grand jury, and they refused to return an indictment" (di Prima, *Bear* xiv–xv; Baraka, *Autobiography* 170). In later years Baraka was to have the experience of hearing his own work read to him by a judge as justification for sentencing the poet to jail time, but in this instance it was Baraka's reading from the canon before the bar that resulted in dismissal of the charge of obscenity against his writing in the vulgate, undertaken to separate himself further from the canon.

This only serves to complicate further Baraka's performance in *The System of Dante's Hell*. If he would claim his place among the hung martyrs of Western writing as a means of self-defense in the material present, it did not relieve him of the feeling that the canon was composed of lying words, or of the sense that he was recording, perhaps even encouraging, "the breakup of [his] sensibility" (9). "If there were a heaven he understood" (16), things might have proceeded otherwise, but from the situated perspective of Baraka in the early sixties, standing on a land made mad by the West's oppressive teleology, surrounded by the cultural debris of modernism's breaking up or down, the horrors organized by Dante's imagination didn't look so bad. "But Dante's hell is heaven," Baraka declares at the commencement of his novel; "look at things in another light" (9). Here at midcentury in America was a hell in which "the FBI showed up to purchase condoms. Nothing interesting was done for Negroes so they became stuck up and smelly" (16); a hell in which people "begged for Oscar Williams" (20) and in which "everybody wanted to be America" (75). It is a preternaturally postmodern hell in which fragments can no longer do anything more than fragment further. All is ruins, and those who hope to shore them up are gross deceivers. It is a hell in which Baraka's persona wakes up "with white men, screaming for God to help" him (152), but there is seemingly no salvation for those who have committed sins of "Violence / against others, / against one's self, / against / God, Nature and Art" (36).

When Baraka speaks of those "who live in blackness," it is clear that "they have no God save who they are. Their black selves" (122). The hell depicted by Baraka holds three broad classes of dead souls: the more or less virtuous pagans, those Western artists of the canon and Baraka's bohemian friends; those like the narrator, who are guilty of various sins of omission and commission with regard to the realities of their own nature and art; and the masses of the oppressed, whose only sin was the original one of being born in hope and happenstance. As was true in an odd sort of way of the *Inferno*, the force responsible for the establishment and maintenance of this hell is largely absent from its portrait; its effects are visible in the tortured lives of the damned, but it assumes no nameable form within the text. "God should be here. Should have his station, his final way of speech. More powerful than our dim halls . . ." (102), but that god is not here. The god terms of Western progress are discernible in their effects upon the dead souls: "Their travels out of hell, hells of the eastern city. Our country grew, its savages were given jobs" (103), but the perpetrators of this misery are an absent cause, somewhere off enjoying the *Paradiso* of their own empty texts.

This is to some extent why the most powerful passages in *The System of Dante's Hell*, those to which most criticisms of the novel inevitably return, are those in which Baraka's protagonist confronts the horrors of his own sin. There may be no ready redemption here, but Baraka must pass through the fires of his past, harrowing the forms of his own narration, before he can emerge as the remaker of the forms he inhabits. It is important when examining these crucial scenes of construction of and confrontation with the self as sinful to recall that this *is* a harrowing of structures. Each of the scenes in question, the notorious chapter "The Eighth Ditch (Is Drama" and the climactic episodes in "The Bottom," takes place within a structure of damnation that bears the imprint of those absent causes, the deific constructors of hell on earth. The action of "The Eighth Ditch" takes place in an encampment, equal parts perverse Scout training camp and military boot camp appropriately enough, as if the tradition represented by Grandfather Russ had been overrun and overruled by the tradition of memorizing the Gettysburg Address in a Boy Scout suit, the tradition of middle-class accommodation to militant oppression. Similarly, the action in "The Bottom" is bounded by the confines of a southern ghetto, the indelible mark of past slavery and present neocolonial constriction. The protagonist's penance, then, is played out within the ever more sin-ridden boundaries of American history, of slavery and ideological racism. Baraka's harrowing of this hell, this cleansing of himself and of his style, is a signifying rescue, a sort of rapture in which the damned are separated out from the damning, in which the expressive vulgate turns the infernal forms upon themselves.

In his 1961 note for the *Floating Bear* on the stage production of "The Eighth Ditch (Is Drama," one of Baraka's earliest theater productions, Joseph LeSeur remarks that "Jones' 'Dante,'. . . taken literally (it shouldn't be, of course), is about a gang bang in an army barracks, with one soldier on the receiving end. It can truly be said that no holds were barred in its staging; in fact, it was so graphic, so specific, that the imagination had no place to go" (*Bear* 168). Truly this most disturbing section of Baraka's inferno, which in its theatrical incarnation again attracted the attentions of the police, is in some ways about what happens to the imagination that is left nowhere to go. Baraka, who had gotten into trouble in the air force largely because of his reading, graphically displays for his audience a system of diabolical repression that enlists those with nowhere to go in its project and then so arranges things that they, in this case literally, "fuck" each other, much as Africans being transported to New World slavery were often placed under the lash of other Africans by the ship's captain. In "The Eighth Ditch," the narrator, who has been chronicling the breakup of his sensibility, becomes two characters, "46" and "64," who are known by their numbers as a sign of the systematic assault upon identity within the postmodern hell. As their numbers/names imply, 46 and 64 are inversions of each other, and their act is an inversion of the ideal of romantic love memorialized in Dante's cantos. 46 is "Brittle youth, . . . dead America" (79), his aesthetic largely borrowed and denatured. He hears, "exclusively," what he wants (85). A poet, his words come from elsewhere, though the details of his young life as he mentions them coincide with Baraka's own ("Even back here. Dey St. is where I live now & I control the Secret Seven" [*System* 81]) and with those recounted in the preceding "Newark" chapters. To the older, cynical 64, 46 is merely an object for him to act upon. "I'll never know you, as some adventurer," he tells 46, "but only as chattel. Sheep. A 'turkey' in our vernacular" (80). Between them these characters share two of the greatest of sins, and a horrific separation of mind and flesh. In Kimberly Bentson's estimation, this is one of those places where Baraka most closely follows Dante's practice: "The drama of Jones's eighth ditch, following the guiding principle of Dante's *Inferno*, inflicts punishment upon 46 that is the same as his sin, a punishment that is in fact a perpetuation of the sin. The schism between body and mind is a violence to both, and 46 embodies the rigidity of a personality condemned to repeat endlessly the gestures of perverse desires" (16).

46 speaks a godly language. He says, "I am as I am" (79), but he speaks, as 64 tells him, "some other tongue" (81), a diction he has schooled himself in as he has moved as far as he could from the likes

of 64. He tells 64, "I delivered papers to some people like you. And got trapped in it; those streets. . . . I could walk out of yr. life as simply as I tossed newspapers down the sewer" (81). 46, inverted as he is, responds to 64's provocations with the weakest kind of braggadocio. He claims to be stronger than people think he is, and challenges 64 to a game of dozens. But 64 wants none of that; he wants to press his hellish existence upon 46 and achieve immortality within him.

When 46 asks who 64 is, the older number replies, "The Street! Things around you" (80). In contrast to 46's elegance and foppishness, 64 posits the concreteness of existence at the core of oppressed life. 46 sits on the surface of his life and appears to 64 to be ignorant and weak. 64 wishes to be simultaneously the disabuser of 46's cherished notions, the abuser of 46's sham innocence, and the bringer of bald knowledge to 46's evasive thoughts. 64 occupies 46's present and his past at once. As an older, disabused version of 46, he knows what lies in store for this ephebe, but like the denizens of Dante's *Inferno,* he is a bit unclear about the present. He is able to tell 46, "It's 1947 and there are at least 13 years before anything falls right for you. If you live" (84), yet he doesn't know in the present of the play if his younger inverse has learned about jazz yet. In an exchange that prefigures the novel's end, 46 and 64 argue about the music, and 64 foretells this novel's writing:

64— . . . Do you know about jazz yet?

46— Jazz? Hell yes. What's that got to do with anything?

64— You don't know yet, so why shd I bother. I don't know really. I never will quite understand.
But I do
know you don't see anything at all clearly. Who's yr favorite jazz musician?

46— Jazz at the Philharmonic. Flip Phillips. Nat Cole.

64— Ha Ha . . . ok, sporty, you go on! Jazz at the Philharmonic, eh?

46— Yeh, that's right. I bet you like R & B & those quartets.

64— You goddamn right . . . and I probably will all my life. But

that's got nothing to do with anything. You'll know that
when you narrate my life. (83–84)

Laughing at 46's preference for the sweetened crossover sounds of
Jazz at the Philharmonic, 64 erupts into 46's present, disrupting his
placid fluency and muddying his future. 64, appearing as an under-
privileged Negro youth in the Boy Scouts, enters into, rapes 46, a
middle-class Negro Boy Scout, thrusting upon the younger character
an illicit, hellish knowledge. Answering his own rhetorical question
in the "Sound and Image" afterward to the novel, Baraka said hell
is "Your definitions" (153). Forcing himself as infernal futurity upon
46, 64 declares, "I know names that control your life that you don't
even know exist. Whole families of definitions" (84). 46's slicked-up
jazz is opposed to 64's funkier fury. 64 shouts, in a passage that looks
forward to the soliloquies of Clay in *Dutchman* and backward to the
lyrics to the spiritual "Nobody Knows the Troubles I Seen": "You
don't have any of the worries I got. I'm pure impression. yeh. Got
poetry blues all thru my shoes. I got. Yeah, the po-E-try blues. And
then there's little things like 'The Modern Jazz Blues.' Bigot blues. . . .
I'm pure expression. White friend blues" (86). 46's strangely detached
and distracted reaction to his violation by 64 underscores something
that is sometimes lost in reaction to the violence of this scene. These
two numeric characters require each other for completion, but it is
a completion that leads nowhere. Like the sodomites in the seventh
circle of Dante's *Inferno* running in endless circles over the Plain of
Burning Sand, these two form an empty circle that offers neither
surcease from his torments. Neither can imagine an alternative, and
neither can find a way out of his own horrific history.

As bad as this is, there is a yet greater sin in Baraka's system, and
he locates it in his version of the satanic city of Dis, "The Bottom,"
one of those southern ghettos America concocted for the sons and
daughters of slaves. This is the one portion of his journey for which
the narrator requires a guide, as Dante did, for he is entering an area
he has not inhabited in this lifetime. Here, where his personal history
is to end, the narrator denies his racial history in an act of heresy and
treason. Jerry Ward has remarked acutely that "within the system of
Baraka's hell, the ultimate sin in the Bottom is the refusal to embrace
the culture that is beyond the pale, the sight, smell, sound, feeling,

taste of Black culture in America" (62). Following his treachery and denial, the narrator will embrace each aspect of African-American culture Ward has enumerated, but while he exits the Bottom at the text's close, he does not exit in a state of grace; he has not yet saved himself, only seen the sins he must expiate.

In stepping off base, the pilot/narrator steps into a world that, while it gave him his grandfather Russ, has become foreign to him. He needs his guide and *is* lost without him. The two are out of place in the Bottom. In a sentence that recalls a conversation between Roxy and her son in Twain's novel *Pudd'nhead Wilson,* we read that "the men didn't dig the two imitation white boys" (128). It is as an imitation white boy that the narrator separates himself from blackness and commits the ultimate act of treachery. Having long passed the point where the last white riders left the bus they are on, the black airmen hop off at a stop a third of the way down the slope to the Bottom. The driver calls out:

> "Hey, son, 'dyou pay for him?" He asked me because I hopped off last. He meant not my friend, the other pilot, but some slick head coon in yellow pants cooling it at top speed into the grass and knowing no bus driver was running in after no 8 cents. . . .
>
> Friday night. Nigguhs is Nigguhs. I agreed and smiled, he liked the wings, had a son who flew. "You gon pay for that ol coon?"
> "No," I said, "No. Fuck, man, I hate coons." He laughed. I saw the night around his head warped with blood. (122–23)

It is this denial of the sign of his racial history that must be assuaged, and Peaches, destined fruit of his accession to knowledge of himself as black, is his final guide.

It is in the arms of Peaches, the "short-haired witch out of [his] mother's most hideous dreams," that the narrator's history ends, his telos is dispelled, his self as "light white talking jig" (129) dies. In losing his white self in Peaches, he is slowly, partially shorn of his sinful violence against his own past. Where before the devil had dropped a book on his head, here he reads in "the streets [he] used for books" (137). Where 46's tastes had run to Jazz at the Philharmonic, now the protagonist listens to "four guys on a bandstand who had taken off their stocking caps and come to the place with guitars," and joins in "dancing like a rite no one knew, or had use for outside their secret lives" (129). His history as an imitation white boy ends when, away from his earlier guide and in Peaches's arms, he finds his own history here. Peaches feeds him watermelon for breakfast. For lunch there are greens, knuckles simmering on the stove, biscuits, and chicken.

It is in the Bottom also that he sees white and black meeting without pretense and reveling in those most creative eruptions of American culture that flow from the gashes in the false bottom of American racial ideology. As the whites the narrator knew in Newark as a child spoke a blackened English ("our fays . . . took their mark from us" [73]), while at the same time coloring his own accents ("When i spoke someone wd turn and stare . . . The quick New Jersey speech, full of Italian idiom, and the invention of the jews" [128]), so white and black meet around the music of African America. In the Cotton Club, a "kind of ditch" named for that club in Harlem that provided black, "jungle" music for white patrons, the white and black working damned touch across the wholly constructed boundary line drawn between them by the racist powers-that-be in hell. The narrator sees a white stripe taped across the floor of the bar, running right up and over the bar itself. But against the backdrop of the music he also watches a black man and a white man standing to either side of the tape: "They talked, and were old friends, touching each other, and screaming with laughter at what they said" (133–34).

There is no salvation here, though, only movement from one level of perdition to another. According to Baraka's account of the real-life model for this episode, his two days AWOL in Shreveport's Bottom, he "finally came back rumpled and hung over and absolutely broke" (*Autobiography* 120). Frederick Douglass proposed in his *Narrative* that slave owners offered whiskey and holidays to slaves so that when the slaves crawled out of hangovers to the resumption of their labors in bondage, it would seem a relief (299). Baraka's narrator, having denied his real history, experiences a kind of death and rebirth in the Bottom, but he doesn't experience election. As Jerry Ward suggests, the protagonist learns to embrace the sight, sound, smell, and taste of black culture in America, but he cannot rest in that embrace. He cannot lose the world "and find sweet grace alone" (150). Rising, he leaves Peaches and starts back up the road out of the Bottom. But what might a prodigal son such as this expect following such a sojourn?

"What is left. If you return? You deserve to find dead slums" (38). For Baraka there is, in the early sixties, no easy step out of torment. There is only the insistence upon his being "a real thing in the world. See my shadow. My reflection. I'm here, alive. Touch me. Please. Please, touch me" (139). He has sounded the underworld of Ralph Ellison's *Invisible Man* and of Richard Wright's "The Man Who Lived Underground." He has been to the Bottom and found that there is no exit there. But he has become palpable as he has made his style, his poem, a black thing made out of words. At the end of *The System of Dante's Hell* he has fallen unconscious with "Negroes dancing around [his] body" and awakened "with white men, screaming for God" to help him (152). If God does not arrive to aid him, at least he can say at the end, "I sat reading from a book aloud and they danced to my reading" (152). In the more optimistic "Sound and Image" note Baraka has appended to this text, he asserts that while he might not have found salvation, "the world is clearer" to him now (154). He knows who the devils are, and having harrowed hell, he has wrested the form of his text from their grasp.

Ralph Ellison rewrote and recast Melville's American epic in African-American modernist terms at the beginning of *Invisible Man.* Baraka's Ishmael has survived the breakup of modernist sensibility; indeed, he seems to argue that African-American modernism was already postmodern. In another text that takes its title from a canonical narrative, "Return of the Native," Baraka writes:

> Harlem is vicious
> modernism. BangClash.
> Vicious the way its made.
> Can you stand such Beauty?
> (*Selected Poetry* 101)

The System of Dante's Hell, with its rewriting of Baraka's poetics within a recasting of Dante's *Inferno,* is one mark of the advent of the African-American postmodern. It is postmodernity with a difference, a difference inscribed along and across the white line taped across our culture by the ideologies of race. When, in *Black Magic,* Baraka speaks of "Death blow Eliot silence, dwindling / away, in the 20th century. Poet clocks crouched in their Americas" (*Selected Poetry* 70), he speaks in the persona of "The Bronze Buckaroo." He is not merely joining a general postmodern assault upon the Eliotic tradition; he is rewriting that assault in terms of racial difference.

"America leads to Africa," writes Homi Bhaba. "The peoples of the periphery return to rewrite the history and fiction of the metropolis" (*Nation* 6). Baraka's return to Dante and his descent into an American hell is a blow against the horizontal homogenizing of American cultural traditions. African-American difference cannot be so subsumed beneath a colonizing critique that enforces sameness, but neither can African-American critique rest within a sameness of its own. Baraka's mode of writing after *The System of Dante's Hell* is the changing same. Having written himself away from white influence by way of Dante, his surface looks remarkably unchanged but is forever altered. His system partakes of what Bhaba refers to as "the *uncanny* structure of cultural difference" that doesn't, as Baraka may have hoped during his period of cultural nationalism, "harbor our most secret selves" but rather "enables us to coincide with forms of activity which are both *at once ours and other*" (*Nation* 313). Always in motion, Baraka is never entirely self-coincident. "I don't recognize myself 10 seconds later," he writes in *System;* "who writes this will never read it" (59). The book the narrator reads from at the close of the book is not the same as the text he is writing as he makes this remark. Baraka's prosody reinscribes the projectivist insistence upon performance and upon the text as scored field within the improvising ethos of the African-American jazz aesthetic. By the close of his fast narrative things have clarified for him. He is not playing someone else's riff but is improvising against the other given, against the cultural lead sheet left to him in the Africanized West. He is at once himself and other in the racial hell of America. In moving against the metanarrative of the American errand he has moved to resituate or resite an African-American expressive tradition: "That when God is killed, talking to oneself is a sign of nuttiness. (Our grandparents suffered" (*System* 105).

The Middle Passage

As I write, our United States are celebrating the recommissioning of the facilities at Ellis Island as a monument to the waves of immigration, mostly from Europe, that gave us ourselves as our histories have tended to portray us. This is everywhere in the news, as it should be. But there has never been on our shores a celebration of similar scale in memory of the millions forced from their homes in Africa across the waters to life in bondage. In the centuries of the Atlantic slave trade, at least 11,345,000 souls were brought alive to this hemisphere against their will out of Africa, at least 523,000 of them to what we now celebrate as the United States of America (Rawley 428). Recently we have determined to set within our nation's capital a museum documenting and honoring the lives lost to Hitler's holocaust against the Jews during his Reich. We have never so honored the memories of the millions who died in bondage in our nation, or the uncounted lost at the bottom of the seas the slave ships traversed, or the inestimable numbers slaughtered in their African homes as a result of the campaigns to acquire human bodies for this traffic. While there is already a museum of African arts next to the Smithsonian's towered castle in Washington, D.C., only now are plans being made to create a museum for the study and perpetuation of the culture Africans created during their sojourn in slavery. The Middle Passage may be the great repressed signifier of American historical consciousness.

But for all our unwillingness to acknowledge this tremendous gap within our thought, we hear the waters of the slave trade's history everywhere lapping at our shores; in our arts the ancient sounds of the songs of the dead reverberate endlessly. Our national culture, in its more attentive moments, is like poet Lucille Clifton when she calls her "name into the roar of the surf / and something awful answers" (*Next* 26). In our search for a past we can carry with us into the future, we are like the apocalyptic horsemen of Amiri Baraka's poem "Legacy":

> Riding out
> from this town, to another, where
> it is also black. Down a road
> where people are asleep. Towards
> the moon or the shadows of houses.
> Towards the songs' pretended sea.
> (*Black Magic* 19)

We are subject to the intervention at any unguarded moment of our most terrible history. Even when we break from our grappling with the worst dreads of the present, we are, like the narrator of John Edgar Wideman's *Philadelphia Fire*, likely to find ourselves back suddenly among the conditions upon which the present is predicated; the people around us "smaller, parts of them lost, stolen by shadow, their voices husky, pitched to night's quiet, movements slowed as if night's a medium like water and they must conspire with its flow. When night's closing down it shuts things in on themselves and that's why you are on a ship with these other men thousands of miles from everywhere else, floating through darkness, and you can't help sensing the isolation, the smallness because night cuts you off drastically

as a knife" (40). Though we have refused to look collectively at the
patterns this past has imprinted on our present, though we have not
wanted as a nation to read the text traced in the wake of the slave ships
making their way across the waters to give us this legacy, though we
have carried ourselves as if we could leave this weight behind, as if we
could walk in a world that doesn't know the difference slavery made
in our souls, our artists have followed these signs for us; the Middle
Passage is everywhere inscribed within the archives of our thought.
Nathaniel Hawthorne, a writer besieged by the power of blackness,
tried to tell us:

> There is an historical circumstance, known to few, that connects the
> children of the Puritans with these Africans of Virginia in a very
> singular way. They are now our brethren, as being lineal descen-
> dants from the Mayflower, the fated womb of which, in her first
> voyage, sent forth a brood of Pilgrims on Plymouth Rock, and, in
> a subsequent one, spawned slaves upon the Southern soil,—a mon-
> strous birth, but with which we have an instinctive sense of kindred,
> and so are stirred by an irresistible impulse to attempt their rescue,
> even at the cost of blood and ruin. The character of our sacred
> ship, I fear, may suffer a little by this revelation; but we must let her
> white progeny offset her dark one,—and two such portents never
> sprang from an identical source before. (319)

Our Puritan divines evinced great interest in monstrous births, con-
struing what they saw there as signs and portents to be read into the
evolving text of the present. Our authors, in reading the monstrous
birth of North American slavery, have often found a fact that few
are willing to countenance even now—that American national culture has its beginnings, as much as in the Mayflower Compact, in the
gaze that passes between African and European on the Mayflower,
in the terrified eyes finding one another in the darkness between
the decks. Hawthorne's hope that one people might "offset" another
marks the monstrous birth of a national ideology of racism, another
sort of Mayflower compact.

James A. Rawley remarks at the outset of his history *The Transatlantic Slave Trade* that "it is not a paradox that the start of the Atlantic
slave trade coincides with the dawn of modern Europe" (9). It was
Africa's misfortune to fall more fully within reach of the Europeans at

the same time that Europe was seizing and developing a huge territory in the Western Hemisphere. While there is no paradox in these events, they have breathed together to produce what may be one of the most ironic histories and cultures ever formed, as Hawthorne's troubled notes on the Mayflower make evident. It is the Middle Passage that irrevocably hinges African and American cultural experience. We have tried in the centuries since to separate our histories into "black" and "white." "White" has attempted to constitute itself as history-as-such, excluding "black" as the repressed other till recently, finally including it as the virtual sign of repression and otherness. But we all arrived by the same vehicle, were delivered out of the same mother ship. There can be no real inside or outside to American history, for we are all, more literally than ever, on the same boat. And if we learn anything from the texts of the *Amistad* rebellion and of Melville's "Benito Cereno," it is that the hatches cannot be permanently secured, that the decks do not demarcate permanent separations of power, that at any moment the repressed and their signifiers may seize the vehicle.

He'd read that sharks trailed the stench of slave ships all the way across the Atlantic, feasting on corpses thrown overboard. (Wideman, *Philadelphia* 60–61)

> atlantic is a sea of bones,
> my bones,
> my elegant afrikans
> connecting whydah and new york,
> a bridge of ivory.
>   (Clifton, *Next* 26)

Memorandum of the Mortality of Slaves on Board the "Othello" while on the Coast of Africa and On Her Passage to the West Indies
   Febr. 6th A Man Jumpt Over Board Out the Long Boat and
      Was Drowned
   Mar. 18th Two Women Lost Over Board Out the Vessell in the
      Nit By Neglect of Sd. Mate Not Locking them up a bad
      Watch Kept
   April 6th A Man Slave Died With the Flux

April 13th A Woman Slave Died With the Flux
April 17th A Boy Slave Died wt. the Flux and Swelling
May 4th A Man Slave Died wt. the Flux
    7th A Man and Boy Slave Died wt. a Flux
June 16th A Man Slave Died at Cape Henry
    21th A Man Slave Died in James River wt. a Swelling
July 5th A Woman Slave Died with a Fever and Swelling
    6th A Girl Slave Died been Sick Two Months wt. the Flux
(Donnan, *Documents* 3:235)

The names of these people trail out across the swelling waters toward Africa. We can never read them in lists in our libraries, nor can we trace their names in stone with our fingers as we do when we visit the memorials to our more recent war dead. But these are our own, and their names own us. A different kind of scholarship may be called for here, a study that listens to seas and is owned by their terrible poetry. When Wallace Stevens listens for "The Idea of Order at Key West," he does not attend to these songs of the dead. "Who remembers the names of slaves?" asks Lucille Clifton in her memoir, *Generations*. "Only the children of slaves" (Clifton, *Good Woman* 227). The slave traders themselves, with their ironically named ships, couldn't be bothered to learn the names among their cargoes. "I suppose they all had names in their own dialect," mused Edward Manning in 1879. "But the effort required to pronounce them was too much for us so we picked out our favorites and dubbed them 'Main-Stay,' 'Cat-Head'" (qtd. in Dow 295). In a reversal of the biblical naming function awarded the first created man, the slave ships' crews sometimes christened the first male and female Africans brought on board "Adam" and "Eve." It is our artists who have determined to tell us whose children we are, to find an art to give names to those such as the Africans who rose up against Captain Hopkins in 1765. According to the *Newport Mercury*'s report, Hopkins's crew had been reduced by illness shortly after leaving Africa, and he'd had to employ some of the slaves to assist in their own transport. They released other Africans and nearly took control of the vessel but were defeated. Captain Hopkins and his remaining men "killed, wounded and forced overboard, Eighty of them" (Donnan 3:213). Illness, however, rather than rebellion, was the usual occasion for throwing live Africans into the ocean. The outbreak of ophthalmia, a common malady on slave ships, struck the French ship *Le Rodeux* on a voyage in 1819. The ship's captain threw thirty-nine blinded bondsmen overboard (Rawley 293). "Perhaps the most infamous atrocity in the annals of the slave trade," according to James A. Rawley, was committed by Luke Collingwood, captain of the *Zong*. He sailed from Africa in 1781 with a cargo of over four hundred slaves, but within two months he had lost seven crew members and sixty Africans:

> Discovering that he had left only two hundred gallons of fresh water, he ascertained that if the slaves died a natural death, it would be the loss of the shipowners, but if the slaves were thrown alive into the sea, it would be the loss of the insurers. He designated sick and weak slaves, and on that day fifty-four were thrown into the sea. On 1 December forty-two more were thrown overboard; on that day a heavy rain enabled the ship to collect in casks enough water for eleven days' full allowance. Even so, twenty-six more slaves, their hands bound, were thrown into the sea, and ten more, about to be bound for disposal, jumped into the sea. (298–99)

Some Africans were killed and disposed of as the result of brutal stupidity. One ship, the *Gloria,* ran into severe weather with 190 slaves on board. The Africans tried to break onto the deck in panic. The captain, fearing an uprising, ordered his men to fire their muskets through the grating "until the negroes became quiet. By this foolish freak forty were killed and wounded and had to be thrown overboard" (Dow 243). The trail of African corpses laid down by these centuries of traffic leads directly to our doorsteps. By November 1805, the slavers' practice of tossing Africans over the sides of their ships had become such a threat to public health and safety in Charleston, South Carolina, that an ordinance had to be enacted to curtail the practice. The *Courier* carried this notice of the new law: "[S]ince the importation of Slaves from Africa, several incidents have occurred of dead human bodies having been thrown into the waters of the Harbour of Charleston; such practices are extremely disgraceful, and ought to be prevented by their severest penalties that can be inflicted by the City Council" (Donnan 4:526n). Such an unutterable past wafts back to us when we stand before the sea:

> Words of fragrant portals, dimly-starred,
> And of ourselves and of our origins,
> In ghostlier demarcations, keener sounds.
>
> (Stevens 99)

One cannot read in the debates over the slave trade without encountering the canonical names of America's founding texts. It is in Captain John Smith's *Generall Historie of Virginia* that we read John Rolfe's note of the first visit of a Dutch slaver to Virginia: "About the last of August [1619] came in a dutch man of warre that sold us twenty Negers" (Donnan 4:2–3). In his memorial "The Selling of Joseph," Samuel Sewall dispensed with one of the earliest arguments raised in defense of the slave trade. "Every War is upon one side Unjust," he wrote. "An Unlawful War can't make lawful Captives. And by Receiving, we are in danger to promote and partake in their Barbarous Cruelties" (Donnan 3:17–18). But even a war considered just in the eyes of most New England colonists could produce startling connections to a trade in African slaves. In a 1645 letter to John Winthrop, Emanuel Dowling asserted:

> if upon a just Warre [with the Narragansett] the Lord should deliver them into our hands, wee might easily have men women and children enough to exchange for Moores, which wilbe more gaynfull pilladge for us than wee conceive, for I do not see how wee can thrive untill we get a stock of slaves sufficient to do all our business, for our children's children will hardly see this great continent filled with people, soe that our servants will still desire freedom to plant for themselves, and not stay but for verie great wages. And I suppose you know verie well how wee shall mayneteyne 20 Moores cheaper than one English servant. (Donnan 3:8)

Few writers, however, put the case quite this baldly in those early years. A discourse was generated that justified slavery on other than purely financial grounds. A hundred years after Winthrop received his communication from Dowling, one of the New Lights of the Great Awakening, George Whitefield, to whom the African-American poet Phillis Wheatley addressed one of her most important elegies, was arguing for the importation of African slaves to Georgia. This gives a horrifyingly ironic sense to Wheatley's heartfelt verses: "Take him, ye *Africans,* he longs for you, / *Impartial Saviour* is his title due" (23).

One can only wonder what Wheatley might have made of White-field's reasoning in proposing the slave trade to Georgia, but we know what the Reverend John Martin Bolzius made of it in his letter of December 24, 1745, to Whitefield:

> I have Considered the Strength of your Arguments by which you seem induced to promote the Introduction of Negroes, as far as it lyes in your power. . . .
>
> Your third Argument was, that you have laid out great Sums of Money for building and Maintaining the Orphan House, which you could not continue without Negroes, and this be the Case of Other Gentlemen in the Colony.
> But let me intreat you, Sir, not to have regard for a Single Orphan House, and Contribute Some thing Mischievous to the Overthrow of the prayseworthy Scheme of the Trustees with Respect to the Whole Colony.
>
> Your Last Argument for Negroes was, as I remember, that you intended to bring them to the knowledge of Christ.
> But, Sir, my Heart wishes that first the White people in the Colony and Neighborhood may be brought to the Saving and Experimental knowledge of Christ. As long as they are for this World, and take Advantage of the poor black Slaves, they will increase the Sins of the Land to a great Heighth. If a Minister had a Call to imploy his Strength and Time to Convert Negroes, he has in Carolina a Large Field. Don't believe, Sir, the language of those persons who wish the Introduction of Negroes under a pretence of promoting their Spiritual Happiness, as well in a Limited Number and under some Restrictions. I am sure, that if the Trustees allow'd to one thousand White settlers so many Negroes, in a few Years you would meet in the Streets, So as in Carolina, with many Malattoes, and many Negroe Children, which in the process of time will fill the Colony. (Donnan 4:607–8)

Thus was the Middle Passage to become a divide within the developing text of American culture. On the one side were those like Richard Saltonstall, whose petition against the slave trade was later memorialized by Charles Olson in his *Maximus* poems, who held commonsensically, "The act of stealing Negers, or of taking them by force, (whether it be considered theft or robbery) is (as I conceive) expressly contrary, both to the law of God, and the law of this country" (Donnan 3:7). On the other, prevailing side were writers such as Governor Charles Calvert who were more motivated by economic self-interest than by a desire to be on the right side of ecclesiastical history. In a 1664 letter to Lord Baltimore, Calvert notes with some frustration: "I have endeavoured to see if I could find as many responsible men that would engage to take a 100 or 200 neigros every yeare from the Royall Company at that rate mentioned in your . . . letter but I find wee are nott men of estates good enough to undertake such a businesse, but could wish wee were for wee are naturally incli'd to love neigros if our purses would endure it . . ." (Donnan 4:9). For almost two centuries this debate continued while the waters of the Atlantic continued to be navigated by those whose purses permitted them to practice the kind of love described by Governor Calvert. The first ship actually built in the North American colonies to engage in the slave trade may have been the appropriately named *Desire,* which for a time traded in both American Indian and African slaves. The *Desire* made a voyage in 1637 to the West Indies carrying Pequot slaves captured in battle. It returned with African slaves bound for Boston (Dow 267). American shipping continued involvement in the Atlantic slave trade even after the importation of slaves to the United States had been banned by law. As late as 1864, ships flying the American flag carried kidnapped Africans over the seas.

Many of our colonial writers urged practical rather than strictly moral considerations upon their readers, arguing for a halt or at least a limitation on the Atlantic traffic. Typical of the tone of these arguments is a letter written by Virginia's Colonel William Byrd to the earl of Egmont in 1736, a letter that serves as a precursor to Thomas Jefferson's writings on slavery:

> They might import so many Negros hither, that I fear this colony will some time or other be confirmed by the name of New Guinea. I am sensible of many bad consequences of multiplying these Ethiopians amongst us. They blow up the pride, and ruin the Industry of our White People, who seeing a Rank of poor Creatures below them, detest work and fear it should make them look like slaves. . . .

We have already at least 10,000 Men of these descendants of Ham fit to bear Arms, and their numbers increase every day as well by birth as Importation. And in case there should arise a Man of desperate fortune, he might with more advantage than Cataline kindle a Servile War. Such a man might be dreadfully mischeivous before any opposition could be formed against him, and tinge our Rivers as wide as they are with blood. . . . (Donnan 4:131–32)

But as the debate trailed across pages of pamphlets and stationery, the Africans went on slipping namelessly into the waters at our shores and into the laboring places and fields of our history. On July 7, 1763, the *Massachusetts Gazette and Boston News Letter* noted that at Hartford, Connecticut, "the Mate of a Vessel lately arrived there from the Coast of Africa, being delirious, took a Negro Boy into his arms, and jump'd into the River, and drowned both himself and the Boy (Donnan 3:70–71).

Those writers who determined the course of the discourse of the slave trade in America seldom spoke bluntly of the actual conditions of the passage. Aside from later abolitionist texts, that task has been left largely to those few who both witnessed the horror and could write. That such documents, few in number as they are, have not till recently been studied and taught widely is a mark of the enormity of our willingness to repress these facts of our nation's becoming. In his introduction to *The Transatlantic Slave Trade: A History,* Rawley argues that "professional historians were long remiss both about engaging in research on the trade and in presenting what was known." Calling this a "virtual conspiracy of silence," Rawley notes that the author of one widely read economic history of eighteenth-century England, D. A. Farnie, makes but one mention of the slave trade, and that mention is "an attempt to mitigate its horrors" (1). This ameliorationist tendency is even more extreme in the texts meant for the general reading public. In 1927, as American ideological racism was enjoying one of its frequent resurgences, Ernest H. Pentecost wrote in his introduction to George Dow's *Slave Ships and Slaving* that

the philanthropic frenzy of the abolitionists, few of whom had ever seen a slave ship with her cargo aboard, created, by their exaggerated statements, a wrong impression of the conditions aboard such craft, which were among the cleanest and best found merchantmen afloat. The common conception of the treatment of slaves aboard slavers, previous to the abolition of the slave trade, is very different from what it really was. In reality the slaves were much better cared for than free white emigrants and their poor passengers were until the second decade of the nineteenth century. (xxi)

Olaudah Equiano had not only seen a slaver with its cargo aboard, he had been a part of that cargo. In his narrative of his life he recalls:

The stench of the hold, while we were on the coast, was so intolerably loathsome, that it was dangerous to remain there for any time, and some of us had been permitted to stay on the deck for the fresh air; but now that the whole ship's cargo were confined together, it became absolutely pestilential . . . each had scarcely room to turn himself. . . . This produced copious perspiration, so that the air soon became unfit for respiration, from a variety of loathsome smells, and brought on a sickness among the slaves, of which many died, thus falling victim to the improvident avarice, as I may call it, of their purchasers. This deplorable situation was again aggravated by the galling of the chains, now become insupportable; and the filth of the necessary tubs, into which the children often fell, and were almost suffocated. The shrieks of the women, and the groans of the dying, rendered it a scene of horror almost inconceivable. (35)

Equiano found that he was unable to eat in these circumstances, but he quickly learned that prisoners who did not eat were whipped hourly. The ship's doctor of another vessel reported having seen slaves threatened with being forced to swallow glowing coals if they did not eat (Dow 145). The memoirs of the slavers themselves, which are considerably greater in number than narratives such as Equiano's but far less likely to be read by contemporary literary scholars, confirm Equiano's recollections. Captain Richard Drake, a nineteenth-century slave smuggler whose career took place primarily during the years when the trade was illegal, provides an account of a voyage that ran short of rations:

Fevers and fluxes soon added to their misery and deaths followed so fast that in a short time at least a hundred slaves were shackled to dead partners. . . . Matters grew worse daily and at last Captain Ruiz ordered the hatches down and swore he would make the run on our regular rations and take the chances with our stock. . . . I began to notice a strange, fetid smell pervading the vessel and a low, heavy fog on deck, almost like steam, and then the horrid truth became apparent. Our rotting negroes under hatches had generated the plague and it was the death-mist that I saw rising. (Qtd. in Dow 243–44)

Even when all went "well," and the captain of the ship took measures to preserve the lives of his cargo, these measures themselves were painful and humiliating. Captain Theodore Canot, whose *Adventures of an American Slaver* was one of the texts Robert Hayden studied before writing his poem "Middle Passage," and who is almost invariably referred to in print as the "infamous" Captain Canot, reports that Africans taken on board his ship were stripped naked and remained nude throughout the passage as "the only means of securing cleanliness and health" (107–9). Each week, according to Canot, the Africans were shaved and had their nails pared "to insure security from harm in those nightly battles that occur[red], when the slave contest[ed] with his neighbor every inch of plank to which he [was] glued" (109). The manner of stowing these human cargoes has been a matter of some controversy over the years. The frequently reproduced diagram of horrific "tight packing" on the slave ship *Brookes* of Liverpool depicts what may have been an atypical situation, considering the size of the vessel. But it is clear from numerous accounts that the captains paid considerable attention to the matter of "packing" and that the results were inhuman. Canot remarks, "[T]he strict discipline of nightly storage is of the greatest importance in slavers, else every negro would accommodate himself as if he were a passenger" (110). The last phrase of Canot's observation serves to underscore the emptiness of comparisons some writers have made between slave ships and other transports. When Dr. George Pinckard compared troop ships with slave ships at the end of the eighteenth century and wrote that "the slaves [were] much more crowded than the soldiers, yet far more healthy" (qtd. in Rawley 300), he was simply missing the largest of points, a point that was not missed by the Americans who interviewed the Africans from the *Amistad*. The testimony of those imprisoned Africans who had risen up and taken the *Amistad* clearly moved their interrogators. One of the whites recorded the memories of Grabeau as he described his transport from Africa to Cuba: "They were fastened together in couples by the wrists and legs, and kept in that situation day and night. Here Grabeau and another of the Africans named Kimbo, lay down upon the floor, to show the painful position in which they were obliged to sleep. By day it was no better. The space between decks was so small—according to their account not exceeding four feet,—that they were obliged if they attempted to stand, to keep a crouching posture" (Barber 19). Cinquez, the rice farmer who led the *Amistad* rebels, again rendered physical testimony by demonstrating for the benefit of the court at New Haven the posture the Africans were forced to maintain between decks.

The slavers also carried further on board their ships the practices they had commenced in Africa and would continue in the New World of setting the Africans against one another in the struggle for survival. According to Captain Canot, "In order to insure perfect silence and regularity during the night, a slave is chosen as constable from every ten, and furnished with a cat to enforce his commands during his appointed watch. In remuneration for his services, which are admirably performed whenever the whip is required, he is adorned with an old shirt or tarry trousers" (110). Olaudah Equiano, who witnessed many voyages, remembers a common scene of racial division that finds its reflection in Melville's account of the battle between May-Day and Rose-Water in *White Jacket* and the "Battle Royal" section of Ralph Ellison's *Invisible Man:* "[F]or the diversion of those gentlemen, all the boys were called on the quarter-deck, and were paired proportionally, and then made to fight; after which the gentlemen gave the combatants from five to nine shillings each" (45).

Equiano witnessed too the vulnerability of female Africans left in the complete power of these crews: "[I]t was almost a constant practice with our clerks, and other whites, to commit violent depredations on the chastity of the female slaves," he writes. "I have even known them to gratify their brutal passion with females not ten years old; and these abominations some of them practiced to such a scandalous excess, that one of our captains discharged the Mate and others on that account" (74). Equiano's pained narrative needs to be read alongside another canonical text, the closing segment of Melville's "Benito

Cereno." Here, in a deposition drawn in part from the real Amasa Delano's *Narrative of Voyages and Travels,* Melville emphasizes Benito Cereno's paradigmatic incomprehension of the Africans' musical expression:

> The negresses of age, were knowing to the revolt, and testified themselves satisfied at the death of their master, Don Alexandro; that, had the negroes not restrained them, they would have tortured to death, instead of simply killing, the Spaniards slain by command of the negro Babo; that the negresses used their utmost influence to have the deponent made away with; that in the various acts of murder, they sang songs and danced—not gaily, but solemnly, and before the engagement with the boats, as well as during the action, they sang melancholy songs to the negroes, and that this melancholy tone was more inflaming than a different one would have been, and was so intended; that all this is believed, because the negroes have said it. (*Piazza* 135)

Black women's songs are almost always heard as mysterious and powerful by white auditors, but the auditors so often seem to listen outside any consciousness of context. They always seem surprised and mystified by the notes that African women sing on the seas leading to America, and afterward on America's shores. James Arnold, in his testimony before a parliamentary committee contemplating abolition of the British slave trade, remembered from his experiences at sea "another time when the women were sitting by themselves, below, when [he] heard them singing other words and then always in tears. Their songs always told of their lives and their grief at leaving their friends and country" (qtd. in Dow 178). It is an ancient song that lingers on the lips of singers long centuries later in America. It is the song that remains in the ears of those who listen to Toni Morrison's *Song of Solomon* as it rides the air. It is the song Pilate and Reba sing near the end of that novel:

> *In the nighttime.*
> *Mercy.*
> *In the darkness.*
> *Mercy.*
> *In the morning.*

Mercy.
At my bedside.
Mercy.
On my knees now.
Mercy. Mercy. Mercy. Mercy.
(317–18)

We were standing on the deck
of the New World, before maps:
tepid seizure of a breeze
and the spirit hissing away . . .
(Dove, *Grace Notes* 23)

Our history begins in division between decks. The texts of our canons are imbricated in the discourse of slavery and race. Our writings are tangled up in one another and implicated in one another. Our authors cannot speak of what we have done, and of what we must do, without calling to one another across the successive waves of historical particularities, without calling one another back to the shared texts, and shards of texts, that compose our consciousness of ourselves. The accumulated lines of our American literature are like the words of the slave-trading skipper in Stephen Vincent Benét's *John Brown's Body,* whose voice was "wholly sincere—an old ship's bell / Hung in the steeple of a meeting-house / With all of New England and the sea's noise in it" (10). In contrast to the national public silence observed as self-induced forgetfulness of the centuries of the slave trade, our literature reverberates with the proceeding crests of reference rising from our past. From the beginning of black traditions of reading, blacks read, among other things, the white texts of and against the slave trade. As white writers indited knowledge of the Middle Passage within the passage work of their creations, black writers reinscribed those texts within the body of their own growing literature, continuing the embodiment of difference that became the corpus of an emergent American tradition. And white writers, reading those texts in turn, wrote new verses of our ongoing epic of struggle in which black creation was reinscribed within the texts of white re-creations of history and of the present.

It is the history of the Atlantic slave trade that informs Americans' readings of Samuel Taylor Coleridge's "Rime of the Ancient Mariner," perhaps Coleridge's most premonitory text for those on this side of the Atlantic. We American readers feel that we are that one of three stopped short by the mariner's discourse on our way to the feast. We recognize in his story a sense of our own fatedness. We feel, like the mariner, that we recognize that spectral ship that he descries on his haunted seas, the skeleton ship through whose ribs "the Sun / Did peer, as through a grate" (*Selection* 126). It is a vision that finds its horrific echo in the shadow cast over American readers by Melville's "Benito Cereno" when a ship turns before us: "With creaking masts, she came heavily round to the wind; the prow slowly swinging into view of the boats, its skeleton gleaming in the horizontal moonlight, and casting a gigantic ribbed shadow upon the water" (*Piazza* 122). According to Wordsworth, the genesis of Coleridge's poem may have been the report of such a skeleton ship that appeared in a dream to Coleridge's friend Mr. Cruikshank (Fruman 404). In a stanza Coleridge added as a manuscript revision in the margins of the 1798 *Lyrical Ballads,* he renders the vision more explicitly:

> This Ship it was a plankless thing,
> —A bare Anatomy!
> A plankless spectre—and it mov'd
> Like a Being of the Sea!
> > (*Selection* 127)

These lines, which sound like Emily Dickinson and read like Herman Melville, call readers across the ages to rekindled memories of the Middle Passage. This, along with Coleridge's activities in the abolitionist cause in England, accounts for the frequency of references to Coleridge in American abolitionist writings, and more particularly in the accumulating mass of African-American literary arts. Indeed, the sole epigraph appearing on the title page of Frederick Douglass's 1855 autobiography, *My Bondage and My Freedom,* a touchstone of classic American writing if ever there was one, is a quotation from the works of Coleridge. Though, as J. H. Haeger has demonstrated, Coleridge adhered to a number of racist doctrines, including a version of the degeneration thesis on the origins of races (340), "hardly a hint of his ideas on race found its way into print during his lifetime" (Haeger 355), and it has been Coleridge's poetic record, and his record as an active abolitionist, to which American literary artists have so often responded.

While "The Rime of the Ancient Mariner" is not *about* slavery in the traditional understanding of "aboutness," its dread lines echo everywhere the weight of sin occasioned by that trade. In describing the deathly, plankless ship that appears in the third part of "The Ancient Mariner," Coleridge alludes to a fact that everybody in the seaport of Bristol knew, "that you could smell a Slaver five (or ten) miles to windward, and that the planks only lasted for five (or ten) voyages" (Empson 30). In his essay "On the Slave Trade" for the *Watchman* of March 25, 1796, adapted from a lecture he had delivered in Bristol the previous June, Coleridge had made use of that general knowledge in a powerful, rhetorical gesture. "Would you choose to be sold?" he asked his audience; "to have the hot iron hiss upon your breasts, after having been crammed into the hold of a Ship with so many fellow-victims, that the heat and stench, arising from your diseased bodies, should rot the very planks?" (*Watchman* 138). The poet had already written a considerable poem in opposition to the Atlantic slave trade. In 1792, as his winning entry in the competition for the Browne Gold Medal for a Greek ode, Coleridge had composed "On the Wretched Lot of the Slaves in the Isles of Western India," portions of which he reprinted in a subsequent note to his part of Southey's *Joan of Arc*. Coleridge's Greek ode sets the tone that he was to follow later in "The Ancient Mariner" and in "The Destiny of Nations," in which he describes a "mad tornado" that

> bellows through
> The guilty islands of the western main,
> What time departing for their native shores,
> Eboe, or Koromantyn's plain of palms,
> The infuriate spirits of the murdered make
> Fierce merriment, and vengeance ask of heaven.
> (*Poetical Works* 78)

Coleridge here appends a note, possibly derived from Bryan Edwards (Fruman 253), explaining that Africans in the West Indies believed that they would be repatriated to Africa in the afterlife, and reproduces the opening of his Greek ode, which also alludes to this belief. This hopeful mythology seems also to have been generally known among the slavers. Captain William Snelgrave, in his 1754 *Account of Guinea, and the Slave Trade,* reports that following the suppression of a revolt on a slave ship the crew cut off the head of a mutineer who had killed a white man and threw the body overboard, because some blacks were thought to believe that dismemberment prevented the resurrected return to Africa (Dow 128). The theme of England's guilt for the slave trade appears in several of Coleridge's poems. In "Ode to the Departing Year" he intones:

> But chief by Afric's wrongs,
> > Strange, horrible, and foul!
> By what deep guilt belongs
> To the deaf Synod, 'full of gifts and lies'
> > > (*Poetical Works* 80)

"Fears in Solitude" imagines that the wretched dead in heaven enter pleas against those remaining on earth who have "gone forth / And borne to distant tribes slavery and pangs" (*Poetical Works* 128). Coleridge was eloquent in his advocacy of abolition, but he fell silent before attempting to detail the full horrors visited upon the Africans. "I will not mangle the feelings of my readers," he cautions in his essay "On the Slave Trade," "by detailing enormities, which the gloomy Imagination of Dante would scarcely have dared attribute to the Inhabitants of Hell" (*Watchman* 133). Amiri Baraka would later follow this line thrown out to Dante in his detailing of the hellish particulars of the lives of slaves and their children, as Robert Hayden would look to Coleridge when he assembled his poem "Middle Passage." Both follow in the wake of Melville, who writes Coleridge into *Moby Dick.* In chapter 42, contemplating the awful whiteness of the whale, Melville names Coleridge, asking readers to think of the albatross: "Bethink thee of the albatross; whence come those clouds of spiritual wonderment and pale dread, in which that white phantom sails in all imaginations? Not Coleridge first threw that spell, but God's great, unflattering laureate, Nature" (190). Ten chapters later, when the *Pequod* meets a ship named the *Albatross,* the skeletal circuit is completed: "[T]his craft was bleached like the skeleton of a stranded walrus" (236). It is in the very next chapter that Ishmael contrasts the "gam" enjoyed by whaling vessels meeting at sea with the spectral passings of slave shipping: "As touching slave-ships meeting, why, they are in such a prodigious hurry, they run away from each other as soon as possible" (240).

For all these reasons, it is not at all surprising that so many have read memories of the Middle Passage into Coleridge's "Rime of the Ancient Mariner." Many readers see in the mariner a familiar, guilt-ridden shade. He resembles somewhat the "Sailor who had served in the Slave Trade and was found bemoaning his guilt in a cowshed outside Bristol" (Empson 29), a figure who was memorialized in a ballad by Southey. More immediately, the mariner's obsessive guilt and need to speak it parallel the West's final inability to elude responsibility for the centuries of the slave trade. What is more surprising is the number of readers who, unlike Robert Hayden, Paule Marshall, Frederick Douglass, and William Empson, find little to remark in Coleridge's concern with the morality of chattel slavery. The indices to many critical studies of Coleridge, including Owen Barfield's *What Coleridge Thought*, include no entries for slavery, slave trade, Africa, or abolition.

Robert Hayden, however, had read "The Rime of the Ancient Mariner" with the same alertness and emotion with which he read *John Brown's Body, Adventures of an African Slaver*, Muriel Rukeyser's recounting in *Willard Gibbs* of the *Amistad* rebellion (Charles Davis 100), and other texts that we find constellated in his "Middle Passage," and the mariner whose log forms part of Hayden's poem is presented as one who has also read Coleridge and who sees in the ancient mariner's guilt-ridden tale a reflection of his own.

Robert Hayden's "Middle Passage," which achieves its most telling effects at a noumenal level of intertextual signifying, is written under the influence of modernism's theories of montage, collage, fragmentation, and juxtaposition, theories Hayden studied in the works of Pound and Eliot during the time he was a student of Spanish at Detroit City College (Pontheolla Williams 14). But by the time he came to compose his "Middle Passage," Hayden may have recognized a certain resonance between the palimpsestic styles of Eliot, Pound, H.D., and other modernists and the earlier prose texts of African-American literary traditions with their embedded layers of actual and fictive documentation. As his wife pursued her studies at Juilliard, Hayden conducted research into the history of the American slave trade at New York's Schomburg Collection (Fetrow 12–13). Here too he no doubt encountered the powerful effects of an intertextual music in the autobiographical works of earlier African-American authors. Later, while studying at the University of Michigan with W. H. Auden, Hayden continued his readings in the history of the slave trade, including the *Adventures of an African Slaver*, in which Theodore Canot's disreputable memories, told to and given final form by Brantz Mayer, again evidenced a disjunct, multivoiced style akin to the narratives edited and reshaped by northern abolitionists from the testimony of former slaves.

While Stephen Vincent Benét's multivoiced epic, *John Brown's Body*, with its call for a poet powerful enough to rise up and sing the "black-skinned epic, epic with the black spear" (337), seems to have been the most immediate influence in Hayden's decision to create the historical collage of his "Middle Passage" (Charles Davis 98), Benét probably did not anticipate that his "white-hearted" call for a black-skinned epic would be answered with most terrible power by a poem that works largely by threading together the words of white participants in the trade in African bodies. Hayden has added what Melvin B. Tolson calls the note of ethnic ambiguity to the already rich ambiguities of textual juxtaposition encountered in both modernist verse and in early African-American autobiography. Hayden's poem recharts American history by means of an African-American recombination of "white" documents within black history and black readings. Vera Kutzinski has observed that "'Middle Passage' as a whole is a careful reading of . . . official texts, one that unravels the threads of their fabric to weave them together in very different ways" (174). I would add to this that "Middle Passage" simultaneously rereads, unravels, and reweaves with a racial difference the official text of modern white verse culture. By respeaking white history and white verse style within the crucible of African-American historical experience, Hayden irrevocably alters all his materials and moves them to a different level of cultural syncretism. His work appears to confirm Houston Baker's assertion that "the most forceful, expressive cultural spokespersons of Afro-America have traditionally been those who have first mastered a master discourse—at its most rarefied metalevels—and then, autobiographically, written themselves and their *own* metalevels palimpsestically on the scroll of such mastery" (*Workings* 42).

In the dialogue between the slave ship captain and his mate that serves as the prelude to *John Brown's Body*, Hayden read texts and echoes of texts, a metalevel of intertextual racial signifying that serves as prelude to Hayden's own work. The captain's voice, emitting biblical justifications for slavery, becomes in Benét's book the "old ship's bell / Hung in the steeple of a meeting-house / With all New England and the sea's noise in it" (10), a disturbing founding image for the nascent republic, one that counters the official text we have written of our Pilgrim fathers. The rhetorical force of guilt and its attendant questions is not faced by this ancient mariner but is displaced to his mate and to their descendants. The mate, echoing Melville, is gripped by "the blackness of black" (11) and in his most Coleridgean moments wonders if he will live to elude his own albatross, whether he will eventually be able to cleanse himself of the stain of his involvement in this malevolent enterprise, or, as he asks himself: "Will my skin smell black even then, will my skin smell black?" (11). It is the mate, too, whose auditory dream of an American future is so haunted. Listening to his captain's texts, listening to his talk of spreading the Lord's seed, the seed of the Gospel, the mate envisions black seed stolen from Africa and strewn on American soil, seed that sprouts a symbol every bit as ominous as Coleridge's albatross, a yoke-shaped tree growing till it blots the seaman's stars. Deprived by guilt of those guiding lights, the mate hears the approaching storm of apocalypse, horses of anger trampling the sky, and wonders: "Was it they, was it they? / Or was it cold wind in the leaves of the shadow-tree / That made such grievous music?" (14). What the mate hears through the tumbling texts of his captain's voice is the "dark sobbing" of an African-American song rising proleptically from below the decks. Benét leaves his readers, Hayden among them, suspended with a trinity of possibility at the conclusion of the prelude. The captain's voice, the founding voice of ringing self-justification, "Trailed off / Into texts" (13). The mate, prefiguring with his action the profoundest American desire to impose forgetfulness upon itself, plans to sling his hammock on the top deck far above his suffering cargo, because "You couldn't smell the black so much on deck / And so you didn't dream it when you slept" (15).

But still rising half-heard from below are black voices singing their "grievous music." Benét completes his prelude's orchestration of texts and voices by transporting back to the slave ship the songs made later by African Americans calling for the Lord's angel and for Jubilee time (14–15). Faced with the problem of saying the impossible, of saying, as a white poet, the sounds of the songs the Africans of the Middle Passage sang into the darkness of their transport, Benét transcribes an example of African-American cultural invention. It may have been here, listening to a white poet trying to say what can't be said, listening to a white poet's rendering of black song, that Hayden began to see what he might do with the workings of racial difference in the ambiguous textual trading of our history. When he came to write his "Middle Passage," Hayden reversed Benét's racial passage. In "Middle Passage" Hayden says the impossible by rewriting white texts with a black pen.

In the stylings of modernist poetics Hayden found replicated the essentially palimpsestic nature of American and African-American cultural experience. The texts of our first worlds are rent by removal and voyage and are overwritten by the multiply voiced texts of our new worlds, providing us with an overironized and polysemous legacy of cultural document. The ironic rupture represented by America's constant renaming of itself and its peoples is bodied forth in the "bright ironical names" (51) of the slave ships that float across the page at the outset of Hayden's "Middle Passage": "*Jesus, Estrella, Esperanza, Mercy*" (48). This ironic nomination continues in the second list of ships Hayden inscribes: "*Desire, Adventure, Tartar, Ann.*" Whose desire is represented by that craft? What terrible guiding star sailed before the *Esperanza*? For whom will *Mercy* finally put to shore? Vera Kutzinski has noticed that the second of Hayden's lists "features names completely devoid of religious connotations" and argues that this change in register "represents the widening chasm between slavery and institutionalized religion" (176). More simply, and perhaps more significantly, the second list indited by Hayden traces the development of an American national involvement in the slave trade and inscribes a legal history prefiguring the arguments over the *Amistad* that Hayden brings into the concluding passages of his poem. The *Desire* was, as already noted, the first American-built slave ship, constructed at Marblehead, Massachusetts, in 1636. The name of this ship, which traded American Indian for African slaves, also forms an intertextual link with Melville; the Indians traded into slavery in exchange for Africans by this ship's masters were all members of the Pequot nation whose decimation was memorialized in Melville's naming of the ship that Ahab captains to its fate. The *Adventure* was owned by Christopher Champlin of Newport, Rhode Island, and traded in the latter part of the eighteenth century. The *Ann*, another Rhode Island vessel, was owned by James DeWolf, a man of wealth and prominence who at one time served in the United States Senate. The *Ann* was captured in 1806 by a British warship and, following considerable legal actions, was condemned along with its cargo as a lawful prize by the Lord's Commissioners in Whitehall (Dow 260). The *Tartar,* owned by Frederick Tavell of Charleston, met a similar fate. Following a voyage to the Pongo River region, the ship was seized near Martinique by the British vessel *Ulysses* on February 2, 1808. In a case clearly prefiguring arguments over the *Amistad,* the *Tartar* was declared a lawful prize "because (1) she was proceeding from Africa to a colony of the enemy (*i.e.,* France) under a false designation, *i.e.,* to Charleston: and (2) because trade in slaves was contrary to the laws of America after Jan. 1, 1808" (Dow 271).

Between the two litanies of ships' names Hayden introduces the ironic and elegiac voice of the poem's organizing persona, a voice that speaks only a few times but that seems to have seized control over the assorted documents written in other hands that Hayden takes into his hands in his poem; it is this voice that announces the poem's defining trope: "Middle Passage: / voyage through death / to life upon these shores" (48). Announcing also its own textual strategy, Hayden's poem immediately embarks upon an intertextual passage that refigures the Middle Passage of its title, voyaging through a textual death to rebirth in a new poetics of a new world. By next adopting the voices of the slave traders themselves and adapting their texts to his own purposes, Hayden accomplishes a scriptural revolution that mirrors the revolt of the *Amistad* Africans. Hayden, in rewriting the words of the slave owners and captains, in ironically voiding them and redeploying them within his historical discourse, effects a metaphorical repetition of the *Amistad* rebellion, a rebellion in which the cargo, the tenor, seizes the vehicle and redirects it homeward. Just before his second list of ships, Hayden transcribes the log of a captain that brings into our reading presence the absent songs of the Africans. The captain, uneasily listening to the African languages rising from his craft, must turn to an intercessor, the ship's linguist, to learn that the Africans' words are "a prayer for death, / ours and their own" (48). He seemingly seeks no translation of the more startling songs his log states were sung as they went under the waters by those who threw themselves overboard.

Then, following the list of ships, the poem speaks again in its own voice, a voice that alludes most strongly to other texts as a means of troping its own renewed source of song, signifying its reemergence in full control of the words it masters and forms. The ships, we read, are "Standing to America, bringing home / black gold, black ivory, black seed." But whose home is it in fact? And do we read the "black seed" as the slave ship captains and their investors did, as seminal capital for their New World venture, or do we read it with Hayden as the same seed dreamed by the seaman of *John Brown's Body:*

Black, shining seeds, robbed from a black king's storehouse,
Falling and falling on American earth
With light, inexorable patter and fall,
To strike, lie silent, quicken.

                              Till the Spring
Came with its weeping rains, and the ground bore
A blade, a shadow-sapling, a tree of shadow,
A tree shaped like a yoke, growing and growing
Until it blotted all the seamen's stars.

                                     (Benét 14)

This latter, more ominously resonant reading is affirmed by Hayden's next passage, an italicized song that points at once to Shakespeare, Eliot, and Benét:

       Deep in the festering hold thy father lies,
       of his bone, New England pews are made,
       those are altar lights that were his eyes.
                       (48)

As Charles T. Davis has pointed out (101–2), these lines enact the sea change described by Ariel's song in Shakespeare's *The Tempest,* a play

that has proved endlessly suggestive to postcolonial poets. Ariel sings
of the father's body:

> Nothing of him that doth fade
> But doth suffer a sea-change
> Into something rich and strange.
>
> (1. 2. 400–402)

Hayden's rerendering of Ariel's song, however, incorporates stunning ambiguity. The song is delivered as a direct address, forcing readers to position themselves with regard to the father's body. Each reader, white or black, must assume a relation to the father described as "Thy father," as there is no specific addressee identified in the poem. As the poet reads the song to himself and transforms both it and its portents, so each reader of "Middle Passage" in turn must be transformed in relation to the song. Stephen Vincent Benét heard in the tolling of New England church bells the awful tones of the self-righteous slaver's legacy. Hayden's poem encrypts slaver and African together in the vaults of American heritage; the father in the festering hold may be either black or white. The legacy of New England's founding fathers was built on the bodies of the founding fathers of African America. The black ivory of the African father's bones was transmuted by capitalist alchemy into the church pews occupied by the Puritan patriarchs. Similarly, abstracted profit transformed the eyes of the African father into the altar lights that are before us in Hayden's poem. The altar lights, like those luminescent devices hung at the prow of a ship, are meant to lead us out of spiritual darkness. But in Hayden's poem the light, as in Conrad's *Heart of Darkness*, merely underscores moral blindness; the light of Christian civilization makes the dark darker. This passage, which prophesies the literal blindness and ophthalmia that arise later in the poem, also summons the darkness of T. S. Eliot's "Waste Land":

> "Do
> You know nothing? Do you see nothing? Do you remember
> Nothing?"
>
> I remember
> Those are pearls that were his eyes.
> "Are you alive, or not? Is there nothing in your head?"

                                                                    But
O O O O that Shakespeherian Rag—

                                                                    (41)

Those who see nothing have been blinded by their own history. Eliot's
disembodied characters, flotsam of the Waste Land, await in darkness the coming of another tempest. Hayden revisits this desolate site
of citation and warped allusion, inhabiting and altering the texts of
both Eliot and Shakespeare, where he will be joined by such later
authors as John Edgar Wideman. In Wideman's novel *Hurry Home*,
Cecil, the protagonist, is transfixed by a one-eyed shoe-shine boy,
by the "Pearl that was his eye. Pearly ball dimmed by the writh-
ing mists" (32). Later, in an African-American revision of Eliot's use
of an African-American allusion (Shakespearean "rag"), Wideman's
protagonist, who has declared that he is a cliché unto himself (144),
engages in a bit of "bathtub shower shaving" poetry: "O O O you
Shagspearean rug cuddled round my chin" (145).

Hayden's African-American revision of Ariel's song is followed directly by a prayerful hymn, one whose lyrics are spaced in such a way
as to highlight the extent to which they mirror the litanies of ships'
names. The first line of the hymn, "Jesus   Saviour   Pilot   Me," repeats the music of the second list of ships, "*Desire, Adventure, Tartar,
Ann.*" The typography of the hymn's placement, flush left, aligns it
with the ships' names and with the first appearance in the poem of the
term "Middle Passage," emphasizing, with the repetition, "*Jesus*"—
"Jesus," the ironic emptiness of prayer and ship's name alike, voiding the Christian imprecation of moral force. But just as African-
American slaves turned Christian songs to their own musical and
signifying ends, deforming and reforming them by their own lights,
so Hayden, as he has done with Shakespeare and Eliot, wrests this text
from the intentional power of its singers on the slave ships. Similarly,
the prayer that comes after the hymn is ironized and answered:

> We pray that Thou wilt grant, O Lord,
> safe passage to our vessels bringing
> heathen souls unto Thy chastening.
>
>   (48)

Hayden's strategy has been from the outset to allow the slave traders'
own language to redound against them, to let their own prayers raise

the questions of who is truly heathen and whose souls are in need of chastening. This white prayer forms a fearful symmetry with the translated African prayers for the deaths of all on board and is answered by the account given in the ship's log that follows.

The "author" of this log entry, a reader of Coleridge, is one who writes to dispel fear and the guilt of his own enterprise. His ship is plagued by ophthalmia, and the blindness has spread from the Africans to the crew. The log entry itself is evidence of both sight and blindness; it eases the writer's fear by demonstrating that he can still see to compose, but it evidences to the reader the enormity of the spiritual blindness afflicting the man. He writes "as one / would turn to exorcism" (49), but he cannot exorcise the evil in which he has enlisted. He asks, "Which one of us / has killed an albatross?" (49), but sees no connection between the voyage's "misfortune" and its purpose. He records that they "have jettisoned the blind to no avail" and still cannot understand that the truly blind are still on board, directing the ship to its dread end. "It spreads, the terrifying sickness spreads," and so it does, so long as these men spread the moral calamity they carry with them. "Its claws have scratched sight from the Capt.'s eyes," the mariner scratches in the page of his log, "& there is blindness in the fo'c'sle." Blindness in the fo'c'sle is endemic among those who would navigate the young American republic, making of its altar lights beacons of depravity and avarice.

The Christian hymn returns: "Thou Who Walked On Galilee" (49). The line, a prayer for salvation from the inevitability of the sea, finds its echoes in Paule Marshall's allusion to legendary Africans who walked home across the Atlantic, and leads to Hayden's use of a deposition in which the deponent, again a seaman who writes *in place* of the captain, describes the horrors of the *Bella J*, a ship that in the end was abandoned by the crew, after it caught fire, with all the Africans and the captain still on board. "Further deponent sayeth not" (50), but his horrific deposition again dramatizes the deliberate immorality of those who have been entrusted with the guidance of the ship of state. The ironic lyrics of the hymn recur to close the first section of the tripartite "Middle Passage": "Pilot   Oh   Pilot   Me."

The second part of the poem furthers the thematics of blindness among the moral leadership. In six monologic stanzas, Hayden, drawing no doubt upon his reading of *Adventures of an African Slaver*, portrays an unrepentant slaver thrilling a young lad with lurid tales of his life and voyages. By placing the reader, and himself, in the position of direct address, Hayden places us in the discomfiting position of youthful audience to this avaricious figure, while he tells us how African kings were seduced into cooperation with the slavers and how traps of war were baited "wherein the victor and the vanquished / . . . / Were caught as prizes for our barracoons" (50). It may be yet more disturbing to witness this braggadocio than to read the terror-laden ironies of the poem's first section, for this tale telling is also a form of catechism to the youth whose position we occupy as audience when listening to this figure. When he boasts at the conclusion of his monologue, "I'd be trading still / but for the fevers melting down my bones" (51), it is plain that the fever is not simply a malaria contracted on his travels but is a sin willingly contracted long ago, perhaps in a scene of instruction identical to that created by these stanzas.

Hayden's poem returns the voice of its framing persona with the third and final section of "Middle Passage," resuming the tone and strategies of the first part and providing a setting for the presentation of the poem's last, and crucial, reformed text, derived from documents regarding the *Amistad* rebellion. Hayden figures the dark slave ships of our past as "Shuttles in the rocking loom of history" (51), and this would seem also to be an apt description of the historical texts he has spread before us. The patterns formed by these texts' motions are like our nation's telos, its "lucent melting shore." They describe "New World littorals that are / mirage and myth and actual shore" (51). Hayden's journey through these documents is a "voyage through death." Turning one last time to his transformations of Ariel's song, Hayden calls down a tempest within the poem. The grammatical ambiguity of this song is heightened upon its second appearance, as Hayden's direct form of address is further complicated. The song begins again with the portentous phrase "*Deep in the festering hold thy father lies*" (51), but this time the song moves to a second stanza:

> *But, oh, the living look at you*
> *with human eyes whose suffering accuses you,*
> *whose hatred reaches through the swill of dark*
> *to strike you like a leper's claw.*
>
> (52)

At one literal level, we may read this as a case in which the speaker addresses us when he speaks of "thy father," and at another, the direct address could be the speaker addressing himself in the general second person. Yet the pronouns continue to shift, permitting additional readings, and Hayden is seemingly aware that the racial politics of American reading practices will cause the meanings of this song to shift with the racial self-identifications and ideologies of his readers. In any reading, this song has the eerie effect of placing its audience simultaneously in positions of suffering and responsibility. The hatred Hayden inscribes haunts the remainder of the poem. The eyes that we encounter here stare out at us from between the layers of texts much as the tormented eyes between the decks of the slaving vessel stare at the "you" addressed by the song. The song is concluded on a note of triumph that will be repeated at poem's end. You "*cannot kill the deep immortal human wish, / the timeless will.*" As Ariel unleashed a storm at Prospero's command, and as Hayden's rewriting of Ariel's song was earlier interwoven with a prayer that called down chastening furies, so now the song is followed by the storm unleashed upon the *Amistad.* Vera Kutzinski has written movingly of the rhetorical effects of this storm in Hayden's reconstitution of the testimony offered in the case. It is a storm that thwarts the intentions of the man who describes it, slave owner Don Pedro Montez, and that redirects the fates of those on board the *Amistad,* and of America itself.

Spain had decreed that any slave transported to America after 1820 was automatically declared free, and the United States, represented in negotiations by its secretary of state, John Quincy Adams, had recognized this as law (Rukeyser 17). And yet, Don Montez in his accounts of the *Amistad* rebellion seemed to believe that both he and Don José Ruiz, the other putative slave "owner," had recognizable rights in property at issue in the court cases. Following an initial examination in August 1839, which proceeded, according to the version Hayden read in Muriel Rukeyser's *Willard Gibbs,* "as if Connecticut and New York had been passionate slave states" (Rukeyser 28), Ruiz and Montez printed a public notice of their gratitude in the local newspapers, acknowledging their "indebtedness to that nation" as well as their "assurance that this act [would] be duly appreciated by [their] most gracious sovereign."

In Hayden's reformulation of the testimonies, Montez views both the storm and the Africans' rebellion as simple bad luck. Storm and rebellion are, in fact, united in his view: "It was as though the very / air, the night itself were striking us" (52). An inhabitant of the same moral universe that formed the authors of the other slavers' logs Hayden has juxtaposed, Montez presents the acts of the Africans as acts of disloyalty and irrational, murderous rage, contrasting their behavior with the "loyalty" of the mulatto Celestino, who fought against the Africans and was killed. To Montez, the Africans are not men at all, though he would hold them responsible as men:

> "It sickens me
> to think of what I saw, of how these apes
> threw overboard the butchered bodies of
> our men, true Christians all, like so much jetsam."
>
> (53)

Coming as it does after the poem's earlier recording of blinded Africans being thrown overboard, this portion of Montez's text is wretchedly revealing. As it happens, following the revolt itself the *Amistad* rebels treated Montez well and promised that once he had guided them back to Africa, he would be permitted to return home (Rukeyser 21). Nonetheless, Montez describes Cinquez, the leader of the *Amistad* Africans, as a "surly brute" (52) and presses his demand for the illegal extradition of Cinquez to Havana.

It is in the final passages of the Montez monologue that Hayden succeeds most masterfully in redeploying the rhetoric of the texts of slavery. Montez's final words are voided of their speaker's desired rhetorical effects, and Hayden, seizing control of Montez's pronouncements, achieves a thorough rhetorical inversion of the Spaniard's desires:

> "We find it paradoxical indeed
> that you whose wealth, whose tree of liberty
> are rooted in the labor of your slaves
> should suffer the august John Quincy Adams
> to speak with so much passion of the right
> of chattel slaves to kill their lawful masters
> and with his Roman rhetoric weave a hero's
> garland for Cinquez. I tell you that

> we are determined to return to Cuba
> with our slaves and there see justice done. Cinquez—
> or let us say 'the Prince'—Cinquez shall die."
>
> (53)

Simply rewriting these words in the context of another age is sufficient to begin the reversal. In the postabolition twentieth century, readers will still find a paradox in the rooting of American liberty in the suffering of slaves. For Africans, the tree of liberty has in fact been a yoke tree blotting out the stars for much of our history. But where Montez hopes to use this paradox to ridicule the arguments of Adams, many will now read Adams's pleas precisely as a blow against that paradoxical flaw in America's founding. Montez argues for a system of "justice" that recognizes chattel slavery and guarantees owners rights to protection *from* their own property, a system in which the system's own laws may be disregarded in the interest of protecting rights to human chattel. To Montez's view, America, as represented in the person of Adams, is in danger of denying its commitment to justice, and he determines to seek justice elsewhere, despite the fact that his possession of the *Amistad* slaves was a violation of Spanish law and treaty agreements with the United States. (The Spanish minister argued *for* Montez.)

John Quincy Adams felt that the initial American response to the *Amistad* case *was* unjust, that America had strayed from the course to which its founding texts committed it, as he read them. He charged that the executive administration "in all [its] proceedings relating to these unfortunate men, instead of that *Justice,* which they were bound . . . to observe, . . . substituted *Sympathy!*—sympathy with one of the parties in this conflict of justice, and *Antipathy* to the other. Sympathy with the white, antipathy to the black" (6). In his revision of the Spaniard's texts, Robert Hayden summons forth as intertexts the arguments of John Quincy Adams as the former president of the United States contends against the appellants in this case, his own United States, who were appealing to the Supreme Court to prevent the freeing of the *Amistad* captives. The poem's reference to Adams's "Roman rhetoric" with which he weaves "a hero's garland for Cinquez" points most directly to a portion of Adams's argument whose classical allusions are both rhetorically powerful and powerfully disturbing:

> Cinque and Grabeau are uncouth and barbarous names. Call them Harmodius and Aristogiton, and go back for moral principle three thousand years to the fierce and glorious democracy of Athens. They too resorted to *lawless violence,* and slew the tyrant to redeem the freedom of their country. For this heroic action they paid the forfeit of their lives: but within three years the Athenians expelled their tyrants themselves, and in gratitude to their self-devoted deliverers decreed that thenceforth no slave should ever bear either of their names. Cinque and Grabeau are not slaves. Let them bear in future history the names of Harmodius and Aristogiton. (86–87)

The condescension Adams shows when speaking the names of Cinquez and Grabeau here is insupportable, even taking into account the evident fact that he here regards them as slave names. His rhetorical renaming of the Africans, no matter the motive, is too reminiscent of the habits among slave traders of christening Africans with ironic names from classical sources. As Nathaniel Mackey has commented in another context, "The discrepant relationship between name and named synecdochically recalls the history of dispossession which haunts the act of naming for the African American" ("Poseidon" 121). Hayden's final version of his poem elides this problematic of renaming by emphasizing the Roman rhetoric and its creation of a hero's garland (Kutzinski 180), and it is Adams's larger argument that seems most representative of what Hayden calls "The deep immortal human wish" (53).

It is the "timeless will" to freedom that forms the rhetorical center of Adams's argument and that he reads, much as Frederick Douglass was to read it, as the noumenal meaning of America's foundational documents. Vera Kutzinski asserts that "Adams's argument does not advocate the abolition of slavery" and that Adams's "rhetorical gesture and the historical analogy on which it so eloquently draws hardly constitute an attack on the system of slavery" (180). It is true that Adams does not, in his address to the Supreme Court, attempt abolition. It is also true that Adams despaired of the ultimate success of the abolitionist movement. In a diary entry written following the freeing of the *Amistad* rebels, an entry Hayden would have read in Rukeyser's *Willard Gibbs*, Adams says:

> The world, the flesh, and all the devils in hell are arrayed against any man who now in this North American Union shall dare to join the standard of Almighty God to put down the African slave-trade; and what can I, upon the verge of my seventy-fourth birthday, with a shaking hand, a darkening eye, a drowsy brain, and with all my faculties dropping from me one by one, as the teeth are dropping from my head—what can I do for the cause of God and man, for the progress of human emancipation, for the suppression of the African slave-trade? Yet my conscience presses me on; let me but die upon the breach. (Qtd. in Rukeyser 46)

Certainly a statement such as this is representative of that immortal human wish Hayden wished to counterpose to the self-assurances of proslavery rationales, and it may be that Hayden felt the surest way to honor Adams was to rewrite the Spaniard's belittling of Adams's brief.

Still, it is the case that Adams's argument, one that Hayden had read, while not explicitly advocating abolition, was a clearly abolitionist assault upon the legal underpinnings of slavery. Prefiguring the arguments of Douglass after his break with Garrison on the subject of the Constitution, Adams offered a brief that destroys the juridical logic of slavery and attempts to shame the Court into a recognition of such a reading of the Constitution. Adams, in moving toward a refutation of the argument that the "legation of Spain does not demand the delivery of slaves, but of assassins" (Adams 39), pauses to deliver his gloss upon the constitutional texts:

> The Constitution of the United States recognizes the slaves, held within some of the states of the Union, only in their capacity of *persons—persons* held to labor or service in a state under the laws thereof—*persons* constituting elements of representation in the popular branch of the National Legislature—*persons*, the migration or importation of whom should not be prohibited by Congress prior to the year 1808. The Constitution no where recognizes them as property. The words slave and slavery are studiously excluded from the Constitution. (Adams 39)

Later in the hearing in what may be Adams's most dramatic gesture, he pointedly calls the attention of the justices to the two copies of the Declaration of Independence that hang on the wall before them. Calling his United States to an accounting before the world, Adams dispenses with another justification for the slave trade:

> That DECLARATION says that every man is "endowed by his Creator with certain inalienable rights," and that "among these are life, liberty, and the pursuit of happiness." If these rights are inalienable, they are incompatible with the rights of the victor to take the life of his enemy in war, or to spare his life and make him a slave. (Adams 88–89)

Any reading of these sentences must recognize in them an attack upon the system of slavery. It is paradoxical that Adams quotes words written by a slave owner in order to refute the claims upon which slavery, and the case against Cinquez, rested. It is equally paradoxical that Robert Hayden most effectively calls our attention and honor to Adams's text by rewriting and deforming the texts of those who attempted to defame Adams.

Samuel Taylor Coleridge, inscribing his own epitaph, wrote: "That he who many a year with toil of breath / Found death in life, may here find life in death" (*Selection* 205). Robert Hayden, joining his collection of disparate and deformed texts around the unspeakable and the unspoken of the Middle Passage, refigures the voyage as a rebirth into life out of death in life. Assuming power over the texts of the slave trade, he assumes power over the historicizing of his own moment. Wresting control of his texts from their place in extant histories, he redirects the signifying motion. From the deathly inscriptions of slavery he evokes new meanings and renewed life; he is able, in the characterization of Vera Kutzinski, "to transfigure the movement from freedom to slavery into its exact opposite" (181). Like Melvin B. Tolson in his *Libretto for the Republic of Liberia,* Hayden reverses the direction of the Middle Passage, making of it a trope for the dual directedness of African-American historical consciousness. Hayden charts the connectedness of African and American cultures. Hayden's poetic reversal returns the Africans to their natal continent *in life, whole* but transformed. He remains here, African American.

At the end of Muriel Rukeyser's account of the *Amistad* case, Hayden might have studied a letter written by one of the freed Africans, Kinna, to Willard Gibbs, one of those who had helped to form a linguistic bridge between the Africans of the *Amistad* and the Americans:

> dear friend
>
> I wish to write you a letter because you have been so kind to me and because you love Mendi people I think of you very often I shall pray for you Dear friend would you pray for me If you love Jesus Christ and Christ will bless you and would you must come sometime to see Mendi people we must want to see you and I see you I am very Glad and Dear friend I pray for you My good love to your wife and all your family I love them very much I pray for them. . . . (Qtd. in Rukeyser 46)

In order to reestablish cultural correspondence with the African and African-American pasts, Hayden had to break into the white writing of the history of slavery. That breaking through was also a reformulation of modernist poetics that looked beyond the fragmentary supports of the Eliotic "Waste Land" toward a salvific view of African-American destiny constructed from Hayden's own archaeological poetics. In the end, it is the African-American poet who reserves the right to speak the last words. In the end, Cinquez, who never appears or speaks in the poem, survives the slavers' representations of him and returns to Africa, to be rerepresented in Hayden's verses. Robert Hayden's palimpsestic negotiations with a perpetually rewritten past chart a "Voyage through death to life upon these shores" (54).

Sea rocks the cradle. Mist wet as rain, heavy as dough, melts the sound. Ten times the bell oozes, the ship plows and bellies and tosses, dropping sounds like a turtle depositing eggs in the gloamy sea. *Deep in the hold thy father lies . . . those were pearls that were his eyes.* A poem written over and over again on the same raw parchment. Cracked, blackened as the hide of a slave's corpse left to rot in the desert. The caravan swims on. (Wideman, *Reuben* 128)

What shall peril hungers
So old old, what shall flatter the desolate?
Tin can, blocked fire escape and chitterling
And swaggering seeking youth and the puzzled wreckage
Of the middle passage . . .

(Brooks, *Blacks* 352)

Avey Johnson and the other characters of Paule Marshall's novel *Praisesong for the Widow* inhabit a discursive universe suffused with verse, from the book's first epigraph, drawn from Robert Hayden, to its last lines, a repetition of oracular, familial tradition. With this poetic swirl of allusion and conversion, Marshall repeats Hayden's and Tolson's reversal of the Middle Passage's direction, once more using the historical structure of the Passage to inscribe a homecoming. This instance of historical recovery, however, does not return to a continental home in Africa but seeks its salvific renewal in the syncretic cauldron of the Caribbean, in the Antillean heart where Africa and America meet.

Praisesong for the Widow opens under the sign of Robert Hayden's poem "Runagate Runagate," which supplies the title for the novel's first section as well as the novel's initial epigraph. The second epigraph is from Amiri Baraka's poem "leroy," and between them these two epigraphs, representing two generations of African-American poetics, seem to produce a textual tension that propels Paule Marshall's novel. "Runagate Runagate" is a free-verse poem launching itself out of the present tense into a meditation upon the will to freedom and the sense of communal responsibility. It is equal parts praise song for Harriet Tubman and gospel-tinged lyric memorial to the millions drawn by the mythic North's fabled freedom. Baraka's poem expresses a wish for knowledge, a knowledge of his mother's thoughts and life when young, when she was "getting into / new blues, from the old ones, the trips and passions showered on her by her own" (*Black Magic* 217), a description that applies to much of the plot of *Praisesong for the Widow*. Baraka looks into the eyes of his mother in a yearbook photograph and feels the power emanating "from that vantage of knowledge passed on to her passed on / to me and all the other black people of our time." The two epigraphs suggest a lyric arc of historical experience through the past into the present moment, and it is that arc that Paule Marshall's novel means to describe. It is the legacy of that lyric tradition that her novel continues in its praise song.

Avey Johnson's life, and her family's lives, are embedded in that tradition of song and of lyric knowledge. Her husband, Jay, learned in his Leona, Kansas, school lines of the black poets, lines that, committed to memory during his childhood in the segregated school, serve him in later life as a cultural touchstone. When he complains that "schools up north didn't teach colored children anything about the race, about themselves" (125), it is evident that he holds this lyric legacy to be the valued transmitter of a race's history and inventive genius. He recites to his young family from the first published poem of Langston Hughes, from the dialect lyrics of Paul Laurence Dunbar, from James Weldon Johnson's *God's Trombones*, which he acts out while striding up and down before his children and which his daughter Sis will recite for her Sunday school in her turn. When an older Avey is stopped cold by her own image in a mirror, startled by the reserve and the "look of acceptability" (49) of her own reversed image, she contrasts that reflection's poise with an image, gleaned from Jay's Sunday morning recitations of Langston Hughes's "I, Too": "*I am the darker brother / They send me to eat in the kitchen*" (qtd. in Marshall 49). When she reflects upon the complexion of her friend Thomasina Moore, she sees in it the witness to historical profanation lyrically recorded by Nina Simone in "Four Women" (Marshall 19). In the 1960s, when the evening's televised imagery of white assaults upon civil rights advocates is rerun as nightmare in her sleeping brain, it is her daughters who are blown up in the Birmingham church bombing, in her dreams, on that same Sunday Sis was to recite her twelve stanzas from James Weldon Johnson's "The Creation" (Marshall 31). Avey's daughters carry forward this habit of viewing their world through the lens of African-American lyric. Marion, a teacher of children "rejected by the public schools as being impossible to teach" (16), considers her pupils her "sweetest lepers," reminding herself of Gwendolyn Brooks's poem "Children of the Poor," a poem she urges Avey to read (16). The narrative itself, with its allusiveness and direct citation, further situates Avey's life in a literary continuum. When we read Avey's memories of her husband's poetic recitals, we read: "oh children, think about the / good times . . ." (126), lines from a poem by Lucille Clifton. When Avey and her husband recall the desperate neighbor whose pain they had regularly witnessed from their window on Halsey Street, the woman "railing loudly to herself" as she roamed the streets looking for her husband till she tracked him to a bar where he was "'Spending [his] money on some stinking 'ho,'" the narration supplies lines from Baraka's poem "Black Art" to represent the shared thoughts and characterizations that reverberate through the text, echoing her rage those dark mornings that "spoke not only for herself but for the thousands like her for blocks around" (Marshall 106–8). Even the incidental characters of Avey's narrative are sometimes reminders of black literary masterworks. "Doctor" Benitha Grant, a practitioner of traditional healing arts on Tatem Island in the South Carolina tidewater, recalls the much younger "Beneatha" of Lorraine Hansberry's *Raisin in the Sun,* whose ambition was to become a doctor.

Avey's full name, Avatara Johnson, suggests that she is an incarnation of an earlier being. Avey Johnson carries within her, along with the poetic traditions of African-American writing and black song, the triumphant tradition of African-American mythos. During her summers on Tatem Island, Avey received the stories by which her ancestors exercised mastery over their own history. In the past of legend, the Middle Passage could be undone. Standing with her father's great-aunt Cuney at a place called Ibo Landing, the young Avey is gifted with a tale of redirection handed on from Cuney's own grandmother, who had been about Avey's age when she "witnessed" the tale. With the singing from the church they have just passed still echoing in their ears ("*Who's that riding the chariot? / Well well well . . .*" [34]), Avey hears:

> It was here that they brought 'em. They taken 'em out of the boats right here where we's standing. . . . And the minute those Ibos was brought on shore they just stopped, my gran' said, and taken a look around. A good long look. Not saying a word. Just studying the place real good. Just taking their time and studying on it.
>
> And they seen things that day you and me don't have the power to see. 'Cause these pure-born Africans was people my gran' said could see in more ways than one. . . . Well, they seen everything that was to happen 'round here that day. The slavery time and the war my gran' always talked about, the 'mancipation and everything after that right on up to the hard times today. Those Ibos didn't

miss a thing. Even seen you and me standing here talking about 'em. And when they got through sizing up the place real good and seen what was to come, they turned, my gran' said, and looked at the white folks who brought 'em here. Took their time and gived them the same hard look. Tell you the truth, I don't know how those white folks stood it. . . . And when they got through studying 'em, when they *knew* just from looking at 'em how those folks was gonna do, do you know what the Ibos did?

. . . They just turned, my gran' said, all of 'em . . . and walked on back down to the edge of the river here. Every las' man, woman and chile. And they wasn't taking they time no more. They had seen what they had seen and those Ibos were stepping! And they didn't bother getting back into the small boats drawed up here. . . . They just kept walking right on out over the river. . . . They just kept on walking like the water was solid ground. Left the white folks standin' back here with they mouth hung open and they taken off down the river on foot. And when they got to where the ship was they didn't so much as give it a look. Just walked on past it. Didn't want nothing to do with that ol' ship. . . . When they realized there wasn't nothing between them and home but some water and that wasn't giving 'em no trouble they got so tickled they started in to singing. . . . My gran' declared she just picked herself up and took off after 'em. In her mind. Her body she always usta say might be in Tatem but her mind, her mind was long gone with the Ibos. . . . (37–39)

But Avey Johnson is at sea when we first meet her, far from the consecrated ground of Ibo Landing, and she is cruising, not walking. Poetry has nearly departed from her life and had begun leaving years before her husband's death. One by one traditions have dropped away from her life under the pressures of trying to establish her family in a place of promise and safety. By the time of her husband's death, the struggles have taken even her name for him from her mouth. For years she had been unable even to think the name she called him in the early days, "Jay," and when facing the corpse of Jerome Johnson in the funeral parlor, she sees staring up at her "that other face with the tight joyless look which she had surprised from time to time over the years" (133). The Jay Johnson who recited Paul Laurence Dunbar lyrics from memory was replaced by the Jerome Johnson who took to saying things like, "If it was left to me I'd close down every dancehall in Harlem and burn every drum! That's the only way these Negroes out here'll begin making any progress" (132). Similarly, the Avey Johnson who used to delight in dancing barefoot on the floorboards of her home to the blues becomes in later age a matronly figure who feels shame when one of her traveling companions joins in a carnival dance. In late life Avey wonders: "Would it have been possible to have done both? That is, to have wrested, as they had done over all those years, the means needed to rescue them from Halsey Street and to see the children through, while preserving, safeguarding, treasuring those things that had come down to them over the generations, which had defined them in a particular way" (139).

Avatara Johnson parted from herself and from her friends. Her husband had come to speak "of his own in the harsh voice that treated them as a race apart" (140), and she came to part herself from her former sources of spiritual comfort. At the opening of the novel she has come to feel an intense separation from her traveling friends, Thomasina and Clarice, a separation marked by the divider that parts Avey from her fellow travelers as they sleep between the decks of their luxury cruise ship. This sleeping separation is one Avey has volunteered for as a means of maintaining her privacy, one that signals the growing distance between herself and her friends and her family, a distance marked by racial measures. Just as the younger, jazz-loving Jay Johnson had become the older Jerome who condemned black dancing, Avey, who once danced for joy in her parlor, has become someone who is shamed by the dancing of her friend. On an earlier cruise when the ship put into Colombia, Clarice had, to Avey's disgust, joined the carnival dance: "And with their fellow passengers watching. White faces laughing! White hands applauding! Avey Johnson had never been so mortified" (25). It is the gaze of the racial other, as much as Clarice's age and "bony hips," that produces Avey's mortification. It is the presence of the white passengers that separates Avey's shame from Clarice's joy.

Avey's daughter had asked her in exasperation, "Why go on some meaningless cruise with a bunch of white folks anyway?" (13), and though Avey at first thought Marion had been wrong to oppose the cruise (15), by the time we begin to read her story, Avey is preparing to jump ship. Though these have been pleasure cruises, the *Bianca Pride,* with its bright ironical name, has begun to manifest its metonymic weight as descendant of the death ships of the Middle Passage. Listening to the seemingly innocent play of the vacationers on the *Bianca Pride,* Avey Johnson is suddenly troubled by a tropic memory: "[I]n the quoit games being played just below where she stood the thud of hempen rings being thrown to the deck reached her ears as the sound of some blunt instrument repeatedly striking human flesh and bone" (56). The sound brings swimming into Avey's consciousness the memory of a night long ago when she and her husband had witnessed from their bedroom window the sight and sound of a white police officer clubbing a black man mercilessly, a memory that, at sea, recalls also the sounds of the slavers clubbing their cargo. In another episode an elderly man in bikini shorts grabs Avey's skirt and invites her to take a seat in the deck chair next to him. The hallucinatory vision Avey experiences as she looks down at this sunning old white man is as ineluctable as the scenes witnessed by Coleridge's ancient mariner: "In a swift, subliminal flash, all the man's wrinkled and sunbaked skin fell away, his thinned-out flesh disappeared, and the only thing to be seen on the deck chair was a skeleton in a pair of skinny red-and-white striped trunks and a blue visored cap" (59). Fleeing in panic and outrage, Avey seeks refuge in the always empty ship's library, and there among the vessel's unattended texts the idea of abandoning the cruise comes to her. Driven by visions of herself and of the other passengers, and by the unsolicited nighttime visitations of her deceased great-aunt Cuney, who had passed to Avatara the familial connection to the transcendent history of Ibo Landing, Avey Johnson becomes an odd sort of Runagate. She wants to return home, and she will. But first she must make the passage through memory to a renewal of her spiritual being and reclaim a past she has put behind her. Before returning to her home in the United States, she must return to the Caribbean landfall, the site where African sojourners first began to create African-American cultures; she must make the passage to reconstitute an origin, to reclaim the work of transformative legacy that she had left behind her in the driven workings of American survival.

Stepping ashore in the Caribbean, Avey at once finds herself in the linguistic interstices of New World signifying, a place where the uncomprehended can be a comfort:

> [R]eaching her clearly now was the flood of unintelligible words and the peculiar cadence and lilt of the Patois she had heard for the first time in Martinique three days ago. She had heard it that first time and it had fleetingly called to mind the way people spoke in Tatem long ago. There had been the same vivid, slightly atonal music underscoring the words. She had heard it and that night from out of nowhere her great-aunt had stood waiting in her sleep. . . . (67)

This "African mix-up something" (75) Avey hears is the first stage of her passage, not to an origin, but to a reclaimed connection to a living language of reinvention and reinvocation. Living out the implications of her name, Avatara learns that she is the twin, even to the way she holds her head, of a woman here, a revelation Avey at first resists (72). She finds that the people of this island immediately strip her of her strangeness, mentally dressing her "in one of the homemade cotton prints the women were wearing" (72), and she is struck too by the sheer Africanness of her new surroundings. The taxi driver she meets "might have stepped off the pages of the expensive photography book with the word 'Masai' on its cover which Marion kept in her living room" (73). She has entered a nominal realm of speaking in which, while all are citizens of the same community, some, particularly among the old, still name and celebrate the African nations and languages from which their lineage has been torn. "What's your nation?" asks Lebert Joseph, Avey's guide to the out island. "Is you an Arada? . . . Cromanti maybe . . . ?" Again Avey resists, but there is a comfort lingering at the border of her confusion: "What was the man going on about? What were these names? Each one made her head ache all the more. She thought she heard in them the faint rattle of the necklace of cowrie shells and amber Marion always wore. Africa? Did they have something to do with Africa? Senile. The old man was senile" (167). In the voices of the people who maintain the traditions of the Big Drum and the Beg Pardon, Avey Johnson begins to hear the overtones of history, theirs and her own. As the memories of Ibo Landing had pierced the carefully nurtured comforts of Avey's leisure cruise, so in the sounds of African-Caribbean song does Avey of a sudden hear the history she has for so long shut away. Listening to a man's falsetto singing,

> without understanding the words, Avey Johnson felt the tragic weight that underscored them pressing her down in the chair. . . .
>
> From the anguish in the man's voice, in his face, in his farseeing gaze, it didn't seem the story was just something he had heard, but an event he had been witness to. He might have been present, might have seen with his own eyes the husband bound in chains for Trinidad, the wife—iron on her ankles and wrists and in a collar around her neck—sold off to Haiti, and the children, Zabette and Ti Walter (he even knew their names) left orphaned behind. (177)

It is in listening to the names that fill her ears, attending to the accumulating connotative values of the language's history, that Avey slowly triumphs over the separations that circumstance and oppression had caused her to feel. Away from the white gaze of fellow passengers, away from the white gaze of America's social construction of race, intent, as it has historically been, upon both uniting black people in oppression and dividing them from one another's powers and visions, Avey is gathered into the heart of an African-American communal expression. In the name of a dance she hears echoes of a great African past:

> [I]t was as if he meant more than just the dance. He might have been also referring to the place that bore the name: Juba, the legendary city, at the foot of the White Nile. And it was clear from his tone that he wasn't thinking of the forgotten backwater it had become, . . . but the city as he remembered it from memories that had come down to him in the blood: as Juba, the once-proud, imperial seat at the heart of the equatoria.
>
> "So you know, you remember Juba," he repeated, giving it the wide meaning. "Come, show me how they dances it where you's from."
>
> She went back to shaking her head. "No one dances it anymore. It's only something you might hear or read about."
>
> "*We* still dances it!" he cried. . . . (178)

Avey and her late husband, Jay, had long ceased to give such names their wide meaning. Given less latitude for spirit than their spirits required, they had constricted to a less resonant lexicon within which they could assure, at least, their children's lives. But as she completes her retrospective passage through her life, as, from the vantage point of late life, she meditates upon what the cost of mere survival has been, she wonders if indeed it might have been possible to survive and to keep that which had once defined her. She sees, in the old out islanders, such a possibility: "All that was left were a few names of what they called nations which they could no longer even pronounce properly, the fragments of a dozen or so songs, the shadowy forms of long-ago dances and rum kegs for drums. The bare bones. The burnt-out ends. And they clung to them with a tenacity she suddenly loved in them and longed for in herself" (240). The ancient forms celebrated here are not the names of origins. They are the names transformed by age, transmuted by history, altered by the accents of a newer place and exchanges with other peoples. They are forms within which a New World art is improvised. Yet, they are forms that carry undertones of origins, tones that tell of ancestral struggle and regeneration, tones that Avey needs to tell again to her children and to others.

In Paule Marshall's novel, as in much of Melville, the places of revival are offshore. To return to Tatem, Avey Johnson must return to the out island, make that last circuit of Middle Passage to the place where the Americas are most African. She has to make a homecoming voyage to the scenes of seasoning and rebirth. Avey Johnson joins the out islanders on their annual excursion home from the larger island to Carriacou. The excursion, for Avey strongly reminiscent of the communal boat rides of her happier years, is a voyage in starkest contrast to the cruise of the *Bianca Pride*. For the passengers of the cruise ship, people such as the out islanders were a spectacle got up for their entertainment, something to be talked about years after at parties on the mainland. For the passengers of the *Bianca Pride*, the cruise was reward for retirement, a chance after years of accumulation to acquire a true relic of the exotic, the tropic, the primitive. Surrounded by the encompassing gaze of the white passengers, Avey had divided herself from the black women with whom she made her

cruise, had worried that they too might become spectacle and sou-
venir. The excursion celebrants on board the *Emanuel C* sing themselves and celebrate themselves and take Avey among them. But she
still has to rid herself of the spiritual detritus she carries. It is her im-
mersion in the experience of the sea that both sickens and saves her.
Taken gravely ill on the tossing boat full of revelers, Avey is violently
purged of her shame. Afterward, recovering in the deckhouse, she is
visited by one more archetypal memory:

> [S]he had the impression as her mind flickered on briefly of other
> bodies lying crowded in with her in the hot, airless dark. A mul-
> titude it felt like lay packed around her in the filth and stench of
> themselves, just as she was. Their moans, rising and falling with
> each rise and plunge of the schooner, enlarged upon the one filling
> her head. Their suffering—the depth of it, the weight of it in the
> cramped space—made hers of no consequence. (209)

When Avatara Johnson is reborn from the bowels of the schooner,
she is prepared for the witness and reconstruction to come. She attends with the out islanders their Big Drum and their Beg Pardon,
and she begs pardon of the past. She bears witness to the cultural
continuity figured before her in the dance, and to the praise songs.
She stands in the place of reconstitution, where old traditions are
honored and new ones brought into being. Long removed from direct
knowledge of her African lineage, Avey is one of those "people who
can't call their nation," but those of the out islanders who still can sing
for her. She can join in the creole dances: "Every and anybody can
dance then . . ." (175). She is drawn into the circle of old folk dancing, completing a circle that had commenced for her at Ibo Landing.
Avey, who had been shamed at the spectacle offered by her friend's
dancing before white tourists, resumes the dancing of her youth. Her
great-aunt Cuney had been expelled from the circle of the Ring Shout
when, with the advent of spirit, she had been caught crossing her
feet. Avey now reinserts her family in the circling of historical signifying, in the creole construction of American identity. Returning to
a long-remembered step, Avey repeats the Tatem Islanders' "dance
that wasn't supposed to be dancing," a step instantly recognized by
the out islanders as their own "Carriacou Tramp." As the dancers

of Carriacou gather her into their midst, Avatara Johnson realizes "she had finally after all these decades made it across" (248), completing her passage and fulfilling her name, "restored to her proper axis" (254).

It is then that Avey Johnson determines to return home transformed with a saving purpose, and it is then that the poetry of her youngest years returns most completely to her. In childhood she had read of an "obsessed old sailor" who detained a guest on his way to a wedding with a harrowing tale of a mystic voyage, primal sin, and spectral, plankless ships. Avey's own marriage, beginning with such great promise and greater hope, had slowly slipped from her grasp, along with her history and her sense of lyric knowledge. She remembers now: "*It is an ancient mariner / And he stoppeth one of three*" (255). She determines to place herself in the path of those swiftly moving achievers, "those young, bright, fiercely articulate token few for whom her generation had worked the two and three jobs" (255), those who "rushed blindly in and out of the glacier buildings, unaware, unprotected, lacking memory." She will, like Coleridge's ancient mariner, delay them with the telling of her voyage and hope that they might take hold of the allegory, that they might learn the value of a lyric memory against the killing embrace of seductive and racist mercantile Middle Passage. She hopes to enlist Marion; "Marion, whom she had tried to root from her body" (255); Marion, who will bring her "sweetest lepers" to Ibo Landing so that they can listen to Avey tell a free story; Avey, who "Rises from their anguish and their power" (Hayden 60), the incarnation at last of the spirit honored in Robert Hayden's praise song "Runagate Runagate." Then Avey shall repeat the lyric of African renascence. "It was here that they brought them," she would begin—as had been ordained. "They took them out of the boats right here where we're standing . . ." (256). Avey Johnson has already found listeners among the attentive young. Filmmaker Julie Dash, for one, has carried forward the intertextual lyric by transposing Avey's received song of Ibo Landing into her film *Daughters of the Dust*. It is the same saving lyric of witness sung in many languages throughout the diaspora:

What Nan told her she had forgotten, along with the language she told it in. The same language her ma'am spoke, and which would never come back. But the message—that was and had been there all along. Holding the damp white sheets against her chest, she was picking meaning out of a code she no longer understood. Nighttime. Nan holding her with her good arm, waving the stump of the other in the air. "Telling you. I am telling you, small girl Sethe," and she did that. She told Sethe that her mother and Nan were together from the sea. Both were taken up many times by the crew. "She threw them all away but you. The one from the crew she threw away on the island. The others from more whites she also threw away. Without names, she threw them. You she gave the name of the black man. She put her arms around him. The others she did not put her arms around. Never. Never. Telling you. I am telling you, small girl Sethe." (Morrison, *Beloved* 62)

━━━━━━━

We were the color of shadows when we came down
with the tinkling leg-irons to join the chains of the sea,
for the silver coins multiplying on the sold horizon,

and these shadows are reprinted now on the white sand
of antipodal coasts, your ashen ancestors
from the Bight of Benin, from the margin of Guinea.

There were seeds in our stomachs, in the cracking pods
of our skulls on the scorching decks, the tubers
withered in no time. We watched as the river-gods

changed from snakes into currents. When inspected
our eyes showed dried fronds in their brown irises,
and from our curved spines, the rib cages radiated

like fronds from a palm-branch. Then, when the dead
palms were hurled overside, the ribbed corpses
floated, riding, to the white sand they remembered,

to the Bight of Benin, to the margin of Guinea.
So, when you see burnt branches riding the swell,
trying to reclaim the surf through crooked fingers,

after a night of rough wind by some stone-white hotel,

past the bright triangular passage of the wind surfers,
remember us to the black waiter bringing the bill.

(Walcott, Omeros 149)

The Great Western Civilizing and Trading Society with branches
everywhere. I was the burden Albert chose to carry. Mongo Al,
supervising the middle passage from darkness to light. But I am
tired of travel, weary of dancing once a day to whip music, nine-
tailed cat songs. I grow old, I grow old. And must I remember old
sorrows, nakedness, hunger. Did they come bearing gifts. Was it
wrong to squat catatonic and die staring at the sea.

There is a storm. I am angry beyond anger. I hear the splash of
bodies heaved overboard to lighten the ship. Some go unnecessarily
because a frightened sailor miscounted and disconnected one black
wrist from another. Waves, thunder, and wind, but the doomed in
one last fatal triumph are heard above the tumult.

I am tossed, tumbled, enraged. But storm settles and for better
or worse some survive. (Wideman, *Hurry Home* 65–66)

An odd crossing of intellectual fashions and prohibitions in recent years has created a situation in which, while more and more of
the best white historians in America have directed their studies to
the era of American slavery and the slave trade, fewer white literary
artists have created works of lasting significance that take this history as their inspiration. There have always been some memorable
white writers who not only spoke of the Middle Passage but made it
a forming structure of their work. Harriet Beecher Stowe included
in *Uncle Tom's Cabin* a chapter titled "The Middle Passage," and one
of her few formal innovations is to be found there. Her Middle Passage is not a voyage from Africa to America but a journey through
the American South on the Red River. In titling her description of
Simon Legree's transport of slaves through the states "The Middle
Passage," Stowe underscores the perfidy and appalling inhumanity of
the continuing traffic in African men, women, and children and provides a historical resonance to one character's observation: "[I]t is you
considerate, humane men, that are responsible for all the brutality
and outrage . . . ; because, if it were not for your sanction and influence, the whole system could not keep foot-hold for an hour" (348).

One of the white writers of the modernist period who employed a scene of Middle Passage as a central element of his work's structure, a scene that prefigures Amiri Baraka's later play "Slave Ship," was Eugene O'Neill, in *The Emperor Jones*. In the sixth scene of O'Neill's play, Brutus Jones, who is attempting an escape into the darknesses of the forests on his West Indian island, experiences a historical regression that O'Neill uses to parallel Jones's rush toward his tragic fate and to foreground the historical and psychological forces that have brought Jones to this pass. Reaching a cleared place in this archetypal forest, Jones finds a space enclosed by creepers, a space that is "like the dark, noisome hold of some ancient vessel" (198). Pausing in his flight, Jones lies down to rest and is soon encompassed within a vision of the Middle Passage, taking his place among spectral rows of seated figures "in crumpled, despairing attitudes, hunched, facing one another with their backs touching the forest walls as if they were shackled to them . . . letting themselves follow the long roll of a ship at sea" (199). Like the work of later novelists Paule Marshall and Russell Banks, O'Neill's figuration of fate and Middle Passage is set in the Caribbean. Here in the Antillean margins of the New World (keeping in mind that margins frame both our entries and our exits), Brutus too finds the present scarred by the past, finds the history of Middle Passage erupting into the moral ambiguities of his present, ambiguities that are only heightened by the racism of O'Neill's text.

Russell Banks is unusual among contemporary white authors in that he sees the historical Middle Passage both as the spiritual hinge of African-American culture and as the vanishing point of American history. He brings this understanding to bear on the writing of his novel *Continental Drift,* a novel that exemplifies the syncretic and palimpsestic modes of composition also adopted by Robert Hayden and Paule Marshall, a novel that mingles languages, religions, and races in a rich *mixage* to voice the tragedies and possibilities of America's unfinished errand in the wildernesses of its own making. Part of Banks's method is to deploy the metaphor of Middle Passage in such a way that its history might serve as an intertext for his title trope, *Continental Drift.* In so doing, he not only uses the Middle Passage to figure the structural center of his novel, he also appropriates African-American syncretic invention to form his epic of national reformation. Where Robert Hayden had seized upon white-authored texts, reconfiguring them to make a black poem, Banks takes into his white hands the sacred symbols of black spiritual signifying to organize his New World narrative.

Continental Drift opens and closes with an invocation and envoi in the italicized voice of the author, passages that set forth the author's intentions and methods. The invocation demonstrates just how this novel will differ from, while honoring, its epic antecedents. Where we would in epic ordinarily anticipate an invocation of the muses at the outset, we find here a crossing of that tradition with traditions at once newer and more ancient. *"It's not memory you need for telling this story,"* we read on the first page. Neither Mnemosyne nor her sisters will suffice for the singing of this song. What's needed instead is *"a white Christian man's entwined obsession with race and sex and a proper middle-class American's shame for his nation's history. This is an American story of the late twentieth century, and you don't need a muse to tell it, you need something more like a loa, or mouth-man, a voice that makes speech stand in front of you and not behind"* (1). Preceding these words is the inscription of a Voudoun vever, a design transcribed on the earth to invoke a loa, and it is the vever of Legba, whom Banks calls upon in his invocation to *"come forward and bring this middle-aging, white mouth-man into speech again"* (2). Papa Legba is the "initial procreative whole" (Deren 96), and within the Dahomean cosmology transmuted into New World Voudoun he is the medium through which "primal energy was funneled to the world," the "God of the cross-roads of the vital intersection between the two worlds" (Deren 96–97). Each of Banks's subsequent chapters is given under the sign of another spirit, invoked with another vever, providing an African-American structuring within which the white "mouth-man's" tale proceeds. As this use of signifying inscription indicates, *Continental Drift* is an act of performative language, directed past the book's covers to bring about an effect in the discursive world beyond. The characters, in their infinite particularities, are not the end point of the narrative. In his envoi, which is pronounced under the sign of Erzulie, Banks explains that, like Leslie Marmon Silko's *Ceremony*, his novel is meant as an action; the reading of it is to accomplish something in us: *"Books get written— novels, stories and poems stuffed with particulars that try to tell us what the world is, as if our knowledge of people like Bob Dubois and Vanise and Claude Dorsinville will set people like them free. It will not. Knowledge of the facts of Bob's life and death changes nothing in our world. Our celebrating his life and grieving over his death, however, will"* (366). The stories of Bob and Vanise, for all their detail, are fictive constructions meant not so much to educate us about the lives of "real" people like them as to cause disruptions in the way we construct our present and our future. Art such as this does not intervene directly in the material circumstances of the world, but it is an intervention in our way of thinking of our world. What Banks hopes to achieve is the destruction of the definitions that currently constrain us. *"Sabotage and subversion, then, are this book's objectives,"* Banks tells us as he concludes. *"Go, my book, and help destroy the world as it is"* (366).

These incantatory edges aside, the narrative of *Continental Drift* is delivered for the most part in the straightforward and conversational modes of mimetic literary realism. It weaves together in alternating sections the stories of two characters we know from the outset are destined to meet, and it is this interweaving that forms in its specifics the larger trope of the novel's title. This is a book about the tragedies of human migration and motivation. In a chapter written beneath the vever for drums and the spirit of Ogun, Banks makes explicit his controlling metaphor: "It's as if the creatures residing on this planet in these years, the human creatures, millions of them traveling singly and in families, in clans and tribes, traveling sometimes as entire nations, were a subsystem of currents and tides, of winds and weather, of drifting continents . . ." (34). This chapter's title, *"Batterie Maconnique,"* names a rhythm, one that, according to Maya Deren, "probably signifies a rapping on the door of the loa world" (326) and that heralds the opening of Banks's primary thematic material. In order to grasp the mass movements of humankind as something more than mere natural, mindless currents without cause in human decision, and hence as something whose shape is not inevitable, Banks imagines two characters whose flights represent both the driven migrations of the present and the past movements that led to them. In creating one character who typifies the sun-belt drift of American workers in the last decades, and another who follows the refugee currents from the Caribbean to the United States, Banks is also tracing the most recent effects of forces loosed long ago by the Middle Passage, another form of American manifest destiny.

Bob Dubois, whose name forms an eerie New England link to

W. E. B. Du Bois, is a man a great deal like those earlier white men who formed the crews of the slave ships and who died working the barracoons of Africa to make other white men rich. Bob Dubois wants very much to think of himself as a good man; he also cheats on his wife, speaks racist epithets, and winds up involved in a number of illegal schemes. Dubois has found that the price of carrying a good opinion of himself is not inquiring too deeply into the logical basis of his moral universe. He is a man who raises no objections to the racist remarks other whites make to him, who says the word *nigger* easily and naturally, who has grown up having virtually no contact with African Americans, who eventually has an affair with a black woman he seems genuinely to love. He is a man who easily accepted the scaled-down version of the American dream offered to laboring people and is thus doubly frustrated when even that modest ambition fails to produce happiness, when, as he suddenly states to his wife, he finds that their lives are nothing but endless bills and evenings spent watching "Hart to Hart" on television. In desperation this descendant of French colonists quits his job as an oil burner repairman for the Abenaki Oil Company, whose ironic name, like Melville's *Pequod,* memorializes another colonial oppression, and joins the millions of others who have headed south in search of better jobs and cheaper living, lighting out for the territory, with its barely civilized promise of easy acquisition.

There he encounters as he never had before the embodied racial otherness that had till then been a hazily glimpsed creature of his own conversations with other New England whites. The southward journey of the Dubois family not only allegorizes the sun-belt drift of American working families, it also accentuates the changing demographics of late twentieth-century America, demographic changes that are here figured as the inevitable outcome of motions made long ago. Driving deeper into Florida, the Dubois family encounters for its first time large numbers of American blacks, Jamaicans, Cubans, Haitians, and the family members sense that they are in another America than the one they had inhabited in their previous lives: "These black-and-brown-skinned people, . . . these working people, who got here first, belong here, not Bob and Elaine Dubois and their daughters Ruthie and Emma. It's Bob and his family who are the newcomers at the Florida trough, and Bob is embarrassed by his lateness" (55). Bob's is a costly embarrassment, and a dangerous one. His willful innocence is the fertile ground of corruption and racism, and he will not be able to maintain that innocence, to go on thinking of himself as a good man, away from the support of the like-minded discursive community he has left behind in the North. For men such as Bob Dubois, the distance between their actions and their conception of themselves as good eventually produces a cognitive dissonance ranging from minor irritation to destructive rage. Often we are told that the intelligence of Bob Dubois is his capacity to form a narrative of his life, that this narrative knowledge, like the lyric knowledge of Avey Johnson in Paule Marshall's *Praisesong for the Widow,* is the source of his solace and understanding. But as Bob's life careens out of comfortable channels it had previously known, as Bob enmeshes himself in patterns of corruption that make his own goodness increasingly an untenable concept, his narrative is constantly ruptured and he is literally at sea.

Vanise Dorsinville is, like Bob Dubois, the child of conquest, slave trade, and colonialism, "the puzzled wreckage / of the middle passage" described by Gwendolyn Brooks (*Blacks* 352). If Bob Dubois in some ways represents those squeezed out of the American dream by the shifting objectives of late capitalism, Vanise Dorsinville is one of those for whom capital conceived but one status, as chattel. Having stolen them from Africa and robbed them of their labor, capitalism has expelled the Vanise Dorsinvilles of this world from its considerations. Haiti, wracked by slavery, redeemed by revolution, and then plunged again into an oppression so deep there seems to be no way out of it, is Vanise Dorsinville's home. But like so many others, Vanise is compelled by circumstance and by desire for a better life to join the thousands of others who, in one illicit craft or another, have set out for Florida, retracing the course of piracy and the Middle Passage.

Adopting a hypothetically plural first person, Russell Banks places his readers in the midst of Vanise Dorsinville's family as they consider the dangers they confront as the result of an almost accidental action of Vanise's nephew Claude, as they slowly determine that their own continued survival requires the departure of Claude and Vanise. In the passages narrating the life of Bob Dubois, the reader stands at one remove to judge the goodness of Bob's decisions, but here Banks places us within the narrative as "we" reach a consensus that "the boy was wrong to insist that we had done nothing wrong, and he was right to be afraid, and Vanise was no doubt right to weep, and we, we were right to do what we did then" (48). What "we" decide is to help Claude and Vanise to reach a "better, safer place" (51) and thus ensure our own safety in this place, Haiti.

That enormous, perhaps inevitable misjudgment of "ours" sets Vanise Dorsinville on her tripartite passage toward her encounter with Bob Dubois and with the United States, her journey from one America to another. The Middle Passage is at the heart of Banks's novel and is explicitly named, almost in the precise middle of the book, in a chapter that is presignified by the vever for Agwe, in whose bark are placed offerings that are set on the sea (Deren 326). In this passage to the America of their conversations, Vanise and Claude are at the mercy of men every bit as corrupt as those who guided their slave ships over the Atlantic, and these men repeat demonically the depredations of their predecessors. The man who has taken Vanise's money to convey her to America instead leaves her and Claude on yet another island, far short of their destination. The second, middle leg of their journey takes them as far as the allegorically named New Providence Island. On the way they are subjected to all the terrors of the Middle Passage of centuries past, held below decks in unremitting darkness, the darkness of the grave, a darkness interrupted only by the flashlights of the seamen who come below to rape and tear: "When the men were down in the hold, their flashlight shattering the darkness, the place seemed tiny, cramped, closed in upon the human beings, as if they were under a huge house; but when the men had gone and taken their light away with them, the place seemed to open up and grow enormous, like a black tent. And with both day and night gone, all of time was gone, too . . ." (182). It is in the telling of this middle voyage to New Providence that Banks names the intertext, the parallel history that grounds his story, the history that first brought all these characters to the New World: "They had come over three hundred miles as if chained in darkness, a middle passage . . ." (188). Claude and Vanise approach New Providence feeling as though "they had returned from their own drownings" (187).

Vanise, however, is not entirely helpless. Like the out islanders of Carriacou in *Praisesong for the Widow,* she maintains a connection to the fertile unbroken practice of African spirituality that constantly improvises out of itself new ways of redemption in the diaspora. Like

Avey Johnson, Vanise feels threads of connectedness to a larger community by which she "connects her sad, suffering moment on earth to universal time, ties the stingy ground she stands on to the huge, fecund continent of Africa, makes an impoverished, illiterate black woman's troubles the pressing concerns of the gods" (209).

Bob Dubois has come unmoored, unconnected, and has not the reassurance of such a system of confronting fate. He too improvises, but each of his nonce solutions is a rebeginning from a moral and historical zero point. Slowly crushed under the weight of his own history, Dubois is unable to take in hand an understanding of the forces arrayed against him, or within him, to change his life in a way that will really matter. Instead he drives himself from one desperate effort at making a masterstroke against his fate to another, till, hoping to make one last killing that will buy him out of the hole his bad decisions, his bad faith, his brother, and his best friend have gotten him into, Bob Dubois undertakes to smuggle human beings from the offshore islands to American Florida.

Bob Dubois and Vanise Dorsinville are both heralds of a history that, insufficiently acknowledged, still moves against us. They should have much to speak to each other about, but they cannot. Both carry in their names the record of drift and conquest, of continents violently in motion. They are both separated from their own tongues by the languages of colonialism and its aftermath. Vanise speaks a language that is at once a sign of her separation from her people's homeland and a tongue inflected and enriched by African languages. What few words of his name's language Dubois has acquired he learned against his father's will, "the half-dozen words and phrases of Quebecois he learned by accident as a child, learned, despite his father's prohibitions against speaking French, from boys at school and old women at LeGrand's grocery store on Moody Street and old men fishing from the bridge over the Catamount River" (302–3). The senior Dubois, fearing that his son's tongue would forever mark him with the wrong signs of postcolonial class and caste, erased a linguistic legacy, and in his hope and shame he erased with it the possibility of Bob's communicating with Vanise across the chasms of color and experience that open between them.

Bob Dubois looks in speechless wonder at Vanise, Claude, and the other Haitians he has undertaken to transport illegally aboard the

Belinda Blue. As they cross the open sea that "stretches straight to Africa, where the eastern sky is born" (300), Bob sees "how astonishingly black they [are], *African*," and wonders: "Why do they throw away everything they know and trust, no matter how bad it is, for something they know nothing about and can never trust?" (305). He sees also, in their quiet gaze at him, a reflection of his own unreadable status in their world: "I'm not their friend, and they're not foolish enough to think it. But I'm not their boss, either, and I'm not their jailer. Who *am* I to these people, he wonders, and why are they treating me this way? What do they know about me that I don't know about myself?" (309). One of the many things that Bob Dubois does not know about himself is that, in the self-interestedness of the moral blankness at his heart, he is to be the instrument of their deaths.

Nearing the coast of the New World, the *Belinda Blue* nears a coast guard patrol, and it is then that Dubois replicates the worst offenses against humanity with which the authors of the slave trade marked the sea-lanes leading to our door. Following the suggestion of his mate, Tyrone, a Jamaican who is positioned in the narrative as, like Bob's brother, a mediator of amorality, a figure who recalls the black overseers placed above their brethren on the slave ships, Dubois gives the order to throw the Haitians out of the boat. It is, like each of Dubois's earlier, unthinking commitments to action, the word that cannot be reclaimed from the air and from history, the word that, once uttered, cannot be undone. To save himself from certain apprehension, Bob Dubois treats his cargo *as* cargo, as things that can be jettisoned, as contraband commodity. He sacrifices the lives of those who, for reasons unfathomable to him, placed themselves in his charge. But, like "puzzled wreckage" of the Middle Passage, one survives, one only is escaped to tell the story, is washed to shore living, a castaway of history and commerce come back to reclaim her legacy.

Bob Dubois can no longer conceive himself a good man and recognizes clearly and distinctly for the first time his need of redemption. Discussing with his wife what they can do to go on living, and living together, Dubois finds the two of them interrogating their lives under a previously absent moral standard. "For the first time, as they make their plans, they are speaking of 'should' and 'should not,' and they do it stiffly, awkwardly, for these are words that make it difficult to mingle fantasy with hope" (398). Before Bob can have any hope, he

knows, there must be expiation. He determines to return the money
he was given to sail the Haitians to a new home, and it is in this moment that Bob Dubois becomes heroic. For he knows that he cannot
make good his debt; he knows that no act of compensation will bal-
ance his life against the lives he has taken. When he enters Little Haiti,
a section of Miami bordered by neighborhoods "where middle-class
Cubans and whites deliver themselves and their children anxiously
over to the ongoing history of the New World" (351), Dubois seems
to understand that he too must deliver himself over to that history,
a history he has reinscribed in bodies scattered across the beaches
of Florida. In the last chapter of Bob Dubois's story, a chapter titled
"Feeding the Loas," Dubois fumbles determinedly toward the fate his
actions have contrived for him. He is led finally to the place where
Vanise Dorsinville, the only survivor of his attempt to save himself,
is, in the company of *les invisibles,* performing her own rites of puri-
fication, sacrifice, and salvation, employing the constantly reinvented
ancient means to make a haven in this terrible New World. At the
close of his quest Bob recognizes that Vanise was

> saved from drowning to come back and move among the living and,
> when the white man presents himself, to name him to himself, that
> he may be judged. She's the woman whose fate now is to say his fate
> to him, that he may live it out. It's she who must endure the sight
> of the sign of his shame, the money clutched in his outstretched
> hands, and must hear him beg her to take it from him. . . . And
> she's the woman who must refuse to remove the sign of his shame,
> who must turn away from him now. . . . (363)

Though Bob Dubois's story is organized under the signs of African-
American spiritual signifying, and centered by the reappearance
within his narrative of the sign of the Middle Passage, determined
circumstance and his own choices have denied him the ability to read
those signs or to learn from that history till it is too late. Denied by the
inexorable progress of capital and its culture the modest place at the
American table he had thought his by birthright, Bob Dubois is also
incapable of entering into the reinvented, syncretic New World he
has drifted across. Vanise Dorsinville, for whom the historical descendants of the inventors of the slave trade can seemingly conceive no
rightful place, survives the depredations of history and in the end is

undeniably present, here in her own text, central to any future we can contemplate, creating that future. Only at the end can Bob Dubois consciously confront the moral shape of the history that has brought him to himself, and only in that end, the narrative implies, can a better beginning be made. Bob must always offer up the sign of his acknowledged sin; Vanise must always refuse to take that sign from him. If the world as it is is to be ended, and if we are not to transcend our own history but to live with it creatively together, Russell Banks tells us through the stories of Bob Dubois and Vanise Dorsinville, we will require, "not occasional heroism, a remarkable instance of it here and there, but constant heroism, systematic heroism, heroism as governing principle" (40). Such heroism requires that, as Banks has attempted in his novel, we own the Middle Passage as the text we have written, as the passage that has brought us to this continent and this time, and that we rewrite it as central to our future as a nation.

We have bred the affliction within our breasts. Each solitary heart contains all the world's tribes, and its precarious dance echoes the drum's thunder. We are our ancestors and our children, neighbors and strangers to ourselves. Fever descends when the waters that connect us are clogged with filth. (Wideman, *Fever* 132)

Had we become such a phantom ship?
(Charles Johnson, *Middle Passage* 158)

> This is the Middle Passage: here
> Gehenna hatchways vomit up
> The debits of pounds of flesh.
> (Tolson, *Libretto* 23)

Curled in the black hold of the ship he wonders why his life on solid green earth had to end, why the gods had chosen this new habitation for him, floating, chained to other captives, no air, no light, the wooden walls shuddering, battered, as if some madman is determined to destroy even this last pitiful refuge where he skids in foul puddles of waste, bumping other bodies, skinning himself on splintery beams and planks, always moving, shaken and spilled like palm nuts in the diviner's fist, and Esu casts his fate, constant motion, tethered to an iron ring. (Wideman, *Fever* 130)

> Feeling predicts
> intelligence. The boats, pointing
> West.
>
> (Baraka, *Selected Poetry* 69)

The revisioning of history and the rewritings of modernism accomplished by writers such as Robert Hayden and Melvin B. Tolson were in their turn revisited and revised with the advent of the postmodern in black American literary arts created by authors who came of age during and after the Second World War. Where Robert Hayden refigured the Middle Passage in his palimpsestic re-creation of the texts of the slave trade as a rebirth, a "voyage through death / to life upon these shores" (48), Amiri Baraka's play "Slave Ship" attempts to shape itself to the presence of the unspeakable. He describes his play as a historical pageant, "a hot note of rage to be expanded, so that the bitterness becomes an environment in which we can all learn to be ourselves, now" (*Motion* 11). It is a play in which the contemporary audience is sunk in the darkness of the slave ship's hold, and in that darkness all times and languages exist simultaneously; the history of African America is evoked with the most minimal but resonant of spoken signs, and the audience is unmoored from its centered attachment to received history. The Middle Passage cannot be reenacted, but it does in this play become the encompassing horizon of experience. Here history is the absent cause of current rage, and a goad to reconstructive action. But if Baraka's "Slave Ship" is an indication of the presence of the unspeakable, an attempt to place us in contact with the absence of the history that has made us, Charles Johnson's novel *Middle Passage,* from the first edition's jacket illustration, which closely resembles contemporary portraits of Cinquez, to its final, postdiluvian phrase, is a postmodern reformation of America's historical texts, a deterritorializing and replacement of all that we have read and "known" of the slave trade, a motion that we cannot follow without finding ourselves finally on different ground, ground that has been racially removed and reconstituted in a continental driftworks. Robert Hayden's virtuoso deformation of form in his "Middle Passage" was achieved by emptying out the texts of the slave trade's history and resiting them to signify in ways their "original authors" could not possibly have intended. That paradoxical motion is remastered and reformed by Johnson, in whose hands the very authorship of the texts is resituated as part of the poetic strategy Houston Baker has termed "deformation of mastery" (*Modernism* 49). In Johnson's *Middle Passage* the texts that tell of the Middle Passage turn out to have been written in an African-American hand all along.

Charles Johnson's *Middle Passage* is a novel whose text proceeds from the interstices of other texts, including the earlier writings of Charles Johnson. The author's page of acknowledgments thanks Russell Banks "for inspiration," and, in another form of acknowledgment, there is an epigraph to the novel drawn from Robert Hayden's "Middle Passage." The African Allmuseri and their intriguing cosmology figured prominently in Johnson's earlier novel *Oxherding Tale* and his short story "The Sorcerer's Apprentice" before appearing in the ship's log of the *Republic,* and the presence in that earlier novel, a mock slave narrative, of a chapter titled "Middle Passage" was virtually a promise of the later novel's appearance. The narrator of Johnson's *Middle Passage,* a manumitted slave whose name, Rutherford Calhoun, inscribes both a political history of early America and its ironic reflection in the name of a character in *Amos 'n' Andy,* has read the poetry of William Blake and much else besides. He appears to be possessed, as is one of the other characters in the book, of "an almost psychotic total recall of everything he'd read" (25), and, as was true of the narrator of *Oxherding Tale,* Calhoun is constantly alluding to canonical works of Western philosophy (written both before and after his "own" time) in such a way as to resite that philosophical tradition in a new context. For example, he remarks at one point, "If you have never been hungry, you cannot know the *either/or* agony created by a single sorghum biscuit—either your brother gets it or you do" (47).

In *Home,* Amiri Baraka writes, "At this point when the whole of Western society might go up in flames, the Negro remains an integral part of that society, but continually outside it, a figure like Melville's Bartleby" (114). For Charles Johnson in 1990, as for Baraka in 1962, Melville's texts are a site upon which the African-American presence in Western culture may be figured. Indeed, while reading *Middle Passage,* one often feels that Johnson's is a textual universe parallel to Melville's, that the characters from each author's fictions haunt one another's thoughts and actions, that the decades separating the fictions of Melville and Johnson are communicating passages in an

intertextual maze. *Middle Passage* is in many ways an orphan's account
of his salvation: At one point the protagonist writes, "Some part of
me was a fatherless child again" (126). That protagonist, Rutherford
Calhoun, was owned in slavery by a man who appears to have been
named for one of the owners of Melville's *Pequod*. Peleg Chandler,
Captain Peleg's namesake and Calhoun's owner, opposes the institution of slavery but owns slaves, and his name seems calculated to
interrogate the very concept of ownership. The captain who figures
at the center of *Middle Passage,* Ebenezer Falcon, is an echo of Ahab.
Like Ahab, Falcon diverts his ship's mission to his own ends, and like
the crew of the *Pequod,* Falcon's crew suspect that their captain "will
sink this ship and take [them] with him. He doesn't *want* to return"
(62). Like Ahab, Falcon's body is marked by his stunted morality and
his twisted ambitions. Like Ahab, Falcon takes the lowly cabin boy
into his quarters with him; but where Ahab offers his cabin to Pip as
a refuge (and offers his hand to Pip in another of the novel's metaphoric marriages), Falcon calls his cabin boy below decks to rape him.
Later in *Middle Passage* Falcon's cabin boy, whose "heartbreakingly
handsome" features recall Billy Budd (26), has an encounter with
spiritual and psychological depths as powerfully dissociating as Pip's
descent into the seas. When the boy crawls back onto the deck, he
seems possessed of only half his mind: "—or could it be it was twice
the mind he had had before. His skin was cold, all one bluish color
as if he had been baptized in the Deep. His face was blank as a pan.
And his words, as his mouth spread and closed like a fish's, were
strange: a slabber of Bantu patois, Bushman, Cushitic, and Sudanic
tongues, and your guess where he learned them is as good as mine"
(68). White Tommy O'Toole, Falcon's cabin boy, as essentially American a character as black Pip, returns from his descent into the depths
of the Middle Passage speaking in the banished African tongues of
the slaves.

Among the Africans taken on board the novel's fictive slaver, the
Republic, are two men named Babo and Atufal, who seem to have
wandered over from Melville's "Benito Cereno." Indeed, at least one
of the crew on the *Republic* seems to have read Melville's premonitory story, or its documentary source, and declares, "[M]ethinks 'tis
scandalous how some writers such as Amasa Delano have slandered
black rebels in their tales" (173). Clearly the web of texts that con-

stitute the tales of Amasa Delano is part of the structure of *Middle Passage*. Johnson's Babo is neither exactly Melville's nor Delano's, and the narratives of the three texts lay athwart one another forming a continuously signifying knot. The Babo of Delano's 1817 *Narrative* had been the leader of the slaves' rebellion, but he had not been Don Benito's servant. Melville, in his 1855 tale, combines features of the "real" Babo with those of Cereno's slave Muri (*Piazza* 235n). Johnson's displacement of Babo from the position of rebel leader appears to be one of several ironic reversals of the predecessor texts. As did Amasa Delano, the narrator of *Middle Passage* observes carefully a young African female slumbering on the decks. At the beginning of his observations we seem to read another trope of exotic primitivism like those we find in Mungo Park or in the works of Ledyard that Delano remembers as he watches a young African mother nursing her child (*Piazza* 87–88). But as Rutherford Calhoun watches the child Baleka sleep, he forms a simile startling in its comedic power to contest Africanist assumptions: "As with other children I'd seen, she looked boneless in her sleep, her body limp, one hand (the right) on her brow like a society woman about to swoon" (107). The overdeterminations of the shaving scene in "Benito Cereno" are compounded in *Middle Passage* when Babo and Atufal grasp the white mate of Johnson's craft, Cringle, and prepare to kill him. Johnson's narrative makes literal the ironic fancies of Delano. When Delano watches Babo enact the charade of shaving Benito Cereno, he cannot "resist the vagary, that in the black he saw a headsman, and in the white a man at the block" (*Piazza* 101). In *Middle Passage* we see Atufal yank back Cringle's head, baring the neck to Babo. "Against this white stalk the little black named Babo placed an English handsaw" (132). It is Ngonyama, the Allmuseri character who appears in neither the text of Melville nor the text of Delano, who intercedes. In fact, Babo turns out to be one of those hatchet polishers Delano sees when he boards the San Dominick: "The little black Babo, who had always seemed so servile before, sat sharpening a hatchet with cloth and stone, a strip of some sailor's coat bandaging half his head so that only one eye was uncovered" (132).

When Johnson reinscribes Babo and Atufal within the text of *Middle Passage,* he is never simply appropriating or reappropriating the African figures from their positions of immurement within the white writing of Melville and Delano. The fictive universe Johnson offers readers does not displace or replace earlier texts; it takes place among them, reterritorializing them along new lines. Johnson demonstrates in the pages of *Middle Passage* the truth of the ironic exchange between Babo and Delano in Melville's text. Babo declares, as if translating his name, "[D]on't speak of me; Babo is nothing." Delano replies in racist innocence, "Don Benito, I envy you such a friend; slave I cannot call him" (68). Babo becomes, as we read between the shifting lines of these multiplying texts, a nothing upon which the others may project the flickering shadow play of racial determinations. In Melville's "belittered Ghetto . . . wholly occupied by the blacks" (*Piazza* 68) Charles Johnson reads the remarkable tale of Babo's people, the Allmuseri. *Middle Passage* logs the tales that live between the lines of "Benito Cereno," transfiguring the racial surfaces of America's imagined shining seas.

This parodic resituation of Western texts typifies Johnson's techniques in *Middle Passage*. Over and over again the reader of this novel finds a familiar tradition reopened in such a way as to reveal the mulatto nature of the Western text, to show that the African American is "always already" there, central, in the position of authorship. The America described in Johnson's novel is one in which whites continually come home to find that black writing has preceded them there. Everywhere, Rutherford Calhoun inscribes his "usual signatures of defiance," a forged letter from a black chambermaid addressed to a local politician but delivered to his "blue-blooded snob" of a wife, or a simple scrawl on the parlor wall in letters written with a coal from the home's hearth: "I can enter your life whenever I wish" (48). In Johnson's novel white mythology proves to be composed in black writing, the white captain of the *Republic* turns out to be the front man for a creole investor, and the white ship of state proves to be an African-American vehicle of release. Rutherford Calhoun can enter the lives of whites whenever he wishes because he is their author. Seizing the ultimate signifying power, Rutherford Calhoun becomes the black author of America's past.

The novel represents itself as a ship's log written retroactively to the events it narrates. The status of this novel's log is thrown into question from the beginning, and in such a way as to submit all other logs and historical texts to similar questions. The log is not written by the captain himself but by the black stowaway Rutherford Calhoun, who has become the captain's eyes and ears and then becomes his author. Calhoun at first resists the captain's request that he take over the keeping of the log, professing, contra the example from his hand in which we read his protest, that he is not a writer and doesn't know how a ship's log is done (146). But in acceding to the captain's dying request, Calhoun determines to tell things as he had seen them. Further, we also read in this retroactive log that no log comes to us as the unmediated and unrevised record of the actual. The captain routinely keeps a "rough" log, and this is the source of some of the information we read in Calhoun's log, but this is not the narrative that the captain presents to his masters. Instead, the captain's investors are presented with "a more polished book" (64), one, presumably, that casts a light more to their liking upon the events of the voyage. However, as the owners of the *Republic* are not all the white investors we and Calhoun assume them to be, it would seem that the captain's intended, more polished log would have been misleading both with regard to the events it recorded and with regard to its "real" audience. Instead of that intended log, though, we have the log written by Rutherford Calhoun, who records as one of his last acts the unmasking and undoing of the man who was to have been among the small, powerful audience for the *Republic's* log, the creole gangster Papa Zeringue, an admired "Race Man" at home (198) who secretly trades in slaves and is the master of the white sea captain and who attempts to master Calhoun as well.

Questions of audience and the log's status within the novel are further compounded by the fact that Rutherford Calhoun tells us that he is a practiced and habitual liar: "As a general principle and mode of operation during my days as a slave, I always lied, and sometimes just to see the comic results when a listener based his beliefs and behavior on things that were Not. But don't judge me harshly; it was one of the few forms of entertainment bondmen had" (90). It's a form of entertainment and self-preservation that Calhoun carries with him into his life as a freedman, and one that memorializes the same tradition of tale telling seen in the "lying" sessions of Zora Neale Hurston's *Mules and Men,* or in the *Conjure Tales* of Charles Chesnutt, or in Paul Laurence Dunbar's "We Wear the Mask," or in any of hundreds of other black texts of invention, reversal, survival, and triumph.

Rutherford Calhoun has masterfully enacted the folk saying: "If I'm lyin', I'm flyin'." These professions are as problematic as the ancient liar's paradox, though. What is a reader to make of the profession, in a novel, by its narrator that he lies habitually? As Charles Johnson's text takes flight, we find, in sum, that we are reading a fictive account of a ship's log begun by a white slave-trading captain, who would have altered his final version to suit his purposes had he lived, and completed by a manumitted black stowaway who from childhood exhibited "a tendency . . . to tell preposterous lies for the hell of it" (3). Any history, Johnson's novel suggests, is a palimpsestic fiction written in many hands, to different ends, and can be read into our accounts of ourselves in any number of ways. Lucille Clifton remembers that her husband told her, "In history, even the lies are true" (*Good Woman* 245). Johnson's novel reveals to us the preposterous truth of our own history, a history whose multiple authorship has been suppressed.

No one could more nearly embody the traditions of American history as it used to be told than the captain of the *Republic,* Ebenezer Falcon, who was born with the American republic itself, the son of a Son of Liberty, a man who follows a puritanical course of self-improvement and "Self Reliance" (51), who dreams of an empire in the West, who is a deformed dwarf who trades in slaves; repeating the course of America's culture, this scholar of self-reliance relies upon the traffic in African humanity for the success of his projects. On his table are laid the symbols and instruments of his power: maps, a quadrant, a chronometer, a spyglass, a Bible, and the log (27). With these implements he can make a world conform to his designs. With these he may project his imagination and his desire upon the globe and record for history his version of events. A subjugator and enslaver of non-Western peoples, this man's enormity of avarice and ambition is parodically mirrored in his dwarfish stature. In fact, he is so short that Calhoun, in one of the novel's most amusing reversals of stereotype and racial custom, finds himself fighting back the urge to pat the diminutive Captain Falcon on the head. Ebenezer Falcon has learned one of the chief lessons of oppression, to set the oppressed against one another. In order to avoid African insurrection on the Middle Passage, he divides the Africans into groups and sets other Africans over them in positions of authority. He enlists Rutherford Calhoun, the African American, to be his eyes and ears on board, spying on the Africans and the American crewmen alike. Calhoun becomes his counterimage, in effect, completing Falcon, and Falcon seals this relationship by giving Calhoun a magnetized ring that, in addition to making it possible to fire Falcon's scientifically elaborated pistol, forms a mock marriage between the two. Just as Calhoun, the manumitted bondsman, is not entirely free in the republic, the master of the *Republic,* as his name implies, is limited by the strings that attach him to his commercial masters. His relationship with Calhoun is a marriage of convenience, in which each of the two half-free men will use the other to accomplish his ends. Falcon may suspect that Calhoun will continue to act in his own best interests, but he exhibits a typically American tendency to underestimate Africans. Speaking with Calhoun in the aftermath of the Allmuseri's successful rebellion, Falcon asks, "Then we underestimated the blacks? They're smarter than I thought?" "They'd have to be," replies Calhoun (146) in one of the great understatements of American literature.

Ebenezer Falcon not only embodies the most awful contradictions of the American past, he is also used by Johnson to demonstrate the vacuity of present-day arguments that derive from those earlier contradictions. Writing Falcon's words into his log, Rutherford Calhoun retroactively records a prophecy of the disfigured mode of debate common to the late twentieth-century discussions of race. In one of their first interviews Falcon regales Calhoun with a disquisition (later Calhoun will express a preference for being birched or keelhauled over having to listen to more of Falcon's lectures) on race and merit, proffering a line of unreasoning rhetoric that will be recognizable to readers of Shelby Steele, Stanley Crouch, George Will, Clarence Thomas, Pat Buchanan, and others, an argument also eerily predictive of debates surrounding the presentation of the National Book Award to Johnson for this very novel (Hale 24):

> I don't hold it against you for being here. Or for being black, but I believe in *excellence*—an unfashionable thing these days, I know, what with headmasters giving illiterate Negroes degrees because they feel too guilty to fail them. Then employers giving that same boy a place in the firm since he's got the degree in hand and saying no will bring a gang of Abolitionists down on their necks. But no . . . not on my ship, Mr. Calhoun. Eighty percent of the crews on other

ships, damn near anywhere in America, are *incompetent,* and all because everyone's ready to lower standards of excellence to make
up for slavery, or discrimination, and the problem . . . the *problem,*
Mr. Calhoun, is, I say, that most of these minorities aren't ready for
the titles of quartermaster or first mate precisely because discrimination denied them the training that makes for true excellence. . . .
(31–32)

Spoken this baldly, the argument collapses as it always should into the
echoing caverns of its own illogic. Spoken as it is in this context by
a man who is, as he speaks, profiting from and perpetuating slavery,
who is speaking to the eloquent bearer before an audience of his
inanities, the comedy of this passage is nearly unsurpassed in contemporary parody. The amorality of Falcon's expression is foregrounded
when, at the end of Falcon's argument in defense of excellence, he
tells Calhoun that he reminds him of a colored cabin boy named
"Fortunata" who was eaten by the captain and his crew on a trip to
Madagascar. Falcon, an upholder of his Virginia traditions and of
Christian decency, abhors cannibalism as a cultural practice, a practice that he attributes to "savage," non-Western cultures, but, as he
patiently explains to Calhoun, "there's not a civilized law that holds
water . . . once you've put to sea" (32). In a subsequent scene, following the seizure of the *Republic* by the Allmuseri it had been carrying
to bondage in the New World, Ebenezer Falcon has a dream that at
once pillories self-satisfied assertions that we have achieved the end
of history and portrays an America that proceeds almost inevitably
from the history we have had:

> It came to me as I lay here, a nightmare that this was the last hour
> of history. Nothing else explains it. The breakdown. I mean, how
> *thorough* it is, from top to bottom, like everything from ancient times
> to now, the civilized values and visions of high culture, have all gone
> to hell in fine old hamlets filled with garbage, overrun with Mud-
> men and Jews, riddled with viral infections and venereal complaints
> that boggle the mind and cripple whole generations of white chil-
> dren who'll be strangers, if not slaves, in their own country. I saw
> families killing each other. People were living in alleyways. Sexes
> and races were blurred. I saw riots in cities and on clippers. . . .

Crazy as it seems, I saw a ship with a whole crew of women. Yellow men were buying up half of America. Hegel was spewing from the mouths of Hottentots. (145)

It is again a measure of Falcon's moral blindness that he sees this future as proceeding from a breakdown of his civilization's hold on things, rather than as the *product* of that civilization's progress, the unanticipated telos of its idea of progress. As he crisscrosses the Atlantic stealing human beings and looting their cultures for the museums and private collections of Western capitalism (even to the point, in scenes that deftly parody the film *King Kong,* of carrying off the theft of the Allmuseri deity), Falcon is in fact producing that nightmare from which he cannot waken, producing history.

Charles Johnson constructs the reader's experience of Rutherford Calhoun's narrative, from the first startlement of finding a freed black man deliberately stowing away on a slave-trading vessel, with an eye to unsettling commonsensical notions of ego and identity, particularly racial identity. The psychological universe of *Middle Passage* is an anti-essentialist space in which the individual character is a shape-shifting construct that, like the captured deity of the Allmuseri, is constantly taking on and throwing off aspects of those who gaze upon it. The gaze across the boundaries of race at first fails even to detect individual differentiation. In another of his comic reversals of stereotype, Johnson writes of the captive Ngonyama, who is on first contact unable to tell one white crewman from another and wonders how their families tell them apart. To the Allmuseri, Europeans were barbarians who had devolved through sin from a higher state of civilization. In fact, the Allmuseri held that Europeans had been members of their tribe before falling into the sin of "failure to experience the unity of Being everywhere" (65). To the Allmuseri, Rutherford Calhoun is more American than African; he is "a crewman like the rest, an American" (135). But he is the point of mediation between the other Americans and the Allmuseri, because he is the only "Negro" on board. As Calhoun explains Ngonyama's view to himself, in the process inventing *avante la lettre,* one of Lévi-Strauss's best-known structuralist metaphors: "The distance between his people and black America was vast—his people saw whites as Raw Barbarians and me (being a colored mate) as a Cooked one" (75). By the same token, while they may resemble one another, Calhoun senses that he and the newly captured Africans are not identical, are not essentially the same people. "Truth to tell," he tells us in his log, "they were not even 'Negroes.' They were Allmuseri" (76). Ngonyama, Babo, Atufal, and the others are still distinctly non-American and distinctly themselves. They have not yet been reconstrued in their identities as "Negroes," and Calhoun's quotation marks around that word indicate the extent to which it is a racial definition that is applied to one by a community outside oneself. Until they experience the transformations of Middle Passage, seasoning, and bondage, they will not fully become either Negro or African-American, and they rebel before that transformation can be forced upon them.

The sea change from African to Negro commences with capture and with the severest physical deformations. Ebenezer Falcon is a "tight packer," and, having branded the blacks with the initial signifiers of ownership, he contorts their bodies against one another into the shape that will prove most profitable. It is upon viewing the contortions of the hold that Calhoun decides the captain is the devil. "Flesh could conform to anything," he notes. But what will would want to press human flesh into such a shape? "Who else could twist the body so terribly? Who else could enslave gods and men alike?" (120). This physical reshaping is followed by other inexorable transmutations of the identity itself, but these transformations occur in black and white both. Forced together on the high seas, the white crew and the black Allmuseri start to become, not one another, but something new all together, or rather two new peoples linked by common sites of formation. Tommy, the cabin boy, already brutalized by Captain Falcon, has a direct experience of the Allmuseri's God that unsettles him as profoundly as Melville's Pip was unsettled by his experience overboard in *Moby Dick*. The crew become, despite bigotry and resistance, Africanized in their culture, and the Allmuseri become "not wholly Allmuseri anymore" (124). Calhoun knows that he has become "a man remade by virtue of his contact with the crew" (124), and long after the events of his narration he finds that he speaks "in the slightly higher register of the slaves," a note that retroactively prefigures Ellison's invisible man, who surmises that, on another frequency, he may speak for us. Calhoun acquires the Allmuseri "accent, brisk tempo of talk" (194). He also begins to see the Allmuseri changed culturally. He learns that they are not "a finished thing, pure essence," but they are "process and Heraclitean change" (124). In listening to the speech of Ngonyama, Calhoun suspected that Ngonyama himself "did not recognize the quiet revisions in his voice after he learned English as it was spoken by the crew, or how the vision hidden in their speech was deflecting or redirecting his own way of seeing" (124). Learning a new language gives the people on board the *Republic* a new world, but learning English does not make the Allmuseri black Englishmen. Calhoun reflects on what is becoming of these Africans in his presence: "The horrors they experienced—were subtly reshaping their souls as thoroughly as Falcon's tight-packing had contorted their flesh during these past few weeks, but into what sort of men I could not imagine. No longer Africans, yet not Americans either. Then what? And of what were they now capable?" (125).

One thing of which they are capable is disrupting the plans of captain and crew alike. In seizing the vehicle of their enslavement and redirecting it, the Allmuseri destroy the givens of power and cultural relationships. "I felt culturally dizzy," Calhoun records in Falcon's log, "so displaced by this decentered interior and the Africans' takeover, that when I lifted a whale-oil lamp at my heels it might as well have been a Phoenician artifact for all the sense it made to me" (142). The Allmuseri will not succeed in directing this vessel homeward; they have disinterred themselves from the premature burial Falcon has subjected them to, but they will not reenter their African lives whole. Neither, though, will those crew members left alive succeed in their plan, paralleling the course of the captured *Amistad,* to steer for Africa by day and end in Long Island. Neither identity nor destination is given and sure. The course of individual and culture alike is a matter of tacking before the constantly shifting winds of difference and change. In the end, Calhoun, writing in his palimpsest log, reads himself as a place of inscription, a site for the intersection and transmission of cultural discourses, a matter of bricolage:

I listened to everyone and took notes: I was open, like a hinge-less door, to everything. And to comfort the weary on the *Republic* I peered deep into memory and called forth all that had ever given me solace, scraps and rags of language too, for in myself I found nothing I could rightly call Rutherford Calhoun, only pieces and fragments of all the people who touched me, all the places I had seen, all the homes I had broken into. The "I" that I was, was a mosaic of many countries, a patchwork of others and objects stretching back to perhaps the beginning of time. What I felt, seeing this, was indebtedness. (162–63)

The *Republic* itself, driven across the waters by the conflicting desires of the remaining crew and the former cargo, moves at the end toward maelstrom. In the swirling waters of history and self we have come to recognize from the climactic narrative surges of Poe and Melville, the *Republic* is torn asunder taking captives and captors both to the bottom of the sea. Calhoun, like Melville's Ishmael, is fished from the ocean along with Squibb (the *Republic's* cook, whose position Calhoun had attempted to usurp before becoming a more literal squibbery for Captain Falcon) and three children, saved by the passing *Juno* and its unlikely Captain Quackenbush. Like Ishmael, Calhoun is forever altered by his voyage, by the white crew, by the African Allmuseri, and by his Atlantic baptism. The long "hangover" of the Middle Passage, he writes, "had irreversibly changed [his] seeing, made of [him] a cultural mongrel, and transformed the world into a fleeting shadow play" (187). But that is what Calhoun, addressing us from the pages of the log he has taken over from its initial author, believes America is:

If this weird, upside-down caricature of a country called America, if this land of refugees and former indentured servants, religious heretics and half-breeds, whoresons and fugitives—this cauldron of mongrels from all points of the compass—was all I could rightly call *home*, then aye: I was of it. There, as I lay weakened from bleeding, was where I wanted to be. Do I sound like a patriot? Brother, I put it to you: What Negro, in his heart (if he's not a hypocrite), is not? (179)

In what may be an accidental pun, Calhoun follows this declaration by telling us, "I was lying where I had fallen. . . ."

But what is America if it is not the lie we have told where we have fallen? If there is a national allegiance, it is to a fiction that is constantly undergoing a recomposition. What the parody of Charles Johnson's *Middle Passage* points to, what its squib is directed to, is the central truth of American culture: that its cultural center is moved with each arrival. The ship of state carries a mongrel crew and will not deliver us to any promised land save that of our own authoring. Johnson's parodic deformation of the texts of the American slave trade reveals the black hand that holds the pen of authorship, reveals the black writing that is American history. In his hands we find a log in which it is recorded that the text of America has always been African-American and that the American text is always reinscribing itself elsewhere, between the lines of the given.

America has never fully heard the vision hidden in its speech, never entirely attended to the lessons of its own languages. Like the personae of Robert Hayden's "Middle Passage," we may wonder which of us has killed an albatross, or, like the boatswain in Charles Johnson's *Middle Passage,* we may swear that the storm of history that rocks the *Republic* proves "the ship was cursed by its black chattel and infernal cargo" (82); but we cannot truly tell ourselves a free story till we tell ourselves that we are truly the children of the Middle Passage. It is a story that brings to bear upon our daily lives the full indebtedness of our identities. When we return to the scenes of telling where whites once sought to seal the signs of ownership in African flesh, we will find always before us the signs of African-American artistry ineradicably embedded in the body of American thought. It is a story that, if told with the constant practice of heroism called for by Russell Banks, could possibly destroy the world as it is and put another in its place. The Middle Passage is a needful narrative knowledge that our authors, like Avey Johnson in Paule Marshall's *Praisesong for the Widow,* try to stop us long enough to tell, to tell to those of us who are "lacking memory and a necessary distance of the mind" (255).

> But their histories are blurred.
> Misread for effect. Booms that shattered the ears
> of schoolboys too young to see in the dark.
> (Which,
> they say,
>
> was their own flesh
> (Baraka, *Black Magic* 61)

James Weldon Johnson's
Impossible Text

The Autobiography of an Ex-Colored Man

When James Weldon Johnson's *The Autobiography of an Ex-Colored Man* appeared in 1912, it met the fate of so many other determinedly original works, critical acclaim and sluggish sales. Generally praised by both black and white critics, Johnson's novel was compared favorably to works by William Dean Howells and Robert Herrick. The *New York Times* praised the book's "calm and judicial tone," something white critics often valued in black writers, and the *Springfield Republican* lauded it as "a human document" (qtd. in Levy 127), as if there

were some other form of document in the world. Typical of more viru-
lently racist responses to Johnson's work was the *Nashville Tennessean,*
which termed the novel a "lie," a characterization whose strangeness
only becomes fully evident when readers accept the fact that the book
is a novel, and an "insult to Southern womanhood." In the midst of its
diatribe against Johnson's creation, the *Nashville Tennessean,* perhaps
inadvertently, registered one of the central problematics of the novel.
Complaining about the book's title, the review argued that there is
no such thing as an "ex-colored man—once a Negro always a Negro"
(qtd. in Levy 127). This is the complaint of a reader confronted with
an impossible object. There had not always been "Negroes" in the
world, but once white people had invented themselves by inventing
"Negroes," they were at pains to see that the integrity of their creations remained intact. Once the "one drop rule" had taken hold in
North America, once it became a fact that a person's identity was constructed as "Negro" if there was any African ancestry in that person's
past, no matter how remote, the conception of an "ex-colored" man
became both impossible and a not uncommon occurrence. As recently
as the 1960s, my own white teachers in various public school systems
(the few black teachers found it a less remarkable factoid) often announced to our classes with the air of imparting a deep and curious
secret the fact that the majority of black Americans had at least some
white blood in their veins. These teachers neither remarked the, to
us youngsters at least, obvious correlative this produced with regard
to white sexual histories, nor did they seem to be aware that this fact
meant that there must be a significant number of "white" people in
our country who had at least some "black" blood in their veins. Then,
as in the earlier part of the century, these thoughts would have registered what was to white society an impossibility, something that, if
not acknowledged, might be assumed not to be at all. The title of
James Weldon Johnson's novel places his text at the very hinge point
of America's most contradictory and paradoxical racial constructions.
In America, the autobiography of an ex-colored man was the most
impossible of ideas, no matter how many such people actually existed.
Johnson's novel is among the most profound texts in America's racial
history because it exists in a state of suspension between racial realms
of cognition. The single text of the novel becomes the multiplied intertexts of overlapping experiences, black and white. The person of the

novel's narrator is divided by his own text, and the text reads itself in and out of black and white history paradoxically and endlessly. *The Autobiography of an Ex-Colored Man* produces the impossibility of a stable reading of its own narrative as exemplary of the instability, the impossibility, of American racial definition.

It would seem that there is no escaping intentional and biographical fallacies when Americans discuss "ethnic" texts. Questions of authenticity and intentionality inevitably arise. It matters to readers of Harriet Jacobs's *Incidents in the Life of a Slave Girl* whether or not the author truly is an ex-slave. It matters to our readings of *Our Nig* that we decide whether or not Harriet Wilson was a black author; in fact, few twentieth-century scholars evinced any interest in the novel until Henry Louis Gates, Jr., produced convincing arguments for the authenticity of its author's perspective. It is usually not enough for today's readers, no matter how sophisticated and critical, that a narrative be a convincing fictive construction of what we now take to be historical reality. Our readings of a slave narrative will be quite different if the putative author is unmasked as a white abolitionist, just as many readers abandoned the recent novel *Famous All over Town* when its author, Danny Santiago, was found to be an elderly Anglo and not the first-person narrator of a Chicano coming-of-age story.

In the case of *The Autobiography of an Ex-Colored Man,* the author cannot be the protagonist, and yet many readers have had difficulty trying not to read the book as Johnson claimed he wanted it read, as social documentation. Johnson and his original publishers were in part responsible for the massive confusions regarding the novel's status. Not only does the book's title seem to promise a work of nonfiction, when published in 1912 the volume carried no author's name on its title page. Johnson had argued that his story would gain in power if the reader believed it actually had occurred. In a letter to George Towns in August 1912, Johnson wrote: "When the author is known, and known to be one who could not be the main character of the story, the book will fall flat. . . . If the book succeeds I shall claim it later, if it doesn't, well there won't be anything lost" (qtd. in Levy 126–27). This suppression of his authorship produced later comic effects. In his actual autobiography, *Along This Way,* Johnson remembers:

The authorship of the book excited the curiosity of literate colored people, and there was speculation among them as to who the writer might be. . . . I had the experience of listening to some of these discussions. I had a rarer experience, that of being introduced to and talking with one man who tacitly admitted to those present that he was the author of the book. . . . I continue to receive letters from persons who have read the book inquiring about this or that place of my life as told in it. That is, probably, one of the reasons I am writing the present book. (238–39)

So thoroughly was the documentary nature of *The Autobiography of an Ex-Colored Man* accepted that Johnson had to write his own autobiography to counter the tendency of his public to read his earlier book as the book of his life.

The preface to the 1912 edition promises a documentary work. The original edition is held up as a "dispassionate, though sympathetic" depiction of "conditions as they actually exist between the whites and blacks today" and refers to the text as "a composite and proportionate presentation of the entire race" (x). There can be little doubt that this is exactly what the first reviewers of the novel looked for in it, and this is part of the reason that the *Nashville Tennessean* so violently wished to brand the volume a lie. Johnson continued to speak of his book as documentation throughout his life. In his nonfiction book *Black Manhattan* he identifies "the club" described in *Autobiography* as having been Ike Hines's establishment and then proceeds to quote his own novel's description of the club as the best available "picture of these places and the times" (75–77). In an interesting reversal of the usual documentary authentication found in early African-American fictions such as those authored by William Wells Brown, Johnson quotes the fiction he has written as an authenticating document within his nonfiction history of black New York.

That is only one of many ironic inversions of the usual pattern of America's racial signifying to be found in Johnson's writings. In *Along This Way* he reports having had a white "mammy" with whom he remained in contact till her death (9), signifying upon the usual southern declarations of fealty to the person of the black mammy. The silver spoon that rich whites find in their mouths at birth is a sort of ironic patrimony for Johnson. His grandfather, Stephen Dillet, the son of a French army officer and a Haitian woman, was placed on a schooner bound for Cuba by his father in 1802. The schooner was captured by a British privateer and diverted to Nassau. Stephen, then about six years old, landed with nothing but the long shirt he was wearing and a silver spoon (3). Where typical middle-class white children of his time might have heard their parents adopt literary black dialects while reading to them from Joel Chandler Harris or Paul Laurence Dunbar (William Carlos Williams records such memories), the young James Weldon Johnson particularly enjoyed hearing his mother adopt Cockney and Irish accents as she read to him (11). In later life, his mother was nicknamed "the Queen" because of the resemblance of her bearing to that of Queen Victoria (18–19).

Houston Baker, in *Singers of Daybreak*, says that "in a sense, *The Autobiography of an Ex-Colored Man* is a fictional rendering of *The Souls of Black Folk*" (22). Johnson did read W. E. B. Du Bois's book upon its publication and reported being deeply moved and influenced by the volume. This was around the time that Johnson first began writing his novel, while he was studying at Columbia University. But like Du Bois's most famous book, *The Autobiography of an Ex-Colored Man* is documentary, if at all, only in the most general, spiritual sense. What studies such as Baker's have demonstrated is that the tendency among readers in the past to focus upon the novel as a social document has diverted attention from the artistic accomplishments of Johnson's novel, which may be most impressive in those portions of the novel that are most fictive.

The title of *The Autobiography of an Ex-Colored Man* signals the extent to which race is a socially constructed category in the United States. The *Nashville Tennessean* was partly right. In the American racial cosmology it is possible to become an ex-racist, an ex-slave, perhaps even an "ex-nigger," but one cannot become an ex-white or ex-colored man, only a "real" black man who has been found out, or a "real" colored man passing for white. At several points in the text the constructedness of our racial identities, and their subsequent instability, are dramatized. The rich white man who becomes the protagonist's patron views the narrator as a man who would have to choose to become black, who would have to reconstruct himself to become a Negro. "This idea you have of making a Negro out of yourself is nothing more than a sentiment," he tells the narrator, identifying blackness with sentiment in a revealing fashion. He asks the narrator, "What kind of Negro would you make now, especially in the South?" (145). The narrator himself observes the extent to which white images of blacks are discursive formations, grown and sustained within the language, perpetrated within the texts of popular entertainments: "[L]og cabins and plantations and dialect-speaking 'darkies' are perhaps better known in American literature than any other single picture of our national life. Indeed, they form an ideal and exclusive literary concept of the American Negro to such an extent that it is almost impossible to get the reading public to recognize him in any other setting" (167). This remark is predictive of the course of the narrator's life, for he is able to move back and forth across racial boundaries because he is unrecognizable to white viewers apart from a determining racial setting. He is impossible outside his racial context. Further, the nameless narrator's critique of literary stereotype has also revealed a type of discursive passing that white writing has unknowingly perpetrated upon itself. If it is true that the literary stereotypes of the "Negro" are "perhaps better known in American literature than any other single picture of our national life," then it must be the case that our literature is a national literature, a cultural product of our national life, to the extent that it is a white construction of blackness. Novels of "passing," thus, may be quintessentially American.

And yet, for all that *The Autobiography of an Ex-Colored Man* is seen as a novel of passing, it begins and ends at the point where most novels of passing, such as Twain's *Puddn'head Wilson,* or Chesnutt's *The House behind the Cedars,* or Robert Penn Warren's *Band of Angels,* take up their primary interest. *The Autobiography of an Ex-Colored Man* is not that much concerned with the usual stuff of stories of passing, incidents of possible exposure and life in the white world. Still, it has everything to say about the white world's life.

E. S. Burt has argued that first-person narratives "take as their horizon the final revelation of the original fold in the narrative: the end, the self developed, has become the beginning, the self being exposed" (197). The voice that greets us at the opening of *The Autobiography of an Ex-Colored Man* is that of the person the narrator has become as the result of the events he is about to relate for us. It is, in this case, the voice of "an ordinarily successful white man who has made a little money" (211). This has the profoundest implications for our reading, for it means that *The Autobiography of an Ex-Colored Man* is the tale of the creation of an ordinary white man. The book whose preface promises to initiate a white readership into the freemasonry of the "colored race" has, in fact, enacted the narrator's desire to "gather up all the little tragedies of [his] life, and turn them into a practical joke on society" (3). It is the autobiography of "an ordinarily successful white man who has made a little money" that is offered to us as an exemplary life through which white readers may come to know the "inner life of the Negro in America" (xii).

The Autobiography of an Ex-Colored Man is, thus, at least in part, a cognitive mapping of a world in which "white" does not "know" the truth of its own blackness—a reading that stands as a revelation, an initiation into the freemasonry of American racial consciousness.

The book begins as revelation: "I KNOW THAT IN WRITING THE FOL-LOWING PAGES I AM divulging the great secret of my life." But the title has already divulged that which most white readers and some blacks would have taken to be the narrator's great secret, and the anonymity of the text would presumably have protected the narrator had this been a "real" narrative. The real secret of the narrator's life is the one that is withheld till the last paragraph of the book, the cause of that "vague feeling of unsatisfaction" (5) the narrator seeks to relieve in confession. The true secret shame that has compelled this narrator to speak his confession, and that makes this an exemplary life in the history of American racial evolution, is the narrator's shame at having forsaken his birthright, a birthright figured matrilineally, a right by birth to participate in, as the narrator puts it, "making history and a race" (211). America, as a national culture, has historically enacted this same betrayal of birth, refusing the responsibilities and possible grandeurs attendant upon acknowledging its multiracial birth legacy. The narrator's shame is that he has betrayed the promise made to his mother, a promise awakened in him by art and oratory and blackness, the promise to assume the prerogatives and obligations of his inheritance. What Americans can read in the black text that unfolds between the white horizons of Johnson's novel is an allegory of historical betrayal and self-denial, a narrative, an intertext, that parts us from ourselves while marrying the ends of our story to one another.

A very young James Weldon Johnson was present at Frederick Douglass's speech in Jacksonville, Florida, and heard Douglass's often retold defense of his second marriage: "In my first marriage I paid my compliments to my mother's race; in my second marriage I paid my compliments to the race of my father" (qtd. in Johnson, *Along* 61). *The Autobiography of an Ex-Colored Man* tracks a journey between two such familial legacies. The narrator chooses to lay aside his mother's legacy of African-American culture, but this leaves him with the impotent tokenism of his patrilineal inheritance. In the most supreme of racial ironies, it is his mother's legacy that assures the narrator's social success among his father's race: it is his ability to play black music, "which was then at the height of its vogue," that renders him a welcome guest in the higher grades of white society (197) and that leads to his meeting the woman who becomes his wife.

This may be the most carefully crafted aspect of the ex-colored man's narrative, despite the seeming affectless style of the writing. As just one example of the care Johnson has taken in creating these patterns of familial and racial movement, I would point to the fact that the narrator's father reappears in his life at precisely the moment that the narrator has fallen in love for the first time. Many readers have remarked the early scene in which the father hangs a gold piece around his son's neck as a precursor of the symbolic structures found in Ellison's *Invisible Man.* Like the invisible man's briefcase, this mark of the father remains with the ex-colored man throughout his life and figures his fate. But this gold of the father's is a strange token. It is the son's legacy, which he receives seated in the lap of the father. It is the only physical token of paternity he has until the subsequent gift of a piano, the only visible sign that he has had a father at all. This, however, is specious specie. Before tendering it to the son, the father "laboriously" (6) drills a hole through it, negating its primary function as spendable coin in order to bind it around his son's neck. The son henceforth carries with him the sign of a legacy that is not his to spend, a token that his father has made it difficult to place in circulation, a sign that has lost its traditional exchange value, and one that recalls the signs of ownership inscribed in the bodies of the slaves.

The white father reappears in the narrator's life at a time when most boys most need a father, but it is a time when the boy "could not arouse any considerable feeling of need for a father" (33). The vision of this seeming stranger, his father, stops the child in his tracks. Portentously, the mother "broke the spell by calling" the child by his given name, a name we never learn, and saying to him, "This is your father" (33). It is the mother who pronounces the relation, the mother who reconnects the golden signifier and the son who is bound by it to their mutual progenitor. And the one moment in which both mother and father show pride in the son they have brought into being is when he plays the music that his mother has given him.

It is not the origin of the son that is shrouded in mystery but that of the white father. The son wonders where the father came from, "where he had been, why was he here, and why he would not stay" (36). The father is unclassifiable, as he does not conform to the qualities attributed to the list of fathers the son has compiled in his wide-ranging reading. He does not fill any known father function, but the occasion of his reappearance is also the occasion of the son's first betrayal of his mother. The father's sudden arrival interrupts the progress of the son's first love and prevents him from meeting with his pale-faced, brown-eyed girl and his music teacher to rehearse a duet. It is as if the first arousal of the boy's passions and "budding dawn of manhood" (37) drew the father across great distances to intervene, though that is not the purpose of the father's visit; as if the father must reappear to prevent the recital, to prevent the romance and duet with its overtones of further racial mixing. Speaking the first deliberate lie he can remember, the son excuses his delay in reaching his appointment, a delay caused by the meeting with the father, by claiming to have been at his mother's sickbed. "I don't think she'll be with us very long" (37), he offers in mitigation of the delay caused by his unspeakable visit with his father, and in speaking that lie against his mother, he later believes, he "was speaking a prophecy" (37).

The ex-colored man was conceived on one of his "impetuous" father's trips home from college (43). In another troping upon the theme of education in the slave narratives, Johnson makes the nexus of intention, ambition, and education the ground upon which competing racial possibilities play themselves out, the territory upon which his final betrayal takes place. The father wants him to attend Harvard or Yale; the mother expresses "half a desire" for him to go to Atlanta University (47). This bifurcated educational ambition is just one of several racially charged choices confronting the ex-colored man, choices that complicate his naturally nurtured desire for a life in arts and letters. In *Singers of Daybreak* Houston Baker asserts of Johnson's narrator that "the progression of his musical tastes is the reverse of his literary development. In music he moves from the songs of his mother's heritage to the Western classics; while in reading he moves from the Bible through *Uncle Tom's Cabin* and the works of Alexandre Dumas and Frederick Douglass" (20). In America it appears one must choose aesthetic legacies appropriate to one's race, and the ex-colored man finds himself going in two directions at once.

The narrator's musical education begins as he listens to his mother "crooning some old melody without words" (8) after he had "helped" her play the piano. (He remembers always having had a fondness for the black keys.) As he had earlier received the legacy of his unspendable token while in the lap of his white father, he receives the legacy of song and lyric in the lap of his "colored" mother. His formal education in music introduces him to the European traditions, but it is his mother's aesthetic legacy that proves always most fecund for him, and part of the ambition he eventually betrays involves the melding of these two musical legacies into a new classical form, a New World invention out of the materials of Europe and Africa. His mother gives him the at first wordless link to an African past; his father gives him that European technological innovation, the tempered scale of the modern piano. His mother's contribution is one of inspiration and soulful tradition; his father's contribution is more purely instrumental.

The narrator continues these patterns into his later life by mastering what the world calls "American music" (87) and by transforming classical standards into ragtime, a transformation that parallels the transformations of autobiographical forms Johnson undertakes in his text. It is the narrator's mastery of this mulatto musical form that earns him the honorific title of "professor" (115), a title that becomes the ironic symbol of his failure to keep his promise to his mother, just as his friend, the ex–Harvard medical student, carries the nickname of "the Doctor" as parodic sign of his failure to complete the very course the narrator's father had mapped out for the ex-colored man.

It is when a European musician, taken by the power of the ex-colored man's playing, takes his rag themes through a series of formal variations that the narrator sees the possibility of carrying out his childhood ambitions (142). His white patron, possibly speaking as the voice of white patriarchy, doubts that "even a white musician of recognized ability could succeed . . . by working on the theory that American music should be based on Negro themes" (144).

The development of the young narrator's ambition is intimately tied to his mother, his race, and his reading. He begins by reading the Bible, *Pilgrim's Progress, Natural Theology,* all volumes gleaned from his mother's library. But it is when he reads *Uncle Tom's Cabin* that he first evinces a sense of racial revelation, and it is over that reading that the narrator, for the first time, is able to "talk frankly with [his] mother on all the questions which had been vaguely troubling" his mind (42). It is also a literary event that first inspires the narrator to form his ambition to glorify his matrilineal heritage. When his school friend "Shiny," the character in the novel who most nearly does resemble James Weldon Johnson, gives a grammar school graduation oration on Toussaint L'Ouverture, the narrator says of his emotional response that "it was like touching an electric button which loosed the pent-up feelings of his listeners" (45). (This episode does resemble Johnson's own description of his response to Frederick Douglass, who spoke at the Sub-Tropical Exposition in Jacksonville. Johnson had won a copy of *The Life and Times of Frederick Douglass* as a school academic prize and says that he "read it with the same sort of feverish intensity" with which he had read about his earlier heroes: Samson, David, and Robert the Bruce [*Along* 60].) In listening to a black child speak in public of the heroism of Toussaint, the narrator is moved to a new desire. Frederick Douglass and Alexandre Dumas replace King David and Robert the Bruce in his pantheon of rhetorical and heroic models, and he speaks to his mother of his newly formed dream: "to be a great man, a great colored man, to reflect credit on the race and gain fame for" himself (46). He later shapes that dream into a vision of himself as an amalgamator of musics, as the composer of American classical forms.

Listening to a black congregation sing, the narrator is lost in marvel at the source of "that elusive undertone, the note in music that is not heard with the ears" (181). In a passage most resonant with the chapter on the sorrow songs in W. E. B. Du Bois's *The Souls of Black Folk,* Johnson describes the ex-colored man realizing, with tears running down his face, that "the day will come when this slave music will be the most treasured heritage of the American Negro" (182) and of America as a body and spirit. In his solitary listening surrounded by the voices of other African-American singers, the narrator envisions a day when the most well known figures of American literature, the coarse stereotypes of Negro life, may be superseded by the actual grandeurs of African-American song.

This is the heritage he dishonors in taking on the father's sterile legacy, the pierced coin of the realm that binds him to a tradition of moneymaking and oppression. When he decides to change his name, raise a mustache, and let the world take him for what it would (191), a position that matches that taken in later years by the author Jean Toomer, it is with the certain knowledge that he will be taken for white. He becomes an ordinarily successful white man, one who entertains other white people at their parties by playing colored music.

The ex-colored man's friend from school days, Shiny, has become, in the meantime, what the narrator once wanted to be; he has earned his title and is one of those "men who are making history and a race" (211). When the narrator looks into the eyes of his own son, who bears the legacy of his white wife's features, he has to wonder what he can contribute to his son's future, what useful coinage he might pass on to him. It is not the image of his father's coin that haunts the ex-colored man at the fold where his narration begins and ends, but the secret remnants of the promise he made to his mother and to his racial heritage. In a nation that will not allow itself to honor and celebrate all of its racial heritages equally, in a nation that will construct anyone who attempts to do so as mongrel and subhuman, the ex-colored man cannot bring himself to the constant practice of heroism that would be demanded if he were to honor both his legacies. It is when he looks at the unplayed music on his yellowing manuscripts that he understands that he has chosen the lesser part, that he has given over the hope and memory of those elusive undertones, "the most thrilling emotions which the human heart may experience" (181), for the mess of pottage that is the legacy of his white paternity, the legacy of a paternity that will not speak itself, a paternity that has owned, but not owned up to, its children. Because he has turned his back upon the promise made to his mother, the ex-colored man betrays his own children, denying them the full value of their history as surely as his own father had denied him. In reading *The Autobiography of an Ex-*

Colored Man, we follow the narrator's reading of the text of his own life as if it were an intertext producing two radically different sets of racial significations, as if its words doubled continually over themselves in the confusions of race that propel American readings. The narrator reads his own life from the vantage point of an ordinary white man, a white man who has suppressed his beginnings in blackness, suppressed them at the greatest price to his own spirit and the lives of his descendants. It is an impossible story, one whose artistry is testament to that which its narrator has denied.

Whose Blues?

In a by now infamous instance in Sartre's *Nausea* we find the paradigm of the white intellectual's seeming incapacity for getting things straight when it comes to things having to do with race in general, and with jazz in particular. Roquentin sits listening to a recording of "Some of These Days," and, in a moment of resonance strikingly like the mood Mezz Mezzrow finds himself in while listening to a record of Bessie Smith, the report of which William Carlos Williams includes in book 5 of *Paterson* (221), Sartre's narrator declares to himself and to us as he attends to the music: "I am so happy when a Negress sings: what summits would I not reach if *my own life* made the subject of the melody" (55). Building upon this moment later, Roquentin moves his imagination to the composition of a fantasia upon the identity of the author of this Negress's melody; he imagines that a Jewish artist has given these blue notes to the black songstress: "That's the way it happened. That way or another way, it makes little difference. That is how it was born. It is the worn-out body of the Jew with black eyebrows which it chose to create it" (236). Here Roquentin hears the stirrings of salvation: "She sings. So two of them are saved: the Jew and the Negress. Saved" (236). Mezzrow's is also a song of salvation in the passage excerpted by Williams. Listening to Bessie, Mezzrow says, "[E]very word she sang answered a question I was asking" (221).

There is a difference, however, between these two narratives of jazz and redemption. Mezzrow was right about Bessie Smith's race, but Sartre's narrator has everything turned upside down. The song he hears, "Some of These Days," was written by a black composer, Shelton Brooks, not by a Jew. And the song was made famous by Sophie Tucker, no one's Negress. Just what difference might this make?

William Carlos Williams was, like many white intellectuals, given to this type of racial mistaken identity. In his historical play *Tituba's Children* he replicates Marion L. Starkey's identification of Tituba as half-Negro, an identification for which there is no historical evidence (Hansen 3), and then proceeds to cast her speeches in a sort of twentieth-century, Amos 'n' Andy dialect. Similarly, the composition of the unfinished novel *Man Orchid*, a collaborative improvisation with a mulatto protagonist, was an idea hatched out of an evening spent listening to Bunk Johnson's jazz band, and its protagonist was modeled after the mistaken identification of the quite white Bucklin Moon as a light-skinned Negro by Williams and his companions, a misidentification apparently based on the knowledge that Moon had published a novel titled *The Darker Brother* and knew a lot about jazz (Mariani 67–68).

Williams's writings on jazz are few and conflicting, but from first to last it is fair to say that they are formulated on the basis of just this kind of white misreadings of blackness. Williams wants to encounter the music of black America divorced from its social, cultural, and historical contexts so that he might make of it what he will, might make his own history around it. As a signifier, jazz floats free from its origins, in Williams's mind, so that he can fix it within his own aesthetic cosmos. I am shortly going to assert that not all the effects of this are negative so long as we do not read Williams's jazz notes as descriptions of external reality but rather read them for the difference they make in American verse.

If, in his prologue to *Kora in Hell*, Williams was willing to reprint the assertion made by others that "the only distinctive U.S. contributions to the arts have been ragtime and buck-dancing" (*Imaginations* 23), he was also able to aver as he does in *The Great American Novel*:

> We are deceived when they cry that Negro music is the only true American creation. Everything is judged from this point of view. But to us it is only new when we consider it from a traditional vantage. To us it means a thousand things it can never mean to a European. To us only can it be said to be alive. With us it integrates with our lives. That is what it teaches us. What in hell does it matter to us whether it is new or not when it is to us. It exists. It is good solely because it is a part of us. It is good THEREFORE and therefore only is it new. (*Imaginations* 210)

And having said this much, Williams would go on in a 1932 letter to Kay Boyle to remark: "The new verse is a new time—'rag-time' is only a penny sample; 'jazz' is excessively limited when looked at thoroughly. Its rigidities are exactly like that of all we have outgrown. Take away its aphrodisiac qualities and it is stale" (*Letters* 136). In *The Great American Novel* he also associated jazz with "impossible frenzies of color in a world that refuses to be drab" (*Imaginations* 200) and borrowed the image from Warner Fabian's *Flaming Youth* of young people "'heeled' by way of petting parties and the *elemental* stimulus of jazz" (*Imaginations* 201, emphasis added). Years later Williams was still associating jazz with sexuality and primitivism but without any of the positive qualities he so often attributed to those elements. In a late interview with Walter Sutton, Williams disclaims his earlier interest in the music in terms that recall Gertrude Stein's denunciations of African art:

> WCW: . . . in jazz music even the saxophone sounds are not
> advanced enough from the primitive to interest me at all.
> I don't like jazz. The artists in Paris rave about jazz, but it's
> too tiresome, it's too much the same thing.
>
> WS: There's not enough variability?

WCW: Not variability at all. Not subtle. And if you've got to be
sexually excited by it, it shows you to be a boob. It merely
excites. There's no subtlety at all. (*Interviews* 55)

It would be more than difficult to derive any coherent jazz aesthetic from this mix. While Williams's observations upon the way that
jazz "integrates" with our lives sound healthy, we must remember
that he posits a jazz that emerges from an ahistorical naught. Like
Gertrude Stein, Williams held that African Americans were beset by
nothingness. For Williams this empty experience of blackness had an
existential quality about it; it permitted blacks a paradoxical, heroic
authenticity. "Nothing," Williams says in *In the American Grain*, "makes
much difference" (210). Ignoring the historical fact that it has been
whites who have made an issue of race most tragically, he says of
African Americans that "when they try to make their race an issue—
it is nothing. . . . But saying *nothing*, dancing *nothing*, 'Nobody,' it is a
quality" (209). This nothing is the basis of the irreducible racial substance Williams awards blacks. This irreducible black hole then emits
the kind of ahistorical improvisation of which Williams can make
something.

What he makes of it thematically is for the most part what other
white artists including Cummings, Crane, Sandburg, Van Vechten,
Lindsay, Stein, and even some of the Beats have made of it, an un-
inhibited libidinal flow. Williams opposes the existential freedom of
black blankness to a white Puritanism. He opposes the manliness of
the jazz musician to an insipid European tradition. He opposes jazz
to the metrical death represented by a poetic nostalgia for lost European origins. He opposes "hot," black jazz to the white, "sweetened"
sounds that overwhelmed classic jazz, and he sees in that opposition
an analogy to his argument against the deathly embrace of Eliotic
measure: "Sweet music was coming in and jazz was through. But I
mean THROUGH! . . . Nobody wants that kind of music any more: . . .
this IS a waste land . . ." (Williams, Miller, and Carlin, *Man Orchid* 83).
Against the overorchestrated strains of Eliot's opus Williams places
the hot spontaneity of black music, but he continually misconstrues
the nature of that spontaneity. As Peter Schmidt has observed in detailing Williams's interest in Dada, Williams felt that "the truly spontaneous moment, after all, would be an unprecedented one, an ahistori-

cal one. Such a moment is the moment of 'relief' and renewal toward which all Dadaist art aspires" (171). But while enlisting jazz in his war on Eliot, Williams rips it loose from its source in the daily lives of a people, and that may be an even higher price to pay than accepting a background of sweet orchestrations. Williams, like Sartre's Roquentin, and like so many other white artists, strips the music of its context so that his own imaginative life might make the subject of the melody. He removes black experience from jazz and in the process creates a white noise that makes much difference. He has, every bit as much as have the white sweeteners of the music he complains about, taken the music away from its classic impulse. Stephen Henderson, in his *Understanding the New Black Poetry,* described a sort of black objective correlative and employed the critical term *saturation* to describe the rooting of black verse in the contextuality of Afro-American experience. Williams, by reducing that experience to an existential nothing, has produced an unsaturated, whitened version of jazz.

I would like here to adduce a poem titled "To a Negro Jazz Band in a Parisian Cabaret":

> May I?
> *Mais oui.*
> *Mein Gott!*
> *Parece una rumba.*
> ! *Que rumba!*
> Play it, jazz band!
> You've got seven languages to speak in
> And then some.
> Can I?
> Sure.
>
> (Hughes 67)

The spirit of this poem is of a piece with the image of multiracial cultural improvisation offered by Mezz Mezzrow in the late pages of *Paterson,* and the multilingual pun in the first two lines sounds like something Williams would want. But the poem is by Langston Hughes, a contemporary of Williams who shared in the internationalist ethos of American modernism. Unlike Williams though, Hughes wrote always, even from Moscow and Paris, from the subjectivity rooted in the experiences of American blackness. He speaks elsewhere of the "undertow of black music with its rhythm that never betrays you, its strength like the beat of the human heart, its humor and its rooted power" (*Big Sea* 209).

Hughes's poem is strikingly like the piece we have come to know as "Shoot It Jimmy" from *Spring and All*. Both poems celebrate the pure productivity of human speech and the improvisational power of jazz rhythm. Both poets seem to agree "that sheet stuff / 's a lot of cheese" (*Collected I* 216). Nonetheless, where the Hughes poem opens out at the end in an invitation to group creation, Williams's poem closes on a note of romantic individualism that seems at first a replay of the hoary notion of the poet as heroic, original genius:

> Nobody
> Nobody else
>
> but me—
> They can't copy it
>   (*Collected I* 216)

Still, there is a saving grace note of irony in this seeming closure. The rhetoric of this poem is such that the last lines give the lie to their own sense; their existence is best evidence that "they" can indeed copy it. The poem, though, is clearly no mere transcription. What Williams has produced is an arrangement, a new setting of the source tune. The words as Williams copies them come to sound and mean differently. If it is true that black and white Americans sometimes speak the same language differently, that the same words mean differently depending on who speaks them and in what setting, it is also true that white jazz provides a different sounding of the American text. The question has never really been "Can a white man sing the blues?" but "What happens to the blues when, as they inevitably will, whites *do* sing them? And what will it make of America?"

As confused as he may have been about the spirit of jazz, and as racist as some of his pronouncements upon black life are, Williams clearly understood the cultural creativity of American racial dialectic. Words he inscribes in other passages of *Paterson* could easily be read into a discussion of the syncretic impulse in American art. In one context Williams writes that "Dissonance / (if you are interested) / leads to discovery" (177), and then, quoting Levy, "antagonistic / cooperation is the key" (177).

In his search for a new measure in the American idiom, Williams was ready to draft jazz to serve in his war against metrical traditionalists. In a 1954 letter to John C. Thirwall the poet traces the development of his discovery of the new rhythms to his childhood. He portrays himself as the "product of a new country" and "a child of a new era in the world." "But," he complains, "the world about [him] still clung to the old measurements." He sees himself as having an innate, New World sense of a saving rhythm that he views as a sort of protojazz sensibility. Reporting his musician uncle's discovery of the young Williams's keen rhythmic instinct, Williams recounts this incident to Thirwall: "Listen! he said and began to beat a drum. At a certain point in the rhythm he would stop sharply and I, to complete the beat, would come in with my, tum tum. I did not have the subtlety of the best Negro drummers, but something fundamental had taken place in me of which I knew nothing" (*Letters* 328–29). The assumption that Negro drummers have a special access to rhythmic subtlety is a racist strategy that has long exercised an appeal to American intellectuals, but what is crucial here again is that as mistaken as Williams may be, the example of jazz aids him in the transformation of American verse.

On the one hand Williams's appropriations of black music may be viewed as another instance of cultural imperialism, of the dominant art colonizing its margins, and the product could be seen as denatured, blank fusion music. But it is more accurate, I believe, to view Williams's sometimes strained relation to jazz as exemplifying the creative modes by which American culture is constantly reconstituted. To the incursions of white appropriators jazz always sets up a resistance. And black music is always in the act of decolonizing American music by entering into and altering the mainstream. The result is a nomadic, deterritorializing musical imperative. "Deterritorialization," as Paul Patton has defined it, "is the operation characteristic of lines of flight; it is the movement by which one leaves a territory. As such, with rare exceptions, it is accompanied by a simultaneous movement of reterritorialization on some other domain, not necessarily continuous with the first" (126). Deleuze and Guattari, in *A Thousand Plateaus*, remark of the relationships of the races *within* the American idiom that "the problem is not the distinction between major and minor language; it is one of a becoming. It is a question not of reterritorializing oneself on a dialect or a patois, but of deterritorializing the major language. Black Americans do not oppose Black to English, they transform the American English that is their own language into Black English" (104–5). Since African musical traditions first encountered Western instruments and tempered scales, there has been a steady movement of boundaries. Just as the whitened, sweetened sounds Williams opposed to "hot" jazz moved the borders of white American music and threatened to drive black music from the airwaves, we had the simultaneous "revival" of classic jazz and the movement by black avant-garde musicians toward a new territory white musicians had not yet glimpsed. The revolution of bop was in part an assault upon colonized music, a deconstruction of American music's major language. As Deleuze and Guattari go on to identify it, the imperative is to "conquer the major language in order to delineate in it as yet unknown minor languages. Use the minor language to *send the major languages racing*" (105). As Dada and Cubism assisted Williams in his search for new means of organizing the poem, the example of jazz sent his language racing and aided in his search for a new time.

Williams's wish to dehistoricize jazz was a replication of the demands the dominant culture places upon minority cultural offerings. Amiri Baraka describes this as "the largely artificial 'upward' social move, demanded by the white mainstream of all minorities, . . . whereby all consideration of local culture is abandoned for the social and psychological security of the 'main'" (*Blues* 191). In this tactic Williams may be seen as assuring continued dominance of white culture by repressing black cultural particulars. But even as Williams is stuffing black music into a white envelope (and we might some other time examine the politics of this), he is mailing a cultural letter bomb. According to Baraka, there is a second, "lateral . . . form of synthesis, whereby difference is used to enrich and broaden, and the value of any form lies in its eventual use" (*Blues* 191). Just as bop phrasings were eventually assumed into the vocabulary of white music, changing its accents and significations, so that altered vocabulary later became some of the stuff out of which new black artists improvised new changes. Under the urgings of Dada, Cubism, Precisionism, and film, Williams helped restructure the image, line, and page of American poetry. The rhythms of jazz filled the air as he worked, and his American idioms were propelled by jazz rhythms. He was largely wrong about jazz, and when he consciously set out to use jazz, he fell into the habits of so many poets who seem to think they have written a jazz poem because they've mentioned a musician. But black music altered the instrument. Williams's rhythmic vocabulary was determinedly American in part because it encompassed the inflections of black music, and his work in turn influenced significant later black poets, Baraka among them. Amiri Baraka, yet another American poet from Jersey, provides this summary of the perpetual motion of musical boundaries among American artists:

> Musically, the Negro's address to the West has always been in the most impressive instances lateral and exchanging. But the mode or attitude characterizing the exchange has always been constantly changing, determined . . . by the sum of the most valid social and psychological currents available to him. Given this hypothesis, the *contemporaneity* of the Negro's music in the context of Western cultural expression can be seen as necessary. (*Blues People* 192)

When Williams addressed black jazz across the crowded room of America's culture club, it was a case of mistaken identity, partly due to the effects of the vocabulary of American racism. Like so many whites he wanted his own life to be the subject of the melody and so subjected black life to white revision and alterations. But his mistake did affect him and helped to change the patterns of poetic improvisation in this country. Black music spoke back forcefully in response to the impersonations of the sweet sound, and in the continued misunderstandings of cultural conversation among America's races we must all talk back to William Carlos Williams.

———

There should be a system of government
based on the music of Charlie Parker
                    (Gardner, "Cover" 91)
    Jazz is
back hand me the flat pack.
                    (Coolidge, *Own* np)

One mode of such back talk, a newer sort of talking blues, may be found in the body of work by Clark Coolidge. Though an enormous amount of writing about jazz and about jazz musicians has proceeded from the pens of white authors in the twentieth century, little of this production has transcended the confusions found in the writings of Williams. Much writing, when it touches on jazz, has borne the racist accents found so often in Ezra Pound, as in his letter of November 18, 1930, to Louis Zukofsky, where Pound, discussing the tensions between the natural accentuation of common speech and the accentuation of verse, remarks: "[A]lle samme jazz etc. depending on whether the guy has nigger blood undsoweiter" (*Pound/Zukofsky* 74). Many white writers, echoing Sartre's pattern of misidentifications in *Nausea*, persist in simply getting things wrong. Jacques Attali, for instance, in his otherwise valuable study *Noise: The Political Economy of Music*, identifies Carla Bley as one of "several blacks" instrumental in the formation of the Jazz Composers' Orchestra (138). (Oddly, he also describes the Free Jazz of the sixties as having been "created with the Black Muslims" [139].) Some readers are surely tempted to respond to poetry announcing itself as jazz verse in much the same way that Kenneth Rexroth, himself a great lover of the music, characterized the demise of the movement toward poetry readings accompanied by jazz, a movement in which he had been instrumental: "It was ruined by people who knew nothing about either jazz or poetry" (qtd. in Feinstein and Komunyakaa, xvii). Clark Coolidge, whose poetics trace one line of descent from William Carlos Williams, gathered an initial impetus from the writers of the Beat generation, a group whose knowledge and love of jazz is legendary, but his writing on jazz, and to jazz, throughout his life, a writing that provides a veritable taxonomy of improvisational possibilities, represents a considerable advance over the, in retrospect, somewhat modest experiments with jazz-oriented aesthetics carried out by the Beats.

Some claims made for the connectedness of Beat writings to jazz may not bear close scrutiny. But, as in the case of Williams, it is probably more important for our understanding of developments in American poetics that we work toward a knowledge of the multiple ways that the idea of black music has altered the sounds made by American poets than that we succeed in locating justifiable technical analogues between jazz and poems. It was the example of jazz that lead Jack Kerouac to his explorations of "spontaneous bop prosody," not a careful comprehending of musical structures. The model provided by jazz musicians, or, more accurately, the model constructed by Kerouac as he gazed upon black musicians, was as important to the evolving techniques of Beat writing as the music itself. This fact is perhaps most clearly evidenced by a passage from *The Subterraneans* in which Kerouac describes a performance by Charlie Parker, one of the few characters appearing in the novel under his own name (possibly because, having become "Bird," Parker was already a novelistic character in the Beat pantheon). Here Kerouac makes eye contact with Parker:

> [I feel Parker digging] directly into my eye to search if really I was that great writer I thought myself to be as if he knew my thoughts and ambitions or remembered me from other night clubs and other coasts, other Chicagos—not a challenging look but the king and founder of the bop generation at least the sound of it in digging his audience digging his eyes, the secret eyes him-watching, as he just pursed his lips and let great lungs and immortal fingers work, his eyes separate and interested and humane, the kindest jazz musician there could be while being and therefore naturally the greatest— (19–20)

This typically Kerouacian cadenza is patently modeled on the rushing flights of notes loosed from Parker's alto saxophone, delivered in lyric phrases improvised against a background structure, and it doesn't matter much to our appreciation of this as a literary technique that Kerouac, who lived intimately with this music, knew little about the actual modes of Parker's music making. What mattered to Kerouac was Parker's seemingly effortless ability to place stunning new phrases in the air at will *and* the woodshedding that went into the feat. That long breath line of practiced improvisation became the key to much Beat writing, and that giving of one's work over to the risks of improvisation is what Clark Coolidge found most liberating in the best work of the generation preceding his own.

Clark Coolidge, an accomplished drummer who is knowledgeable about a wide range of musical forms, was in the audience at Hunter College Playhouse the night that Jack Kerouac presented his talk "The Origins of the Beat Generation" at a forum sponsored by Bran-

deis University. In what must have been a startling gesture even to a
fifties forum, Kerouac at one point wandered to a piano at the back
of the stage and began picking out an accompaniment to the remarks
of one of his antagonists at the forum, Kingsley Amis. According to
Coolidge, Kerouac moved to the piano "in a friendly way, to kind of
back [Amis] up, and get something fresh going" (qtd. in Nicosia 24).
As he has remarked many times over the intervening years, Coolidge
found in Kerouac an emancipating model not unlike that located by
Kerouac in Charlie Parker. In a recent interview Coolidge recalls:

> When I realized I could write, it was when I put jazz playing
> together with Kerouac's work, reading Kerouac and realizing he
> was improvising. He was not doing like Hemingway or like some
> teacher I must have had in highschool English instructed. In other
> words, the whole pedantic notion that you know what you're going
> to say and then you find the right word for it. That there's only
> one, and you find it and put it down. If you don't get it, you go and
> search and you can't go on until you do find it. All that just gave
> me a blinding headache. I could never conceive of being a writer
> that way. But when I read Kerouac, I thought this guy doesn't know
> where he's going, he's improvising, he's winging it. And that was
> the big discovery that enabled me to be any sort of writer at all.
> (*Talisman* 24–25)

This free-style oral response is interesting in its formal resemblance
to the free-flowing improvisation of Kerouac's description of watching Charlie Parker watch him, for when we turn to Coolidge's writing,
we find that it is only the improvisational impetus that has come from
Kerouac. Coolidge's poems are in most other ways as unlike Kerouac's
writing as might be imagined, and in Coolidge's art jazz is surrounded
by none of the exoticism and primitivism we so often find among the
Beats. The liberation Coolidge finds in the model of jazz is that freedom that comes to the intensely practiced. It is not the freedom to do
anything but rather the freedom to replace the given of a melody line,
the freedom to play over the bar lines, the freedom to supply inter-
chords and counterrhythms, freedoms successfully embraced only by
those who are already familiar with their instrument and with its
repertoire. It is the Free Jazz evolved by Ornette Coleman or Cecil

Taylor, not the freedom of the technically ignorant so often conjured by early critics of those musicians.

In a conversation with Lee Bartlett, Coolidge remembers: "I started out as a musician playing drums, which transformed eventually into jazz and be-bop. If I don't get a certain kind of movement, a literal moving forward in time in my work, I don't feel it's really happening" ("constant" 2). While it is nearly always a mistake to attempt a literalizing move toward tying the pronouncements of poets regarding the effects of jazz upon their poetics too tightly to specific technical instances in the music, it is not too much to say that Coolidge here presses further than the free-verse revolution of the Imagists. If Pound advised poets to break with the metronome and its line-end heave, to compose in the rhythms of the musical phrase, Coolidge, under the influence of postmodern black jazz, seeks a still more propulsive rhythm. Jazz drummers are valued for their abilities to invent, and to respond to the inventions of others, while "keeping" time. Coolidge's verbal constructions "take" time, they press consciousness forward in time-space figuring, like Charles Olson's projective verse, a constant "outward," an intentional movement counter to the given of an existing line limit. Similarly, Coolidge, who is familiar with atonalism and serial composition as well as more traditional tonalities, observes that he thinks "of the sentence as something like the key center in a piece of music" ("constant" 11). As Cecil Taylor's music mobilizes its harmonic inventions against a tonal gravity rather than within a traditional "key," Coolidge adopts and adapts the sentence as a motivating work space. But in the same way that Taylor demolishes the standard syntax of jazz jamming to reveal and refigure the musical values that have become mired within it like dead metaphors (and what could be more clichéd than the predictable cycle of chorus and solo that composes most jamming), Coolidge subjects the comforting syntax of traditional lyric to a radical torque as a means of discovering new possibilities of song. At the same time, Coolidge links a conception of poetic tonality resembling Frost's "sentence sound" to the determination of line breaks. As he remarks to Bartlett, "I can hear certain tones of voice saying certain words in certain line lengths" ("constant" 6). Coolidge is possessed of a drummer's understanding of pitch, touch, time, and space. He likens the effect he seeks to the "magic cymbal" of Kenny Clarke's trap set. Kept level, Clarke's cymbal presented a challenge to other drummers who tried to use his set when sitting in. In Coolidge's recollection, contained in his explanatory note to his contribution in Sascha Feinstein and Yusef Komunyakaa's *Jazz Poetry Anthology*, when other drummers touched Clarke's cymbal, "it would sound like the top of a garbage can, but when he played it, it was like fine crystal" (255). In his own work as a writer Coolidge shuns the metric feet of the newer formalists, but he does not shun the steadying hand of rhythm. As he writes, he listens for "the unceasing teem of that top cymbal at the back of [his] room" (255). Coolidge is a poet who has Max Roach, as much as Milton, "imprinted on [his] nervous reflex," and he feels "the space between people (voices) in terms of tempos" (255). Again, it would be rash to seek exact correspondence between the recorded practice of Coolidge's jazz models and his published forms; what is crucial is to think with Coolidge the difference African-American music makes in the verse of our time, and in the time of our verse. "These days," Coolidge notes in *The Jazz Poetry Anthology*, "I ask myself again and more acutely the relation (if there is one?) between language forms and the wordless shapes of time. Perhaps there is no direct exchange. All I can be sure of is that I am able to possess them both within one body and one mind" (255). In practice this has propelled Clark Coolidge to produce a body of texts incredibly varied within itself and endlessly reshaping itself. While it might be too much to de-clare his work jazz poetry, it is clear that jazz supplies a most signifi-cant intertext for Coolidge's writing. Few white writers in America have ever worked so insistently and so creatively under the signs of black music; few white writers have conducted such a sustained and fecund exchange with the lyric inventions of American culture made by black hands.

At moments Coolidge's poems sound much like drum solos, or per-haps like the improvised mouth-percussion sounds favored by some street corner rap artists over the less emotive electronic drum ma-chines heard on so many recordings. The poems of *Polaroid*'s first part, with their sharp bursts of monosyllabic vocables, strongly re-semble the drum fills played under a vocal in a jazz band. They also call to mind the virtuoso scat singing of artists such as Sarah Vaughan and Ella Fitzgerald, who, having established the melody with the given sentimental lyric, proceed to improvise stunning solos whose notes are formed of seemingly nonsignifying, but potently recognizable, syllables. These poems simultaneously carry forward the semantic and syntactic experiments of the Objectivist poets. Louis Zukofsky spent much of his life exploring the possibilities offered by such small words as *a* and *the*. In *Polaroid*, Coolidge places the most familiar words of our language in strange paratactic streams. The syntax that inheres between the seemingly unrelatable words works like the "blue" notes in jazz to create the sense of sounds that aren't wholly there, creating a kind of melody of sound and sense as the reader naturally intones a rising and falling phrase sound. The first words of the third page of the book first promise a familiar sort of song, something on the order of "There Will Never Be Another You." But by the time the eye falls upon the fifth word of the first line, the mind registers the fact that this lyric will not follow the anticipated itinerary. The two opening lines set up a kind of verbal chord, which is broken apart and explored by the subsequent, shorter lines; the reader hears an effect akin to John Coltrane's "sheets of sound" while moving forcefully through the poem. The shorter lines hurry us past the balladlike opening into a region of scatting syntactic flight:

> never will those means what of it's true
> on either kind yet often only all
> above even
> same when where
> it's what's
> a not so yet
> still often all must
> this that hence evens
> till once onto about once
> downs which ever some those
> do and the it
> such as such
> while once

Still, writing is not drumming, nor is it singing, no matter how musical the effect upon reading aloud. Coolidge's writing in poems like this is, though, a material, signifying movement taking place in time, arranging space tonally, and is, to that extent, drumming lyric.

In other works Coolidge's jazz inventions take the shape of formal lyric allusions to and tropes upon familiar songs. Just as Paul Blackburn wrote portions of his "Torch Ballad for John Spicer" quite recognizably to the tune of "Bewitched, Bothered, and Bewildered" (*Collected* 365–66), so Coolidge on occasion twists a tune out of its comfortable place in the nearly public domain, as in the poem "Doubts in Kilter," where readers encounter the line "Nobody knows the numeral troubles I shine" (*Solution* 216). In many poems Coolidge's allusions serve to insert the work at the intertextual intersection where the poet's musical models meet with his literary predecessors. A direct connection back to William Carlos Williams is available in part 3 of Coolidge's long poem *At Egypt* when it "towers out of the coffee whorl / to see Bunk Johnson's Blackstrap Papyrus Lab near Garden City" (30). The literary line we can draw from Williams (*in* New Jersey) through the Beats (also *in* New Jersey in the case of Ginsberg) is inextricable from the musical line that connects Bunk Johnson with bebop, and Coolidge maps this territory in his poem "Kerouacy": "the litanies of bop and salt on their freight trains / I'd saw it go glow in the window" (*Own* np).

Where Williams persisted in primitivizing the black musicians he heard, seeing in them the exotic other as mark of some desired libidinal free flow, Clark Coolidge finds among the musicians he listens and alludes to an opportunity to sit in, a free-flowing interplay among improvisers. Coolidge's contributions sometimes seem a playing out of Mezz Mezzrow's message in that portion of his *Really the Blues* that William Carlos Williams excerpts in *Paterson:* "You didn't have to take the finest and most original and honest music in America and mess it up because you were a white man" (qtd. in *Paterson* 221). Coolidge seems to understand, though, that the invitation jazz extends to white artists is not an invitation to be black, or to assume musical and literary blackface, but rather it is an invitation to bring what one has in hand as culture to bear upon the collective composition. Coolidge's poems invoking the works of particular jazz artists are improvised responses to the recorded call of the greats who have ministered to their instruments, their muses, and their audiences. One of the most frequently appearing musicians in Coolidge's texts is Thelonious Monk, whose work forms a bridge between the revolution of the bop generation and the younger generation of Coolidge's contemporaries. The book *Own Face* owes as much to Monk as it does to Floyd Collins, whose face gazes out from the volume's cover, and the poem titled "Rhymes with Monk" provides a semantic rhyme to the walls of the cave that held Collins to his death: "Music a matter of walls. / Breathing in the place of record" (np). Just as this poem offers no means of determining whether the title indicates that a rhyme *for* Monk is to be found here, or whether the poem is an act of rhyming in concert with Monk, so it refuses to supply readers with a reason to decide whether the "Breathing" of the poem is in, or on the record, or whether it is a breathing that supplants the record, a breathing in the place where the record is, or a breathing in the officially designated place of history. In any event, resounding music is, in the poem, a matter of walls, which was evident to Monk, the composer of "Brilliant Corners." The walls of a record's groove (we may have to find another analogue for this in our present, digital age) attempt to contain the music *and* to bring it to us. Additionally, music is sometimes a matter of breathing in the place of record, in the space where recording takes place, within the walls. Toward the end of the poem, Monk, Coolidge, and the reader all wake "clear of the bop." A long-distance reader with the recall of a master jazz musician who drops snatches of old tunes into new improvisations will find Coolidge rhyming himself years later in his long meditative poem *The Crystal Text,* a poem that often joins the poet's interests in jazz and geology:

> Otherwise than sound afternoon, exceptional of
> false grasp at type of tongue, and if rhymes
> with Monk the crystal pinks, the emergent brothers
>
> (124)

The language play of this later passage also rhymes with the earlier poem. In the phrase "the crystal pinks," it is impossible, perhaps undesirable, to determine whether we are hearing an adjective followed by a plural noun, or a singular noun followed by a verb. This lack of semantic and syntactic determinism, in turn, is strongly reminiscent of the tensions created by the unusual melodic rhythms and sometimes unresolved chords of Monk's music. The poet composing within the walls of his room, attuning himself to the quartz crystal that occupies a place upon his recording desk, picks up a frequency laid upon the air much earlier:

> Monk strike key, and all presumed
> depth to shoot out later? He likes
> the sound in the room, nothing now to be
> patched. Ring. Ring be the mineral
> quotient of blocks to move?
>
> *(Crystal* 52)

Here blocks of mineral, block chords, the memory of music, and the crystal as muse all ring changes within the stanza. Each room, as Monk knew from unending nights on stages around the world, has its own sound. Each stanza rings to its own resonant frequency. Each object, each word is a key to be struck. The poet's improvisation is a return to the place of an old tune to record a new chorus:

> The music levers into brain, insists
> I listen to it. That I have no other
> life I am a listener. (Am I lighter?)
> He plays an old text, he
> does it. He plays on
> a text otherwise lifeless.
>
> *(Crystal* 69)

All texts are lifeless save we play upon them by reading, but sight reading, though a valued skill, is but a beginning. The reader, like the poet, must be a listener prepared to play the text, to do it. The jazz musician must be at once the most attentive of listeners and a consummate composer. Jazz requires the mastery of clichés, riffs, old texts, and the ability to respond to the call of the moment with a novel turn of phrase. To paraphrase Wallace Stevens, each jazz performance is the cry of its own occasion. We do not paraphrase music; we join it. We answer and talk back to it. In another text conjoining textual strata of geology and jazz, the book-length poem *Mine: The One That Enters the Stories,* Coolidge visits the mountaintop: "We could sandwich talk on the mountains noontimes. Talk over music, how does it last, how does Monk pause. Now I muse away from the music, missing its hardness" (71). We could be talking about music over our sandwiches or talking across to one another over the music we have brought with us, but our musings in any event come around to those at first hearing unexpected openings in Thelonious Monk's texts. Monk's music, like

Coolidge's poems, points beyond the inherited limits of the form. We never really know where the boundaries are till someone transgresses them, demonstrating in the process that the boundary isn't an unnavigable border, but limits always call back to posited origins. Cecil Taylor's piano playing insists, against the complaints of some early critics, on the traditions out of which his compositions unfold. Monk always, no matter how far he left behind "good" piano technique, took the blues with him:

> Monk took the blues upon the surpassing swing
> but doesn't understand when someone puts them back in a bag.
> How does that big bag adapt?
>
> (Coolidge, "Registers" 59)

Coolidge's capacious line measures the pliability of stanzaic form while taking Monk, himself as well as his name, as a key in which to work, as the title of this poem, "Registers (People in All)," suggests. Linguists as well as musicians use the term "register" to indicate a possible vocabulary, and Coolidge sees that each person demands a different set of possible pitches. The ability of the blues to remain recognizably and productively the blues in eight-bar, twelve-bar, sixteen-bar, and no-bar configurations figures the adaptability of language, thought, to material experience. Included among the "order of regions" that would compose a journal of the procession of his work *Quartz Hearts*, Coolidge notes "Thelonious Monk's (solo) I Should Care" and provides readers with the Columbia Records catalog number for the side (57). Other regions so noted include "Gerry Mulligan's earliest-fifties Quartets rediscovered, [and] Kerouac's Desolation Angels." Like favored keys in which artists know they can bring forth their best improvisations, these are registers in which the poet's tone is assured and in which his technical facility is most evident.

Coolidge is a poet for whom "words have no safety zone" (*Crystal* 146), but he is also a poet for whom technique, jazz technique, may offer the dream of a common reassurance. In *The Crystal Text* he records a dream:

> in which I'm playing in a group
> with Lee Konitz (a quartet?) and we've just
> done taping a tune. Listening to playback we

discover that a single note by everybody
    (simultaneously!)
in the whole piece is wrong, will have to be corrected.
Lee says we'll just have to replay that one note
and drop it in at the exact moment on the existing
tape. This seems to me as if it will be
extremely difficult, and I look at Lee for
confirmation but his expression, a slight smile,
leaves no doubt that this is the only way.

                                              (145–46)

It is always possible, even in improvisation, to be mistaken. ("Brubeck, / Just how long were your mistakes?" [119], Coolidge asks elsewhere in *The Crystal Text*.) But such mistakes are corrected in the same way that they are made. The precision Coolidge dreams of is not the kind of precision that presents itself as the right words in the right order, for it assumes no a priori orders of rightness against which its productions might be measured. The improvisations generate and demonstrate the orders of their own measure, as did the earlier improvisations of Gertrude Stein and William Carlos Williams, and the words composing them cannot be detached from their contingent orders for measurement against something outside. Still, they are measurable against their own construction. Theirs is always the rightness of these words in this order. In a 1965 discussion with Nat Hentoff, Cecil Taylor offers his understanding of this call to precision:

> If a man plays for a certain amount of time—scales, licks, what have you—eventually a kind of order asserts itself. Whether he chooses to notate that personal order or engage in polemics about it, it's there. That is, if he's saying anything in his music. There is no music without order—if that music comes from his own innards. But that order is not necessarily related to any single criterion of what order should be as imposed from the outside. Whether that criterion is the song form or what some critic thinks jazz should be. This is not a question, then, of "freedom" as opposed to "nonfreedom," but rather it is a question of recognizing different ideas and expressions of order. (*Nefertiti* np)

Taylor's aesthetic in this exchange sounds strikingly like Williams, and Taylor has in his time received just as much uncomprehending criticism as Williams ever did while he was alive. Some musicians refused to perform with Cecil Taylor early in his career, for long stretches of time he was unable to secure opportunities to present his work to the public, and many jazz critics simply dismissed his works as nonmusic and noise. But Cecil Taylor's improvising units became a musical laboratory for some of the most exciting artists of Clark Coolidge's generation, including Archie Shepp, Andrew Cyrille, Jimmy Lyons, and Sam Rivers. Cecil Taylor's works are in many ways a continuation by other means of the revolution in piano vocabulary brought about by Thelonious Monk, and Taylor's work has long been a fertile source for the always listening Clark Coolidge. One of Taylor's accomplishments has been a renewed emphasis upon understanding the piano as a percussion instrument, and this no doubt bore particular interest for Coolidge. Taylor himself has always been actively interested in the avant-garde literary scene. In his early days he sometimes helped Diane di Prima and the then LeRoi Jones get out their mimeographed newsletter, *Floating Bear*. In recent years Taylor's own poems, as they have more frequently appeared among the liner notes to his recordings, have looked a good deal like Coolidge's poems, perhaps an indication of the similarity in poetics arrived at by two artists mutually listening to their music. There's not much possibility of mistaking the poems of Taylor for those of Coolidge, but neither is there any mistaking their shared understanding of what improvisation might mean in a verbal art construct, as may be exemplified by this excerpt from Taylor's "Scroll No. 1":

> Whistle into night
> Recognize exorcism
>   blue's history
> Whittled whispers while
> city technique wrung
>   awakened needs
> Spring cotton answer
>   Recognition
>   Carver's oil estranged

>   outer earth's garments
>   Scorched exclusivity
>   Shining Bandanah

Taylor's orders of expression differ from those of Coolidge, but both artists are committed to an aesthetic practice that construes the materials of their arts in difference.

Jacques Derrida has reminded us that it is always possible for a letter not to be delivered to its addressee. Clark Coolidge reminds us that even when we have the number right, our call can be placed on hold. Coolidge's major poem to date evoking the work of Cecil Taylor is part of a long text titled "Comes through in the Call Hold (Improvisations on Cecil Taylor)." These improvisations, like the poem "Rhymes with Monk," may be read as improvisations upon that body of work signed with the name "Cecil Taylor," improvisations upon the name itself, and improvisations upon the person of Cecil Taylor. Coolidge answers to his calling as a poet, responds to the call of Taylor's compositions by placing a call, which is held. Within that seemingly infinite space of waiting, we hear and read, as it were, deep background. What comes through to us as our reading is held up is the noise, the interference, which communications science might attempt to filter out. But in art the art is the noise, and what we hear in the rests of the music, as our instruments are on hold, comes to us out of the distance of language. On hold we hear the residue of all calling as it washes back and forth through the endlessly internetworked systems.

The very first thing we hear is the crashing of a sonic wave set in motion years earlier. The first words of "Comes through in the Call Hold" are "Fell to this, house markings" (9). The first poem in one of Coolidge's very first major books, the volume titled *Space*, published in 1970 by Harper and Row during that rare bright moment when major American publishing houses experimented with editions of experimental verse (an experiment quickly abandoned, not yet replicated, placed on hold), begins with these words: FELL FAR BUT THE BARN (came) up & smacked me" (3). That falling motion carried through the line enters the ear all these years later, breaks against the desire never to have heard, and rushes into the open space of the hold, a rest in which any rhythm might emerge;

Fell to this, house markings, the will to unhear
it broke off, let to us without hold up, mean us
and bearing on the time heat sulks, marchers, matches
a gone cell in haste repeats, replace that cap on
oversets the rhythm . . .

(9)

This is far more than mere misconnection, not simply a wrong number. (All musicians introduce their pieces as numbers, but only bad musicians play by the numbers.) Coolidge, in the act of creation, writes, "creation makes it hard and I / the post has failed, my number, your answer, he staid / the running out and the swearing." When the posts fail and our calls are placed on hold, there is only the waiting, swearing, and listening left.

One of the things that comes through is snatches of music. When we hear a soloist refer to an earlier piece of music, we don't step outside the club to check up on the health of the referent. We place the reference, listen to it, hold it to the emerging orders of the new music. The difficulty Coolidge's work presents to traditional close reading is not that the referent is dead but that the overwhelming volume of reference makes that kind of critical discourse and distance difficult to maintain (another of Coolidge's books is titled *The Maintains*). When Coolidge writes here, "I too would rather than listen not listen," I hear "The Orchestra" of William Carlos Williams in the referential distances of the poem:

> The purpose of an orchestra
>   is to organize those sounds
>   and hold them
> to an assembled order
>   in spite of the
>   "wrong note." Well, shall we
> think or listen? Is there a sound addressed
>   not wholly to the ear?
>   (*Collected II* 250–51)

If we think and listen while on hold with Coolidge's text, we will hear a "home boy tune / goes out with the latest flatten," and not far from that flattened note we will hear "white man sleeps" (10), which, in addition to describing a racial slumber, is the title of a composition by Kevin Volans that has been recorded twice, in original and revised versions, by the Kronos Quartet, a classically trained string ensemble given to performing arrangements of works by Thelonious Monk. Later still in Coolidge's poem we read that "the quartet in encoupling weights doubts / and is in panel seed" (10). By this point we can agree with Coolidge that "the house of sound fell ill" (9), and we too may rather than listen not listen, but we are still on hold with the will to unhear broken off. Clearly Coolidge has our number. But this poem is not about Williams or the Kronos Quartet or Cecil Taylor's quartets any more than Cecil Taylor's composition "Nefertiti, the Beautiful One Has Come" is about Nefertiti. "Comes through in the Call Hold" is an improvisation written under the signs of the jazz of Cecil Taylor. The swirl of referential possibilities constitutes the overtones heard as the reading touches on the materials of the poem. We may re-enter the poem by means of any of its referential openings, but what counts is the shape and generative force of the improvisation. What Amiri Baraka says about Cecil Taylor's work in *Black Music* provides an analogous description of Coolidge's verse: "It is an orchestral language that Cecil is pointing towards; a language that still conceives of verb force, i.e., the solo exclamation made fierce by improvisation" (107). In Baraka's estimation this art is "as exact in its emotional registrations and as severely contemporary in its aesthetic as any other Western art" (109). What this severely contemporary art produces in Coolidge's work is a "home boy tune," an unaddressed calling in the echoing holding pattern of our language:

> Too much whisks away, has your name wrong and thus waits
> another day of witchery alone
> shorter things, the timing of which
> waits long in the lights

> (9)

Coolidge's is "a marginal score, new vocabulary needed legs" (10), which awaits renewed reading in the holding space of marginal writing, writing that takes place in the margins of American literary practice in much the way that jazz erupted in the margins of American popular song. Coolidge's poems are to official and officious verse culture what bebop was to "Moonlight in Vermont."

For Clark Coolidge, poetry can never be fleshed out by source hunters because, as Amiri Baraka reminds us in the title of his early essay on poetics, "Hunting Is Not Those Heads on the Wall" (*Home* 173–78). In Coolidge's listening and improvising practice one must attend to the forms left by the passing of sound and by the passing of the hand across the page, "hear / what's missing there / music is the core of the missing" (*Sound* 13). In the poem "The Great," Coolidge listens to the core of the jazz traditions he has drawn upon. Like John Ashbery's poem "Into the Dusk-Charged Air" (*Rivers* 17–20), which is ordered by the enumeration of the world's great rivers, a technique that lifts the rivers' names from the register of geographic denotation that they might sound anew in the reading, Coolidge's poem is organized as a riff built around the names of Bud Powell, Thelonious Monk, Miles Davis, Carla Bley, Lester Young, Ornette Coleman, Art Tatum, Cecil Taylor, and Charlie Parker and whose sounds sometimes produce, like overtones, the names of those missing from the list, such as Billie Holliday. In Coolidge's writing the music recorded is the "core of the missing" in the same way that for Williams a book is "not the flames / but the ruin left / by the conflagration" (*Paterson* 123). The music walled in by recording is a technical effort to hold still the always-in-motion composing of the artist.

> The greatness of music
> > and it won't hold still since only you heard it
> > > that mind doubles itself faster than seconds
> Perfect rate
> > > > > > (*Sound* 13)

These lines from a book whose title enacts Coolidge's jazz aesthetic, *Sound as Thought*, record the wondrous sense of invention that attracted Williams to Bunk Johnson. But where Williams was constitutionally incapable of wholly unlearning the racist significations in which his hearing of jazz was held (here was a rigidity Williams could not seem to outgrow), Coolidge has inserted himself within the shifting streams of jazz tradition and found his way to a double writing that owes as much to the double time of jazz drumming as to the double science of Derridean textuality. Oddly, the names of drummers are mostly missing from "The Great," perhaps so that we might listen for them in the rhythm section, perhaps because Coolidge himself is on the ride cymbal for this date:

> I turn over my hands more times than are thought
>   and sheathe of the all
>   the seething things
>   a breathing star.
>
> (14)

Like a drummer in his room, headphones clamped to his skull, the poet can keep time with "The Great" of several generations in one session. The speed of language need only measure itself against the reference point of the tradition as it registers the materials of the poem:

> I only want to make midnight mast to my song
>   in shivered and tracing words in other words
>   the Miles off further from the phantom he is
>   blow back
>
> (13)

Thelonious Monk wrote "'Round Midnight." Miles Davis schooled himself with Thelonious Monk (he'd already been to Juilliard) and made "'Round Midnight" a mainstay of his repertoire. What Miles Davis has had to say about Monk could also be said of those such as Cecil Taylor and Clark Coolidge who have furthered the motions Monk made part of the jazz vocabulary:

> [H]ardly any of the critics understood Monk's music. . . . [Y]ou had to be quick with Monk and be able to read between the lines, because he never did talk too much. He'd be doing what he'd be doing in that funny sort of way that he had. If you weren't serious about what *you* were doing and what *he* was *showing* you—not telling you—then you'd be saying, "What? What was that? What's he doing?" It was over for your ass if you found yourself in that place. The shit done passed you by. And that was that. It wasn't no coming back. By that time Monk was somewhere else. (80–81)

Clark Coolidge seeks no fragmentary hold against the ruins; he doesn't call upon the tradition as shoring. He makes midnight, and the music for which it stands, a device for catching the full force of propulsive sound as thought.

Coolidge has attended carefully to the revolutions marked in American poetics by William Carlos Williams and Gertrude Stein, but he has also learned from black American music in ways that they never could, for they never really listened. Coolidge takes jazz as his text and his aesthetic, but in this taking jazz too is transformed. He seeks "A tune of / such device it could collect all the chords" (*Solution* 367), as he writes in his meditative poem "Of What the Music to Me." In the midst of this poem, which includes the history of the music in the only appropriate way, by improvising upon its arrangements, the poet responds in astonishment at the accomplishments of the greats: "Damn, what haven't they played!" (369). In the same vein, there is astonishment in the reading, astonishment at the constantly self-renewing impulse to inscription, to scoring: "How could you go on for liquid pages!" (370). These gestures sign the rhetorical structure of the entire poem, for its lyric stanzas are spun out of rhetorical questions that punctuate the text like rim shots and that are really exclamations of perpetual surprise:

> How can I say about the music, how can I
> deal with all the musics, after they've lasted?
> The linch pin is on the snare. And is When
> the point?
>
> (366)

Practiced soloist that he is, Coolidge launches himself from this beginning onto an extended lyric passage that uses reliable riffs in transformed contexts to make new shapes. Sometimes it's a matter of a single favored note around which the solo makes a turn, as in the lines: "Bird's arrayed for / us to pass this point (if not all fell points)" (372). Many musicians have certain notes they return to as anchors for their improvisations. Here the note is "fell," but its position in this line causes the word to sound with a different inflection from the one adopted by Coolidge when he placed that note in the initial position in poems like "Fed Drapes" and "Comes through in the Call Hold." In other stanzas the familiar riff is a repeated phrase that brings with it a repeat of its connotative thematic strands. One passage of this poem addressed directly to the "shrugging listener" promises "impossible dates," recorded sessions "featuring guys / who never met in life" (368). That phrase picks up on an earlier line, from *Mine:*

The One That Enters the Stories, which records another dream date:
"I awake believing I know the exact fiberboard location in the base-
ment of racks wherein the impossible to classify jam-date LP may be
located. Those guys never even met in real life. Which is why dual
piano sessions never work out" (9). In other instances the riff is taken
directly from the hands of another improviser, for the purposes of
commenting upon and within the tradition:

> Bop never fell out of anybody's mind.
> Once they faced up and trod those unfastened banisters.
> And "the rooftop of the beatup, tenement, on 3D &
>   Harrison,
> had Belfast painted." (a Kerouac that Williams couldn't
>   hear?)

(371)

Some individual notes allude to bodies of music and text whose memories hover like massive, shimmering chords against which Coolidge
solos. The line "But in Ascension the bits come therming down"
(374) summons the massed instruments of John Coltrane's 1965 large-
group recording *Ascension,* and Coolidge becomes a vicarious con-
tributor to the memory of that breathtaking event that alternated
scheduled solos with free-blowing ensemble passages. Similarly, the
line "At the john door / of the Five Spot the skimmers throttled" (374)
not only memorializes the literal proximity of the men's rest room to
the bandstand in that legendary club, it also memorializes the best-
known memorial poem by Coolidge's predecessor poet, also a jazz
fan, Frank O'Hara. That same john door is the climactic listening
post, midnight mast, against which O'Hara is leaning in memory at
the end of "The Day Lady Died." His recollection of leaning against
that bathroom door listening to Billie Holliday as she "whispered a
song along the keyboard / to Mal Waldron and everyone . . ." (325) is
the point toward which all forces in O'Hara's poem point. That same
head door, in turn, becomes the fulcrum for Coolidge's stanza. In
music, even in program music, composers must be finely attuned to
the colorations, nuances, and cultural histories of notes and chords
if they wish to guide the signifying effects of their music within a
potential audience. Poets must also minister to the tonalities and ety-
mologies of the words they use if they are to give shape to the massive

referential apparatus of even the simplest phrases. Coolidge does not content himself with a poetry of reference. "But what is this becoming, an excuse for inroads?" (374), he asks. His is a poetry that, like the tone poems of Duke Ellington, avails itself of the capacities of each constituent in the orchestra to achieve an amazing grace of ever-shifting form: "Music bending different. Abrasions of amazing / pockets" (375).

The answer to the question I find myself wanting to ask William Carlos Williams when I read his scattered characterizations of jazz, the answer to the question "Whose blues?", is a response America is making to the call of black music, a response to its own blackness. It is an answer growing in the interstices of racial subjectivity as Americans hum to themselves and read one another's charts. Clark Coolidge has listened to the deep song of black music, and his poetics have been shaped in that listening. Listening to the music and to the percussive sounds of his own writing, Coolidge always hears a new line, because the music is never finished with itself or with us, never arrives at a final address. The answer to the question "Whose blues?" is always awaiting our arrival at the next session, the double session, the all-night session, always to be read, as Coolidge writes, "Last bars, frantic postcards. Linings of the road" (*Solution* 375). Well, shall we think or listen?

"Baraka as a text"

—Paul Hoover, *Novel*

Amiri Baraka

LeRoi Jones as Intertext

At the close of a long list of personal dedications in his collection of poems titled *In. On. Or About the Premises,* Paul Blackburn adds the kind of note generally reserved for the deceased: "And in memory, to Jim Johnson and LeRoi Jones." The second of these memorials is Blackburn's humorous way of recording the transformation of LeRoi Jones to Imamu Amiri Baraka, and of elegiacally invoking the working friendship that had been theirs during Baraka's early period. (This dedication has acquired a tragic uniqueness in the intervening years. It is one of the few such dedications whose subject has outlived its author.) A less amusing and indeed critically bigoted notice of Baraka's evolution of the mid-sixties was recorded

by Kenneth Rexroth, who wrote: "In recent years [Baraka] has suc-
cumbed to the temptation to become a professional Race Man of the
most irresponsible sort. . . . His loss to literature is more serious than
any literary casualty of the Second War" (qtd. in Harris, "Introduction" xxvi). It is difficult to regard this reaction as anything more
than an unthinking rant. Within America's black communities, to be a
race man was precisely to leave irresponsibility behind and to assume
one of the greatest of responsibilities to one's nation. Rexroth, interestingly reflecting the racial determinism of some of Baraka's own
aesthetic statements during this era, simply substitutes a racial characterization for critical analysis. If Rexroth truly believed that Baraka's
politics had irreparably damaged his poetics, he is a long way from
offering any critical demonstration in this comment. Both Blackburn's
humor and Rexroth's assault indicate the extent to which Baraka's
remaking of himself, and his adoption of a politics of cultural nationalism, were deeply and personally felt among white writers who had
come to value his work, and whose reactions, as in the case of Rexroth,
sometimes give testament to their incomprehension. That Baraka anticipated such reactions is clearly registered in poems such as "Will
They Cry When You're Gone, You Bet," where he hears:

> muses, singing
> to us in calm tones, about how it is better to die
> etcetera, than to go off from them, how it is better to
> lie in the cruel sun with your eyes turning to dunes
> than leave them alone in that white heat,
>
> (*Black Magic* 63)

When Donald Allen compiled his anthology *The New American
Poetry,* he included only one African-American poet, LeRoi Jones.
While this inclusion did have the positive effect of bringing Baraka's
work in poetry to the attention of a much larger audience, it simultaneously suppressed signs of the existence of a significant community
of black writers, many located in New York, who were pursuing aesthetic experiments similar to those of the white poets anthologized in
Allen's benchmark book. That there was such a community of black,
avant-garde writers, one that interacted extensively with the white
bohemian communities, was no secret among the poets themselves at
the time. John Ashbery, for example, in his prose poem constructed

entirely from names of poets, included in his collection *The Vermont Notebook,* lists David Henderson and Tom Weatherly along with LeRoi Jones. The exciting works being produced by black poets were widely known among writers, but, as in the case of Allen's anthology, they were kept from a wider circulation among critics and readers by the publishing practices of the time. While most of the tendency among white critics to see Baraka as a lone figure of black experiment at midcentury is attributable to the white public's historical unwilling-ness to hear the voices of more than one or two black writers in an era, it is also true that Baraka's tireless efforts as a publisher and propagator of the newer poetics, coupled with the original quality of his own radical approaches to writing, rendered him one of the most visible nonacademic poets of his time well before the popular success of his play *Dutchman* brought him the kind of recognition seldom accorded to American poets. Amiri Baraka may be the first major postmodern black poet, and he became one of the central fig-ures in the development of the Black Aesthetic Movement. Though the importance of Baraka's contributions to black writing is almost universally recognized, few have publicly noted the fact that Baraka is one of the first African-American poets whose works were also enor-mously and almost immediately influential among white poets. The ability of a black writer to influence whites is, of course, no measure at all of the quality of that poet's work, but the extent of Baraka's influence among the most interesting white poets of his generation marks a turning point in the history of racial politics in American writing. Probably not since Langston Hughes had any black poet been so widely read by his contemporary artists, and probably never be-fore Baraka had any black poet been so instrumental in the early careers of white poets, so integral a player in the development of the emerging poetics of his time.

In his autobiography, Baraka summons up the excitement with which he discovered the first works of those poets who would eventu-ally appear together in *The New American Poetry:*

> I learned about Charles Olson's work and began to read it. Also Robert Creeley and Robert Duncan. I got hold of copies of *The Black Mountain Review* and witnessed real excellence not only of content but design. . . . I took up with the Beats because that's what

I saw taking off and flying somewhat resembling myself. The open and implied rebellion—of form and content. Aesthetic as well as social and political. . . . I could see the young white boys and girls in their pronouncement of disillusion with and "removal" from society as being related to the black experience. (156)

Always an activist, Baraka became an ardent promoter of the talents joining in what he came to view as a united front among the various emergent schools of poetry that shared an oppositional stance against the dominant, supposedly "academic" mode encouraged by Eliotic New Criticism and the better-known literary journals and that also tended to assume a position of opposition to the political hegemony in the United States at midcentury. Socially, Baraka viewed the bohemianism of the Beats and of the New York school, and the counter-hegemonic poetics of the Black Mountain school, as being at the time at least loosely analogous to the rebellious aesthetics of the marginalized within the African-American community. He also saw that the New American poetries were in at least some ways more central to that which is most vital in "the traditions" of American verse than the narrowness of vision enforced by the leading journals and critics. That narrowness of vision that marginalized the works of Baraka and his early associates (and in many ways continues to do so) had, in earlier generations, marginalized the aesthetics of Whitman, Melville, and Dickinson. The more American traditions, in Baraka's view, were found in texts such as black blues and the poetry of William Carlos Williams. It was Williams's lifelong advocacy of an American idiom that Baraka found fruitfully taken up within each of the more interesting of the New American poetries: "Williams was a common denominator because he wanted American Speech, a mixed foot, a variable measure. He knew American life had outdistanced the English rhythms and their formal meters. The language of this multinational land, of mixed ancestry, where war dance and salsa combine with country and Western, all framed by African rhythm-and-blues confessional" (*Autobiography* 159). (Baraka's use of the word *confessional* in this context seems a rescue of that much-abused term from the more world-weary and sometimes facile confessional modes of those poets who became the most critically acclaimed during this period.)

With his first wife, Hettie, and with Diane di Prima, Baraka began publishing ventures that provided a means of circulating the works of these new poets, and these publications, *Yugen* and the *Floating Bear,* became a kind of correspondence school in their own right. Baraka's home quickly became a magnet for musicians, painters, and writers, black and white, who were attempting to accomplish something fresh outside the constrictions and clichés of official art venues in America. Just as artists would visit the Five Spot to hear the latest improvisations of Thelonious Monk, they would drop by Baraka's place to share their own works and ideas (and drinks) with one another. "My own poetry was much influenced by the Olson-Creeley Black Mountain hookup," Baraka writes in his autobiography. "In the BM crowd that hung around my crib that was normal. Williams and Pound were the greats to that crowd and Olson and Creeley their contemporary prophets" (160).

The depth of the loyalties other artists came to feel for Baraka is attested to by their readiness in subsequent years to rally to his assistance when needed. Julian Beck, in a piece titled "acrostic for the community of poets" that appeared in a 1964 issue of the *Floating Bear,* provides one such instance in which the artistic community's willingness to help Baraka, who had done so much to help so many of them, became a sign for Beck of an ideal communitarian spirit:

> l is for leroi jones for whom a benefit was
>   given at the living theater last june when leroi
>   and hettie were in need after a complex siege
>   of hepatitis and bills l is for the community
>   of love in which the poets are charter members and
>   on whose help i rely when i have become the
>   abomination
>
> *(Floating* 355)

Subsequent issues of the newsletter record the artistic community's efforts to assist in the legal defense of Baraka following his arrest during the Newark uprisings. Issue number 34 carried a notice soliciting contributions that were to be sent to Diane di Prima's address for forwarding (477). The next issue reported that Allen Ginsberg's Committee on Poetry had raised eight hundred dollars for the LeRoi Jones Defense Fund; the defense fund now had its own address in

Newark that the *Bear* supplied for those wishing to make direct contributions (503).

Baraka's eventual break with his colleagues among white artists occurred over a number of years and is amply documented in his published writings of the period of his adoption of cultural nationalism. That the evolving separation caused pain and concern among some of his old friends was evident to Baraka. He speaks of it in his autobiography: "These white men saw that I was moving away from them in so many ways and there was some concern, because it wasn't that I didn't like them any longer, but that where I was going they could not come along. Where that was, I couldn't even articulate" (192). On one level it had simply become the case that the pain white people might feel at being excluded by black people attempting to organize themselves for their own salvation paled into insignificance in the face of the tasks that Baraka and other African-American artists faced in the effort to achieve liberation within an oppressive society. If Baraka couldn't articulate with precision where he was going, he could articulate in some of his most powerful verse the spiritual imperative he felt to move beyond:

> The don'ts of this white hell. The crashed eyes
> of dead friends, standin at the bar, eyes focused on actual
>   ugliness.
>
> I don't love you. Who is to say what that will mean. I don't
> love you, expressed the train, moves, and uptown days later
> we look up and breathe much easier
>
> I don't love you
>
> (Selected 77)

In the same way that many white artists came to see Baraka's departure from the "united front" as paradigmatic of the Black Power movement's politics of self-determination, some came to view the absence of the former LeRoi Jones as a sign of poetry's inability to encompass all experience within a commonly communicable language. Stephen Rodefer, in an interview with Lee Bartlett, speaks of the sense of disappointment felt by many younger poets when Baraka decided not to participate in the now nearly mythic Berkeley Poetry

Conference of 1965. During the period leading up to the conference, Baraka had been lecturing with Ed Dorn, Charles Olson, and Robert Creeley in a program at the State University of New York at Buffalo, a program whose students became some of the most interesting new writers of the next generation. Rodefer, who was a student at Buffalo at the time, had headed west and attended the marathon sessions on poetics at Berkeley:

> It so happened that that was the summer of the Newark riots, and LeRoi Jones was transforming his identity to Amiri Baraka, dropping out of white culture. In fact, he ended up sending a telegram to Berkeley which said in effect that he wouldn't attend the white man's poetry conference. His lecture was to be entitled "Poetry and Murder," very dramatic. He had been at Buffalo with Ed Dorn, and we were disappointed he would not come. So you realized again that this poetry business was a bit of an isolating event. ("I inhabit" 191)

It has been characteristic of Baraka's career that the question of what he has come to stand for in people's minds has sometimes seemed as significant as his poems themselves. His life has been "read" as a signifying event of equal importance with his verse, and the deliberate ferocity of his transformations of himself has rendered that life even more polysemous and ambiguous than most. At the Berkeley Poetry Conference the name "Amiri Baraka" arrived to displace the scheduled appearance of "LeRoi Jones," who had become more literally than usual the absent signified in the thinking of white poets. The name "LeRoi Jones" became an endlessly signifying intertext in the writings of those white poets with whom he had once formed a united front, a sort of populist modernism in revolt against the dominant poetics of their time. These poets came to read "Jones," and the absence of "Jones," as a sign of racial poetics and politics and as a sign of their own evolution as artists in America. Many poets of different races and nationalities have written significant poems dedicated to and about Amiri Baraka in the years since his move from Greenwich Village to Harlem, the move uptown figured in the poem "I Don't Love You" and troped in his change of name. But those poems are written, as it were, from the other side of the unpronounceable slash that divides Amiri Baraka's signatures, that graphic divide that marks the site of Baraka's division from his earlier self, that marker erected above the textual site where LeRoi Jones absents himself, and thus those poems belong to another, equally crucial intertextual study. What will be addressed here will be a reading of the varied intertextual readings *of* LeRoi Jones by those artists he broke with when he became Amiri Baraka. For some of these poets the break was permanent; for others the relationship resumed, with a radical difference, when Baraka rejected cultural nationalism in favor of an internationalist Marxism. In Julia Kristeva's formulation of intertextuality, the process, and it is always a process, is the transposition of sign systems into other sign systems:

> This process comes about through a combination of displacement and condensation, but this does not account for its total operation. It also involves an altering of the thetic *position*—the destruction of the old position and the formation of a new one. The new signifying system may be produced with the same signifying material; in language, for example, the passage may be made from narrative to text. Or it may be borrowed from differing signifying materials. . . .
> (59)

In the often disjunct signifying systems of racialized languages in America, the same words may signify differently when written from "black" or "white" subject positions, words may be passed from one system to the other with explosive force, the use of a word within one system may lead to its disappearance in the other, and signifying repertoires of gesture and stance may be read variously from differing racial perspectives. As Amiri Baraka left behind the name "LeRoi Jones," that name continued to signify within various communities of language that had taken it up. The name "LeRoi Jones" passed from its position within the nominating discourse of black naming practices and continued to exercise new and different meaning effects within white discourse. Thus "LeRoi Jones" could be viewed as lost by Kenneth Rexroth even as Amiri Baraka found himself in his new name. The passage of these signs back and forth across the nomadic border lines of American racial discourse is mimicked in the continuing appearance of both names, conjoined, in the publishing of Baraka's works, and in the disruptive reappearance of both names as signs of Baraka's textuality in this essay. For each of the white poets Baraka had befriended during his early years as a poet, "LeRoi Jones" would soon mark a site of radical rupture and absence, an even more highly politicized site of rereading America. For each of them, "Jones" was a sign of black life in white America and a mark of American blackness within their own lives and texts.

In the life of Frank O'Hara we can trace both the closeness of Baraka to the early sixties art scene in New York and some of the reasons he felt the need later to extricate himself from his circle of white fellow artists as he began to work out just what a black aesthetic might be. Scattered throughout O'Hara's poems are passages that evidence his proclivity for objectifying African-American people, for viewing them as exotic pigmentation on his urban palette. In a 1950 poem titled "Poem" both blacks and whites are reduced to O'Hara's imagined essentials, but the particular way that O'Hara presents African Americans as being removed from the supposed natural state is unnerving:

> The flies are getting slower now
> and a bee is rare. Negroes walk
> around the fountain with too many
> clothes on and whites have lost
> already their faint contact with
> the sun.
>
> (*Collected* 24)

In "A Step Away from Them," written in 1956, a similarly anonymous "Negro stands in a doorway with a / toothpick, languorously agitating" (*Collected* 257), a stereotype as immediately recognizable to today's television viewer as any that might be imagined. Whenever blacks *as* blacks appear in O'Hara's writing, they are announced by their imagined aura of primal exoticism, but these accents tend to recede from O'Hara's texts when he specifically addresses individual black people. It may appear somewhat less surprising, then, both that O'Hara and Baraka became friends during Baraka's early days in New York and that O'Hara so clearly inscribes the very whiteness of much American writing that Baraka later rejected. Looking back on those earlier times, Baraka remembers that it was Don Allen who first brought him together with O'Hara:

I started meeting Frank for lunch some afternoons at joints near our workplaces. . . . We'd meet at some of those bar restaurants on the Upper East Side and drink and bullshit, exchange rumors and gossip, and hear the latest about the greatest. . . . I found myself going to the ballet, to cocktail parties, "coming over for drinks," to multiple gallery openings. . . . With Frank O'Hara, one spun and darted through the New York art scene, meeting Balanchine or Merce Cunningham or John Cage or de Kooning or Larry Rivers. Frank, [Allen Ginsberg] and I even had a few notable readings together at the old Living Theater . . . Another at Princeton with Diane di Prima. (*Autobiography* 160)

O'Hara's wit and sophistication impressed the young Baraka, as did his breadth of knowledge and his generosity toward other artists. O'Hara was at the time perhaps the most prolific of the emerging New York school of poets, and his blend of French surrealism with American subject matter and open form exercised a great appeal for Baraka.

It was O'Hara's custom to write poems during his lunch hour (but then, when wasn't he writing poems?) and to turn all of his experiences, including lunch dates, to use in his art. A 1959 composition, "Personal Poem," makes a record of O'Hara's lunches with LeRoi Jones. The poem was first published in 1960 in Baraka's journal *Yugen* and was later joined with other products of O'Hara's midday musings in his book *Lunch Poems*. The piece is typical of O'Hara's walking around poems, the works he called his "I do this; I do that" poems. Like "The Day Lady Died," written in the same year, the poem rushes across the surface of its own experience with minimal pause for punctuation, according each element in its composition equal weight. It opens with a stanza describing the two lucky charms O'Hara carries with him as he walks around on his lunch breaks, and registers the fact that he is "happy for a time and interested." In the following stanza we are witness to O'Hara's happy break as he passes the House of Seagram and arrives at Moriarty's, where he is to meet "LeRoi," whose first name, as so often is the case in O'Hara's poetics of "personism," becomes a character in the text. While waiting for LeRoi, O'Hara hears the latest gossip about "who wants to be a mover and shaker," and thinks about his own humbling batting average. Then:

> ... LeRoi comes in
> and tells me Miles Davis was clubbed 12
> times last night outside BIRDLAND by a cop
> a lady asks us for a nickel for a terrible
> disease but we don't give her one we
> don't like terrible diseases, then
> we go eat some fish and some ale it's
> cool but crowded we don't like Lionel Trilling
> we decide, we like Don Allen we don't like
> Henry James so much we like Herman Melville
> we don't want to be in the poets' walk in
> San Francisco even we just want to be rich
>   (*Collected* 335–36)

In a peculiar way, LeRoi Jones enters this poem like William Carlos Williams's black "ambassador / from another world" (*Collected II* 287), carrying news of an oppressive place that O'Hara's poem only half inhabits. It is almost as if LeRoi Jones and O'Hara live on planes at right angles to each other, intersecting in Moriarty's. They go about the business we all go about when establishing friendships; they search out the common ground of their shared interests and mutual dislikes. They gossip about "the latest and the greatest." Despite the structural similarities to Baraka's early verse, however, it is impossible to imagine LeRoi Jones writing this poem. In O'Hara's wry presentation, none of the details of the poem stands out from the depthless surface of the text. One of the reasons for the aesthetic success of "The Day Lady Died" is that the poem's recitation of quotidian particulars is transformed and made memorable by the enunciation within the poem of the news of Billie Holliday's death. In reading "Personal Poem," the consciousness is constantly pulled back to the news of the beating of Miles Davis, and the poem acquires power insofar as the ordinariness of the day is rendered abominable by the fact that such racist acts occur behind that featureless curtain of the mundane. Nothing else in the poem changes, and perhaps that very lack of consequence within the plane that O'Hara inhabits is one point of the poem. Miles Davis is beaten by the police; we don't like Henry James so much in Moriarty's.

What is on O'Hara's mind as he takes leave of LeRoi Jones, shaking hands in parting, is his need of a new strap for his wristwatch and his wondering if "one person out of the 8,000,000 is / thinking of me" (336). While we must be grateful that O'Hara's poem does not close on the kind of curtain line epiphany telling us what to think about all this that has become the stock-in-trade of the dominant modes of contemporary poetry in America, it is O'Hara's own happiness at poem's close that makes LeRoi Jones's news all the more terrible. O'Hara returns "to work happy at the thought possibly" one person in the naked city is thinking of him as he shakes "hands with LeRoi." For many readers, the way that the poem leaves Miles Davis behind, battered at Birdland, is as breathtaking as Billie Holiday's absent voice at the close of "The Day Lady Died." In "Personal Poem," LeRoi Jones is a friendly messenger of destruction. He carries word of the racist assault from the world in which such things occur into the world of O'Hara's text. "LeRoi" is the intertext linking the realm in which Miles's creativity is attacked by the authority of white domination to the realm of O'Hara's (and Baraka's) poetic revolution. LeRoi Jones's news is a sign transposed from the signifying system employed by the ideology of racist domination for the purposes of speaking power to black people, into the signifying system of O'Hara's new poetics and aesthetics. Part of the terror of "Personal Poem" is our understanding that the very placid surface offered to the 8,000,000 is in part underwritten by authority's battery of Miles Davis. The poem's rush past LeRoi Jones's news is a reenactment of the authoritarian silencing of black creative expression and the racist blanketing of blackness. O'Hara's poem, in that reenactment, reinscribes for readers that systematic terror that is always elsewhere, terrorizing someone else, some other. In this, O'Hara's poem is a far more effective testament against racist outrage than many more direct protests by poets. But it is difficult to read all of O'Hara's texts without wondering if the same modes of thought that present readers with objects such as "Negroes languorously agitating" are not at the root of the thinking whose authority is manifested in the beating of black people. O'Hara's "Personal Poem," while recording an important friendship between poets (and incidentally helping us to historicize the development of the New American Poetries), also implies a calling of readers to a re-

sponsibility for the worlds the text lives inside. It may be that a form
of that responsibility led to LeRoi Jones's removal of himself and his
name from such circuits as were traveled by Frank O'Hara.

Allen Ginsberg, too, seemed to turn sometimes toward psychic territories of blackness constructed out of his own desire for a refuge
from the life that white America had laid out for him. In the first
line of the poem that will forever first come to mind at the mention
of his name, "Howl," Ginsberg sees the best minds of his generation
"destroyed by madness, starving hysterical naked, / dragging themselves through the negro streets at dawn looking for an angry fix"
(126). Though some residents of these poetic streets might have wondered, not only what they had done to be so black and blue, but what
they had done to be so favored by the attention of America's disaffected young, it was this poem that drew Baraka to Ginsberg and that
gave Baraka a sense of the possibilities of the directions he had been
finding in his reading:

> I'd come to the village *looking*, trying to "check," being open to all
> flags. Allen Ginsberg's *Howl* was the first thing to open my nose,
> as opposed to, say, instructions I was given, directions, guidance. I
> dug *Howl* myself . . . I'd investigated further because I was looking
> for something. I was precisely open to its force as the statement of
> a new generation. As a line of demarcation from "the silent genera-
> tion" and the man with the (yellow) grey flannel skin, half brother
> of the one with the grey flannel suit. (*Autobiography* 156)

Along with their oppositional politics, their exploration of open
forms, and their activist roles within the community of artists, Baraka
and Ginsberg shared an abiding love for jazz of all kinds. Ginsberg's
"Elegy for Neal Cassady" records as part of his New York vision:

> Listening to a wooden Radio,
> > with our eyes closed
> Eternal redness of Shabda
> > lamped in our brains
> at Illinois Jacquet's Saxophone Shuddering,
> > prophetic Honk of Louis Jordan,
> > Honeydrippers, Open the Door Richard
> > to Christ's apocalypse
> > > (488)

Baraka, who had also grown up in New Jersey glued to some of the same frequencies, used his own early poem "In Memory of Radio," among other things, to memorialize these shared listenings with their mutual friend Jack Kerouac, and another early piece, dedicated to Ginsberg, "One Night Stand," also evokes that history of radio that links them in a world in which "We *are* foreign seeming persons," in which "We have come a long way, & are uncertain which of the masks / is cool" (*Preface* 21–22). Ginsberg also shared Baraka's attentiveness to all that was new in jazz, celebrating those artists who, to "(yellow) grey flannel" ears, might sound most "outside." Ginsberg's late "Ego Confession" includes among its imagined marks of what it would be to be the most brilliant man in America, being the man "who went backstage to Cecil Taylor serious about chord structure & Time in a nightclub" (623).

It would seem at times that Baraka and Ginsberg have been locked in some strange orbit, two bodies traveling a common plane but always looking across to each other from opposite sides of the circumference. They write to and of each other early and late, and they continue to provide the most engaged form of critique possible upon each other's work, other poems. At the time of Baraka's movement into cultural nationalism he set down a number of scalding references to Ginsberg's life and positions. But a reader can't help thinking that Ginsberg attracted such heated attacks from Baraka precisely because of the depth of Baraka's feelings for him, and, in poems such as "The Burning General," Baraka, though rejecting Ginsberg's mode of response to America, seems to view Ginsberg's very existence as a chastisement of American society:

> Smoke seeping from my veins. Loss from
> the eyes. Seeing winter throw its wind
> around. Hoping for more, than I'll ever
> have. Forgetting my projects, and the projected
> sense of order, any claim to "sense" must make.
> The reason Allen and the others (even freakish
> pseudo dada mama) in the money jungle of uncontrolled
> pederasty
>   finally bolted.
>   (*Black Magic* 27)

Among his later poems, following his adoption of a Third World Marxist politics, Baraka revisits the metaphoric analyses of the American way of oppression he and Ginsberg had put forward in their earliest works. One poem in Baraka's late-seventies collection "Poetry for the Advanced" is allusively titled "Reprise of One of A.G.'s Best Poems!" "A.G." is, of course, Baraka's usual shorthand way of referring to Allen Ginsberg in his texts, much as most white poets who knew Baraka during his early years as a New York artist simply identify him within their texts as "LeRoi" or "Roi," and it is evident from the first line of Baraka's poem that the work of Ginsberg's being reprised is "America," from the collection *Howl.* The exclamation point of Baraka's title indicates the extent to which Ginsberg's poem has held up for Baraka throughout the several shifts in his working life. Ginsberg's "America" is a hilarious send-up of American political mores at midcentury, one that bears with it faint echoes of Langston Hughes's "I, Too, Sing America" (*Selected* 275) and stronger echoes of everything Whitman ever wrote. In his Whitmanian voice, a voice calculated to confound McCarthyites, Ginsberg declares, "America, I am the Scottsboro boys" (147). In a voice Whitman might have found more perplexing, Ginsberg satirizes America's Russophobia:

> America its them bad Russians.
>
> .   .   .   .
>
> That no good. Ugh. Him make Indians learn read. Him need big
>   black niggers. Hah. Her makes us all work sixteen hours a
>   day. Help.
> America this is quite serious.
> America this is the impression I get from looking in the
>   television set.

$$(147-48)$$

When Baraka reprises this moment in Ginsberg's text, he declares Ginsberg one of America's prophets, "blind & crazy / metaphysical" (*Selected* 282), and he deftly updates Ginsberg's raucous humor:

> America
>   Maybe you need to be
>   investigated

>   for yr unamerican
>
>   activities
>   (283)

But like Ginsberg's fifties America, Baraka's reprise two decades later is deadly serious in its humor. Bringing his reprise of Ginsberg together with a reprise of the gospel songs that served as a medium through which African America communicates with itself its own lyric saving grace, Baraka writes:

> We wade in the water
>   America
>   America
> We wade in the bleeding
> We wade in the screaming
>
>   .   .   .   .
>
>   in the anger of its
>   workers
>   its niggers
>   its wild intelligent
>   spics
>   its
>   brutalized
>   chicanos
>   its women out of work, again
>   (283)

"A.G. thought you was 'America' / because that was yr myth-name" (285), Baraka writes, recalling also the Moloch passages of "Howl" and calling for America to transform itself in revolutionary explosion.

In this lifelong poetic exchange, LeRoi Jones enters the verse of Allen Ginsberg as an intertextual sign, marking transpositions of race, rebellion, and political courage. Ginsberg's poem "Nov. 23, 1963: Alone" is a macabre elegy modeled partially upon the technique of Frank O'Hara's "The Day Lady Died." Ginsberg's poem catalogs in Whitmanic stanzas all the things Ginsberg is doing and not doing when news of President Kennedy's assassination comes to him. Like a hyperbolic twist on the cliché that everyone remembers what he or she was doing on that day, Ginsberg lists in rhythmic anaphora all the commissions and omissions during that period of "the television continuous blinking two radar days" (333). Among the things Ginsberg is unable to undertake as he sits alone is attention to a newly received work from his friend LeRoi Jones. Dazedly recording the sadnesses and happinesses on his mind that day, Ginsberg sits "with LeRoi Jones's white-eyeballed war-cry unread, babbling in postmortem blue-sneer / with myself confused shock-fingertipt on the rented typewriter" (233). Baraka's own poem on the Kennedy assassination, "Exnaugaral Poem," is an equally unusual effort, with its subtitle "for Jackie Kennedy who has had to eat too much shit." His own response to the assassination disturbed him, as he remembers in his autobiography: "I was trying to move to a revolutionary position, but I was still ready to weep for Jacqueline Bouvier Kennedy" (185).

As Ginsberg, in radical motion himself, witnesses the transit of his friend toward an ever more actively revolutionary position, he begins to read LeRoi Jones as a mark against which to measure his own commitments and trepidations. In his lengthy meditation growing out of his pilgrimage to Angkor Wat, published as a separate illustrated volume, Ginsberg begins to satirize his own presumptions and fears, in the form of a confessional to his poet friend of the early years:

> Nothing but a false Buddha afraid of
> my own annihilation, Leroi Moi—
> afraid to fail you yet terror those Men
> their tiger pictures and uniforms
> dream to see that Kerouac tiger too—
> Helicopter to—Sh, spies with telescopes
> for seeing the bullets that shoot—
> Leroi
> I been done you wrong
> I'm just an old Uncle Tom in disguise all along
> afraid of physical tanks.
>
> (*Collected* 310)

Ginsberg's adoption of dialect and his assumption of the "Tom" stereotype racialize and deepen the nature of his sensed betrayal in loss of nerve, a strategy that renders the humor of the passage yet darker. In addressing "Leroi Moi" Ginsberg addresses his failure to achieve his own spiritual goals and acknowledges a sense in which his spiritual preachments may at times have imploded his political commitments. Still, this gesture of speaking to the "Leroi" within himself, even in the midst of his questionable "tomming," shows that Ginsberg feels a political responsibility to all that which is represented by his signing of his friend's name across this stanza, "Leroi Moi—." The note to this at first perhaps cryptic signature identifies "LEROI MOI" for readers of Ginsberg's *Collected Poems* as "The American radical poet Leroi Jones, later known as Amiri Baraka," thus simultaneously underscoring Baraka's radical work *as* a poet and resigning the younger Baraka with a signature somewhere between the name as given to him by his parents, "Leroy," and the name as restructured and aestheticized that he signed to his first books, "LeRoi."

In later years the name of LeRoi Jones figures in Ginsberg's text much as Baraka's news of the assault upon Miles Davis appears in Frank O'Hara's "Personal Poem," as a sign of the systematic brutalities of American racism. In the 1968 poem "Chicago to Salt Lake by Air," Ginsberg surveys the logics of American political violence, connecting the individual atrocities carried out by state authority against America's own citizens to the global violations carried out by the state in the name of those same citizens:

> Mind is fragments . . . whatever you can remember from last
>   year's *Time*
> *Magazine,* this year's sunset or gray cloudmass over Nebraska,
> Leroi Jones' deep scar brown skin at left temple hairline . . .
>   . . . Don McNeil emerging from Grand Central w/6 stitches in
>   Forehead
> pushed through plateglass by police, his presscard bloodied.
> Deeper into gray clouds, there must be invisible farms, invisible
>   farmers walking up and down rolling cloud-hills.
> "A hole in its head" . . . another World, America, Vietnam.
>
>   (491–92)

Here Ginsberg sees a political relation between the forces that scar the landscape of Vietnam and those that scar the skull of LeRoi Jones. The event alluded to in the poem occurred during the rebellion in the streets of Newark, New Jersey. Baraka and companions were pulled over by police and accused of carrying guns. As if ensuring the possible ironies of the situation, one of the officers, who had attended high school with Baraka, clubbed the poet over the head with the barrel of his gun (*Autobiography* 262). Thus did the hegemonic power of the state inscribe itself upon the newly renamed Amiri Baraka. Few prominent American poets bear such visible signatures of state authority, and the memory of that recent sight is carried forward in the text of Ginsberg's poems. The same episode figures in another nomadic Ginsberg poem, "Crossing Nation." This time Baraka's name appears in a gathering of the silenced, those who have fallen silent through choice or who have been impeded in their practice of free speech by the state apparatus of enforcement: "LeRoi on bum gun rap, $7000 / lawyer fees, years' negotiations—" (499). Thinking of the state's mostly successful efforts to make miserable the lives of those who struggle to speak truth to power, Ginsberg confronts himself with the kinds of questions that had troubled him at Angkor Wat: "What do I have to lose if America falls? / my body? my neck? my personality?" (500). Almost as a marginal meaning effect of the question of personality, this poem, as Jones has become Baraka, transforms Ginsberg's signing of Baraka's name from "Leroi" to "LeRoi."

Ginsberg's quiet rewriting of Baraka's rewriting of his name is echoed elsewhere in the texts collecting around the figure of LeRoi Jones/Amiri Baraka, reflecting in curious ways the aesthetic of compositional speed and written perception advocated by many writers of the New American Poetries. The appearances of Paul Blackburn's poem "Motivations I," for example, strangely move about the words drawn from Baraka's "Crow Jane's Manner" that serve as an epigraph to Blackburn's poem. Almost a surfeit of intertextuality, Blackburn's poem is constructed in the same number of lines as the two epigraphs to the poem drawn from Louis Zukofsky and Baraka. Baraka's lines appear in *The Dead Lecturer* in this form:

> Crow. Crow. Where
> you leave my
> other boys?

(50)

Blackburn's "Motivations I" as it appears in the collection *In. On. Or About the Premises,* that collection partly dedicated in memory of LeRoi Jones, alters both the word order and the lineation of "Crow Jane's Manner" significantly:

> Crow. Crow. Where
>   leave you
>   my other boys?
>
> (np)

Blackburn signs the epigraph "—L.J." In his posthumously published *Collected Poems*, edited by Edith Jarolim, Baraka's justified left margin is silently restored, but Blackburn's reordering of the words is retained:

> Crow. Crow. Where
> leave you
> my other boys?
>
> (343)

Blackburn's versions of these lines raise interesting questions about motivation themselves. Did Blackburn draw his epigraph from a misprinted or interim state of Baraka's poem never reproduced in Baraka's books, was he simply careless in transcription, or does Blackburn's text continue the sly joke begun in the dedication? Around the time of the composition of "Motivations I," Baraka played a part in the abrupt termination of Blackburn's poetry program that had been airing over radio station WBAI from 1964 to 1965. As Edith Jarolim recounts the episode, the show "was terminated a few weeks before the completion of its contract because of the—even more than usually—'strong' language of one of his participating friends, LeRoi Jones" (*Collected* xxix). Whether Blackburn's misprinting is merely a mistake or a mischievous playing upon Baraka's lines, the intertext suffers a sea change as it is lifted from its position in *The Dead Lecturer* and floated into position at the head of "Motivations I." This bibliographic peculiarity, with its embedding in the ruptured broadcast and friendship of Blackburn and Baraka, gives an additional resonance to the last lines of the prematurely evicted Blackburn's poem: "What he misses in the street / the street" (343). This context also lends an even greater air of prophecy to the poem's epigraph from Zukofsky: "each animal / his own gravedigger."

For Diane di Prima, as for so many other white poets of her generation, Baraka, coeditor with her of the *Floating Bear*, represented the successful melding of an activist poetics with an activist politics. But

for di Prima, who was also at one time Baraka's lover, and with whom
Baraka had a child, Dominique (now a popular figure on television
in the San Francisco Bay region), reading LeRoi Jones and his life is
inevitably bound up with a reading of her own works and days. In a
1960 photograph taken at the Cedar Tavern, Baraka and di Prima
look less like revolutionary bohemians than like any earnest and open
young couple embracing whatever the world brings their way. But by
1962 di Prima was married to Alan Marlowe, and Baraka, already
married to Hettie Cohen, and the father of two daughters, was increasingly restive about his involvement with the bohemian counter-
culture of white artists. Nonetheless, the work that di Prima and
Baraka had undertaken together, including formation of the *Floating
Bear* and the New York Poets Theater, left a lasting legacy in American art, and residual traces of each poet's work are inscribed in the
texts of the other.

In her work as a poet, Diane di Prima revises both herself and
LeRoi Jones. In "For the Dead Lecturer," di Prima's title substitutes
LeRoi Jones *for* the dead lecturer of the title of his book of poems.
It is an easy substitution to make when looking at Jones's book, since
a photograph of the poet looks out at the reader from beneath the
volume's title, *The Dead Lecturer*. But the title poem of Jones's 1964
collection is actually "I Substitute for the Dead Lecturer," and the
poem's first line might be read as a rebuke to di Prima's revisionary
poem: "They have turned, and say that I am dying" (*Dead* 59). Di
Prima's poem summons a vision of Jones and addresses him as the
dead. In part this gesture is a response to the epigraph of "For the
Dead Lecturer," words also written by LeRoi Jones: "We must convince the living / that the dead / cannot sing." These lines, drawn from
another poem in *The Dead Lecturer*, "A Guerilla Handbook," speak a
rhetoric of rescue. It is a poem calling upon those still alive to the
possibilities of more humane ways of organizing the world to take
upon themselves the work of saving others from the deathly illusions
fostered by an all-encompassing hegemony, a poem calling for:

> Silent political rain
> against the speech
> of friends. (We love them
> trapped in life, knowing no way out

except description. Or black soil
floating in the arm.

(Dead 66)

But in di Prima's poem there is a double reversal. In "For the Dead
Lecturer" it is Jones who is, by his absence, dead. Still, he does,
through his inscription within di Prima's consciousness, continue to
sing. In her poem di Prima both ignores the direction of the rhetorical gestures of the Jones poems upon which she draws and redirects
the logic of their metaphoric structures. "THE DEAD CAN SING / and
do" (52), di Prima insists against the assertions of her epigraph. The
dead relationship with Jones stirs to life and song again in her verses,
and, writing in opposition to the materials she has taken from Jones,
di Prima writes a love song to the dead. Adopting direct address, she
says to Jones:

> I have heard you creaking
> over the roof at night to steal my books
> coming in thru the telephone wires
> just when my head
> was empty
>
> (52)

In this vision there is an afterlife for the illicit romance of their youth.
They steal to each other in the eerie dark of the imagination. Di Prima
hears Jones's singing "start / out of the skull of [his] daughter" (53)
sleeping in her arms, and asks "why not talk of these things?" (53).
The talk itself becomes a kind of counterexorcism. At the close of her
poem di Prima describes an intertextual singing in which the lines of
both poets intertwine to image forth a new sign. But, continuing the
oppositional logic of her poem, rather than save the living from the
unmusical oppressiveness of the dead, di Prima writes that she must
complete Jones's death in order to have his song more fully:

> I'll tangle my crest with yours, like scorpions,
> and kill you for love
> I'll kill you yet
> so your song can fill my life.
>
> (53)

Di Prima dreams that Jones still steals into her life and makes off with her books, but in this instance she has effectively stolen Jones's stanzas. She has filled his song with her life (as all readers must do), only to make it signify a radical difference. Aside from the effectively touching image of their Dominique, di Prima has here constructed one of the weirdest poems in her life's work. Such a thorough redirection of Jones's rhetoric seems, in the end, an effort to respeak LeRoi Jones, an effort to find within his signature works another saying, one more comforting, her own signature. All such efforts succeed, which may account for some of the vehemence of the rejection recorded in Baraka's "Will They Cry When You're Gone, You Bet," a poem that describes madmen and saints:

> sand packed in their mouths
> eyes burning, white women serenade them
> in mystic deviousness, which is another
> way of saying they're seeing things, which
> are not really there . . .
>
> (*Black Magic* 63)

Di Prima's and Baraka's poems appear locked together in an intertextual tangle of mutual incomprehension. Di Prima's poem is an attempt to reread LeRoi Jones that Amiri Baraka's poems repel.

A quite different kind of rhetoric is engaged in di Prima's "Note to Roi," the third section of "Ode to Keats." Here di Prima muses upon Jones's present activities and wonders, "How much of it *is* pride, or ambition," and then questions the status of her own imputation of motives, "As we so easily say" (59). Memorializing the suicide of choreographer Fred Herko, their mutual friend, di Prima recalls a moment of mediation when Herko served as messenger:

> I remember the message I gave Freddie for you
> That I would see you again at the end of this
> (Meaning my marriage and yours)
> Not dreaming how far that would take us:
> Freddie dead
> You living in Harlem where you'll surely be killed.
>
> (59)

We shouldn't be surprised that so many images of the death of LeRoi

Jones, a poet in whose work death is a frequent caller, appear in the verses of others. Still, there is a troubling sense here that di Prima is rushing Jones toward a premature martyrdom. She imagines a fate for him like that of Malcolm X, imagines that he will fall in the struggle: "Without my having told you you were my love / Among the adventures & common sense of my life" (59).

Baraka, of course, did not die, despite the assaults upon him, but he continues to meet death in a later poem by di Prima, "To the Spectre of the Lecturer, Long Dead." Di Prima, like Ginsberg, measures herself both against the commitments and adventures of her youth and against her sense of the revolutionary commitments of Baraka. "I wd be ashamed / to face you," she thinks:

> lines
>   around my eyes
> low breasts &, just now
> big belly for the fifth time, I go
> over it, in this S.F. room,
>   big fog
> coming in, grey sky, grey street, shouts
> of black kids, playing late, now
> 8 years after
>
>   (90)

In the midst of this surprising self-deprecation, the rolling fogs of San Francisco call to mind another text, a cinematic text in which a fog-bound leave-taking takes place against a backdrop of war and awesome responsibility. Here we realize that di Prima's harsh shame about her appearance is not so much despair at physically aging as it is pain at the distance between the life she now leads and the heroic ideals of youth:

>   for the first time it comes as pain
> comes clear
>   what I walked out on
> to turn one's back on love
>   & walk away
> like Casablanca
>
>   (90)

When Ingrid Bergman turns her back to Humphrey Bogart (and to the camera) and walks to the waiting airplane at the end of *Casablanca,* we know that she goes with a man who is already a hero and whose leadership is essential to the safety of his nation. But we also know, in the irrefutable logic of Hollywood romance, that Bogart, in his suicidal act of self-denial, is the real hero of the piece. At the end of "To the Spectre of the Lecturer, Long dead," as she acknowledges eight years later the pain that she had "never touched," di Prima also hears, against the imagined engines' roar of *Casablanca,* Jones's agonies: "I hear the roar / of yr pain" (90), and she tells Jones that she is no longer at all what he would remember. Within the analogy to *Casablanca,* di Prima presents herself as the one who walked away, and wonders what intensities she walked away from. Within the workings of that cinematic allusion, Jones is again portrayed, as he was in "Note to Roi," as the willful martyr, he whose possibly romanticized giving of himself to struggle is perhaps suicidal but heroic. The absence of Baraka in this poem signs LeRoi Jones as a marker of the absence of heroic danger in di Prima's life. It will be in other poems, without Jones, that she locates the heroism of women in America, a heroism unconstrained by the needs of a heroic man.

While Charles Olson was clearly a kind of elder statesman of the New American Poetries, the young LeRoi Jones was as instrumental in propagating Olson's texts and assisting his career as Olson was instrumental in the early development of Jones's poetics. At a time when Olson often had difficulty getting published, Jones opened the pages of *Yugen* and the *Floating Bear* to him. As for Olson's value to Jones, Jones states flatly in his autobiography, "His Projective Verse had been a bible for me" (192). The two had much in common despite the difference in their ages. Both had come from families that included men who had fought against injustice and suffered for their stands. Both of their fathers had worked in the United States Post Office. Olson alludes to this shared background in the third volume of the *Maximus Poems* in a passage that compares the difficulties that were faced by the Swedish immigrants in his family and the injustices dealt to black Americans (496–97). The counterhegemonic political stances of Jones and Olson were a particular point of commonality; it was Olson's political engagements and his contextualizing of his work in history that caused Jones to remark that, of the Black Mountain poets, "Olson had the broader sword, the most 'prophetic stance.' His concerns touched me deeply" (*Autobiography* 158). In his memoirs, Amiri Baraka testifies:

> What fascinated me about Olson was his sense of having dropped out of the US, the "pejoracracy." He said in his poems we should oppose "those who would advertise you out." It was a similar spirit that informed the most meaningful of the Beats, and Olson was a heavy scholar. . . . It was Olson, because of his intellectual example, and Ginsberg, because of his artistic model and graciousness as a teacher, whom I thought most about in terms of the road I was moving along. (192)

It is that prophetic stance against "those who would advertise you out," Olson's insistent speaking of truth to power, that is most evident in his major poem directed to LeRoi Jones.

Olson's "The Hustings" exists in at least three versions. *The Collected Poems of Charles Olson* includes both an early version written on November 10, 1960, and the final, much modified version completed on November 16. George Butterick has included an important intermediate draft of the poem in his valuable collection of Olson's "Supplementary poems," *A Nation of Nothing but Poetry*. As the dates and the title indicate, Olson composed this work shortly after the election of John Fitzgerald Kennedy to the presidency, and with that year's campaign very much in mind. Olson had more than a layman's interest in the progress of the campaign because he had been an assistant to Howard Mumford Jones at Harvard when the future president was enrolled in Jones's course on the novel. (Olson reports having given Kennedy's work "a gentleman's C" [*Nation* 207].) The first version of the poem, while not directly addressed to LeRoi Jones, is clearly a response to discussions the two poets were having during this time of enormous political ferment. Jones had recently made the trip to Cuba that forms the basis of his essay "Cuba Libre," and he had written at length to Olson regarding his experiences and observations on the trip.

According to George Butterick, there is no evidence yet uncovered that Olson ever mailed this poem to Jones (Butterick does not indicate if he has asked Baraka about this), though Olson did in at least one letter to LeRoi Jones mention the poem's existence. In a later letter to

Ed Dorn, Olson's remarks reveal the extent to which Olson had come to regard Jones's evolving political positions as a sign of the transformations awaiting America. "I in fact wrote a long poem the day Kennedy won addressed to Leroi," he tells Dorn, and then remarks that Jones "seemed then and seems now the 'key' to that very sort of politics which goes way ahead of the obviously transposed events of the sd present" (*Nation* 206). "The Hustings" is an election day poem in the tradition of the Jeremiads preached by Puritan divines of New England as election day sermons. At a time when leadership is changing hands, when the people are supposed to be acting in the interests of the nation's future, it is time to reexamine the covenant entered into by our ancestors and to measure the progress of the body politic against the covenant. In 1960, when the Kennedy forces presented their candidate as the torchbearer of a new generation poised on the cusp of a new frontier, it was time to reinspect the state of our cultural legacy. It was time for Olson to ask, mockingly and metaphorically, "is New England wealth / Robert Creeley / or John Fitzgerald 35th President of / Sweet Adeline" (*Collected* 530–31). While the advent of the new frontier (and what a pale, third-generation catchphrase "new world order" looks like next to that so recent advertisement for the powers that be) was being celebrated by *Time, Life,* and the powers of the air, Olson complained in the early version of this poem:

> we
> look forward to the new Frontier as though Nothing
> was what the Open Ended Portfolios yes That's
> what China Cuba the Soviet Union Algeria Africa one
> Great Business Partnership
>
> (*Collected* 531)

Olson is responding as much to the challenging questions of his young correspondent, LeRoi Jones, as to the media buzz on election day: "lies sd Jones this nation is lies on / the face of the people" (*Collected* 530). The older poet feels on this election day a responsibility to provide a serviceable answer to younger writers with whom he joins efforts such as Jones and Robert Duncan. He chides himself at the close of the early version: "What do you have to say, Poet? What do you have to / say What do you have to say What do you have to say to Leroi / Jones   to Robert Duncan" (*Collected* 532). The enjambment here as Olson conducts a Williams-like experiment with the lineation and rhythm of his question brings to the surface almost accidentally the typical street-English response to unbelievable assertions like the promise of a new frontier, "say what?"

The later revisions of this poem reveal the question "The Hustings" is meant to address. Olson has read in his friend, lately returned from a country attempting the most dangerous of social experiments, a despairing interrogation. Olson, who had himself left a promising future in Democratic party political work, finds himself called to account for his country:

> on a day when Leroi Jones
>
> has asked me
> it seems to me
> to say why
>
> one should continue
> to live
> in the United States
> (*Collected* 534)

Like other Jeremiads, this poem will gather in at the end notes of covenant renewal, but first it will levy scathing assessments of America's dire drive against its own promise; how the mighty are fallen.

"The future sucks," Olson begins, casting enjambed lines that once again render the colloquial judgment of the average citizens, they in whose name the state governs. "The future sucks / all forward, the past / has been removed / by progress" (*Collected* 532–33). "Progress," too often the name for government guarantees of the right of capital to accumulate more capital without restraint, has decimated the physical trace of America's cultural legacy (which is *not* the same thing as its cultural capital) and brought us a science in the pay of endless commercial expansion, a science that may have contaminated even the moon, as Olson notes in his poem. The much vaunted new frontier is, as Olson characterizes it near the end of the intermediate draft of the poem, "decadence and the future / is the race's future / all over the place" (*Nation* 137). If LeRoi Jones "spits out the Nation / for its lies," Olson joins him, but with a different response. "I do too / I stay at home" (*Collected* 533). The reasons Olson supplies for not abandoning

America are as problematic as the new president's primary victories. The new generation, here or abroad, is now joined together in the inescapable international grasp of capital and advertising. As he tells Jones in a 1964 letter that George Butterick quotes in his notes to the poem: "The power of the Negro is in fact the power of numbers of non-Whites now . . . and the only dreadful corollary is the one you seem not to keep alive, that Soviets and Chinese and Mexicans and Negroes and Whites will all wear watches" (*Nation* 207). One implication is that anywhere one might go on the globe, the same fight will eventually have to be engaged. In hindsight Olson's poem appears particularly prophetic on this point, as all over the world artists and rebels strive to assert difference against the smothering uniformity of what has euphemistically been termed "market forces," the enforced absorptive powers of multinational capital. The Whitmanian vision of American democracy as humankind en masse has given way before the vision of democracy as the masses acting upon a single vision, all listening to the same sponsored messages. "Do you believe / in the promises / of the use / of human beings?" (*Collected* 534–35), Olson asks Jones, "democracy / en masse on / transistors?" Olson's first volume of the *Maximus Poems,* sounding much like Thoreau, cautions:

> In the land of plenty, have
> nothing to do with it
>
> > take the way of
>
> the lowest
> including
> your legs, go
> contrary, go
>
> sing
>
> > > (*Maximus* 19)

In "The Hustings" Olson asks Jones to remain American, to sing his contrary lyrics at home:

> The open-ended character of the future Leroi Jones
>
> says stay in the age
> of your nation
>
> > (*Collected* 534)

These lines look to the openness of the nation's future, and to the open-ended nature of the future LeRoi Jones, and posit both as reasons for a poet to stay.

Olson thought of many of his works as letters. This poem, addressed in its final dedication to LeRoi Jones, never reached its addressee as it wasn't properly posted. On eventual delivery, in published form, the addressee no longer existed, having been displaced by Amiri Baraka. How much postage due might have accrued in the ensuing years as this poem made its circuit? Olson signs his unsent letter with a return address and a political declaration:

> Leroi Jones
>
> > my name is Charles Olson
> > I live at 28 Fort Square
> > in Glocester Massachusetts
> >
> > in the world. I would like to die
> > with my eyes open as I imagine
> > God's eyes are
> > > *(Collected* 535)

Both the interim draft and the final version end, in the opening out of projective forms, in the renewal of covenant, as befits a projective Jeremiad, and in a calling to Olson's correspondent. The canceled passages of the draft include a reminder:

> > > Our life
> > Leroi Jones
> >
> > is not an energy
> > like the sun's   Our life is a purpose
> > > *(Nation* 137)

The last stanzas of Olson's final version of "The Hustings" telegraph a plea for a united front against the pejoracracy, a call for a homecoming and a promise that America can be called back to itself. Olson goes contrary to the siren songs of the new frontier, as he'd eventually walked out of the margins of the New Deal, but he issues his own challenge to the younger generation to join him in that contrary song that, as Williams had shown us, was truly in the American grain, a challenge to join in making it new:

> . . . you and I are as much examples
> as crowds demanding
> youth taking
>
> and the new inventing—

Olson's last call is a promise that America can be America again, can be reclaimed from usurpers and contaminators, that it will answer to those who call out in its wilderness:

> I don't think there is anywhere
> Where I am nearer, and I wire you
>
> Please come immediately
> There is no need to worry
> We shall all eat   All is here
>
> (*Collected* 535)

Olson sounds remarkably Frostian at the outset of this passage ("I don't know where it's likely to go better," Frost says of earth in the poem "Birches'), which may mark just how much at home Olson is in his poem. He wires his reassurance to LeRoi Jones, but the message is finally undeliverable. LeRoi Jones did go home, to Harlem and then to Newark, but he returned as Amiri Baraka. Like those letters in Bartleby's dead letter office, Olson's missive misses its mark, is misdirected, arrives too late; it ends in other hands issuing its call generally, calling us all to our covenant responsibilities and our promised home. It is yet to be seen if all is here in America for Amiri Baraka.

According to Amiri Baraka's first wife, Hettie Jones, LeRoi Jones once told her "that Ed Dorn was the only white man who understood him" (212). Dorn, who had been a student of Olson's, is also the author of an unmailed letter. At the end of his poem "A Letter, in the Meantime, Not to Be Mailed, Tonight," Dorn begins to address the separation that has grown between himself and Baraka and the way that separation has come to act as a metaphor signaling the separation of the races in an increasingly untenable body politic. Dorn writes:

                                    of Buffalo
and that air so dry in the eye of its wetness and infertile
to an extreme we almost drunk ourselves to death with
who because he could not other wise explain left
                                              the next day
and took all the gods with him
                                      however
this letter is to a black man from whom I have become separated
in the newest of all land with the oldest hyphen of the
    western world
hot wet rooms where everyone ages rapidly, and we said
    pragmatic
goodbyes,
        a tension of action which all things become in forlorn places
    where some outcast people find a place at last and others wander
    with an open and unplaceable heart in this most enforced of all
    wildernesses.   (101)

The same program that had invited Charles Olson asked both Dorn
and LeRoi Jones to teach at the State University of New York at Buffalo, and the two poets and their families shared a rented house. (In
her memoir of the period, Hettie Jones tells of having to fight off the
owner's attempt to oust this poetic encampment once he learned of
the extra family.) But that was also one of those "long hot summers" of
urban rebellion, and when Harlem exploded, according to *The Autobiography of LeRoi Jones/Amiri Baraka*, "it was like proof that the ticking
inside our heads had a real source" (192). Jones left Buffalo, and his
friendship with Dorn, despite a flurry of correspondence, entered a
wilderness of its own.

   Jones had been instrumental in the publication of one of Dorn's
important early books, *Hands Up!*, which was brought out by Totem
Press in association with Corinth Books as part of the same series that
published Jones's own *Preface to a Twenty Volume Suicide Note* . . . . One
of Dorn's most significant early works, the long poem "Idaho Out," is
dedicated "For Hettie and Roi" Jones, and *The Dead Lecturer,* a book
that remains one of Baraka's most important publications, bears a
dedication to Ed Dorn. (The dedication includes a crucial epigraph,
Green Lantern's Oath.) Jones has remarked, "I liked Ed so much be-

cause he had (and has) an intellectual toughness that perceives the worst in the US, but he has the energy needed to survive that worst" (*Autobiography* 192). As the development of his political analyses and the ever-escalating climate of racial crisis in America pushed Jones farther along the path toward cultural nationalism and the break with his white colleagues, Dorn was insistently in Jones's thoughts. Dorn was located in Pocatello, Idaho, a place, in Jones's estimation, "so American it didn't understand itself" (*Autobiography* 192). In the middle of his poem "The Burning General," a poem whose rhetoric forces us to a choice between active political response and those bohemian diversions an oppressive social apparatus is only too happy to permit its disaffected intellectual classes, Jones addresses a question to Dorn, calls to him across the country's midsection:

> What do you think, Eddie, out there in Idaho shivering
>   against
> the silence, the emptiness of straight up America? What's it
>   look like there?
> Can we ask a man to savor the food of oppression? Even
> if it's rich and full of mysterious meaning?
>
> (*Black Magic* 27)

In the midst of these correspondences that cross in the mails, or that stand unmailed, which we read before their addressees, the increasing distance from Dorn to Jones becomes, for Dorn, a space filled with texts that tell of the peculiar institution of New World madness that inextricably imbricates race and class, that lodges the objects of oppressive progress in epidermal determinism.

At times Dorn wishes to remove race as the determining instance, because he recognizes, as Olson recognized, the ways in which race had been constructed in the modern West and employed in the race for empire and dominion. In yet another letter, his "Epistolary Comment," which constitutes the fourth section of the poem "Oxford," Dorn incorporates a text that is sadly as timely now as it was when he transposed it into his verses:

> We are *all* in the sarsen circle.
> We are *all* in the *da nang*. Even the Shades

> *All*
>
> of our numbers come up
> Russia and china jockey,
> it is not race, "Le revolte
> de Los Angeles
> est une revolte contre La Marchandise
>   contre le mode de la Marchandise
>
> .   .   .   .
>
> "Les noirs Americains
> sont le produit de l'industrie
> moderne . . .
>
>   (201–2)

But in the modern world brought into being by commerce, the Negro was created *as* merchandise. Race had nothing to do with the ultimate objective of domination and commodification, but race was refigured as the determining, motivating feature of the commodification of human beings. In the contemporary world that Dorn describes, a world in which "the ugly faces of the news / determine what you shall know" (202), the determination of what shall be known is at the same time a determination of what shall be unknown. The hegemony of "the news" operates to mystify the origins of racial oppression and the realities of the lives of African-American peoples. It is precisely because of our history that we cannot now argue that "race has nothing to do with it," because that argument invariably leaves the inherited structures of racism in place, their meaning effects inscribed, as literally as the scar on Amiri Baraka's forehead, upon the lives and bodies of black people. The argument that "race has nothing to do with it" is finally a disingenuous refusal to see its own complicity in the continued mystifications of racial discourse. It is not as unmistakable as Dorn would have it, in the fifth part of "Oxford," that there is no longer any cause,

> that DeGaulle
> Ho Chi Minh, Chou en-Lai,
> LeRoi Jones, Dean Rusk
> are all doing the same bit:

> pressing
>   and they are
>   all correct—it is their thing
>   against anybody else's
>   (209–10)

This attempt to subsume race within a yet more petty classification of motivations signals a cynical turn toward conservatism in Dorn's thought less remarked than Baraka's loudly proclaimed shifts in political philosophy.

Even as Dorn's "Oxford" tries to read Jones's texts into a metatext of relativism in which the specifics of discrete struggles are submerged in an ascription of power hunger that regards all as equally corrupt, and hence all as essentially incorrect, other passages in Dorn's work detail the difference that operates between the arguments of a LeRoi Jones and a Dean Rusk. "Oxford" is part of the volume *The North Atlantic Turbine,* a text that ranges across history discovering the sources of New World rage, a project similar to Williams's *In the American Grain* and Olson's *Maximus Poems.* Near the opening we find "A Theory of Truth / The North Atlantic Turbine," in which Dorn finds that the modern rediscovery by Europe of the rest of the world was not itself an opening: "not *includes* west africa / *goes* to west africa / rum slaves and crude molasses." Dorn's poem tropes the Middle Passage as the perpetually grinding movement of trade:

> There is no beginning
> unless the end
> has been reached. First.
> The second is the middled
> and that may be people
> or some other material.
> Molasses or molasses skinned persons.
> The turbine is only movement.
> The current of the atlantic
> swirl
>
>   (186)

The Middle Passage is designed for an end, not implicit in the West's cultural beginnings. The Middle Passage is the movement of product, "people / or some other material," and the people become materi-

ally identified with the objects of trade. The people are only worth
what they can produce for trade, or what they can bring in trade, and
their darkness is defined as the mark of their status *as* material for
trade. This particular signifying genie will not go back in its bottle just
because we tire of it. Dean Rusk produced a discourse that, while advancing the signs of equality under the banner of liberal humanism,
served to obfuscate the still operating structural engines of inequality,
mechanisms whose effects continued, and continue, to be inscribed as
race. LeRoi Jones, whatever his errors, was clearly advancing a discourse that would have different effects, even if those effects were still
to be racially determined.

In some ways the discourse of cultural nationalism spoken by
Baraka during his middle period was a result of the discourses of
commerce and nationalism produced historically by people like Dean
Rusk. In Oxford, thinking of Hardy's *Jude the Obscure,* Dorn despairs
over the results he anticipates from this evolution:

> that the stone *would* not
> and *could* not admit him remains just too lamentable.
> The stone
> itself, is common
> as america is a creation via common art
> will men always be hurled back
> until they destroy the stone
> itself. That's what
> the black men back in my land
> propose to do,
> tear every
> pillar of it
> down, and tear the world,
> the neat world, down,
> It wasn't Jude's thwarted ambition
> that's the dullest meanest part
> of Hardy's mind, it is the condition
> which *permits*
> *such a hopeless plot* we're still stuck with
>
> the new
>
> world was an evil world—
>
> (215)

Sampson is, obviously, the intertext transposed through the texts of Hardy, Dorn, and Jones here, and hovering behind this passage is the chorus of that ancient American Jeremiad of the gospel traditions: "If I had my way, If I had my way in this wicked world, I would tear this building down." Dorn despairs over the endless replication of this endless plot of martyrdom and recompense, but what counternarrative can he offer his correspondent? Is there a conceivable plot he could post in time to save us from ourselves? This letter, too, remains unmailed, sidetracked by the history it indites:

> We have had race
> and color and oppression / oppressor
> shoved up our asses so long
> we don't even see that, *even poets*
> are no longer in communication.
>
> (214)

Certainly Dorn knows that no one would be readier to deconstruct this most wearying of all binary oppositions than the oppressed themselves. But it seems that there are no tools with which to tear down the master's house *but* the tools of the master. What Baraka undertook was a liberating transformation of his discursive chains; Dorn feared the suffering inevitable in the collapse of the master's house of discourse, but he saw no way to avert the tragedies that would follow in the collapse. There is something inherently conservative in Dorn's despair, and if he has found another language in which to speak of these things, he has not yet posted it. Wandering within the geographies of American racial discourse, Dorn and Baraka have never again found themselves inhabiting the same house of poets. They may remain more like each other than any readers would be comfortable contemplating, but the once united front is now united only by a common sense of the deadly consequences of America's ideologies of race. At "The End of the North Atlantic Turbine Poem," Dorn readdresses his nation with what we may read as his answer to Baraka's "What do you think, Eddie, out there?" Having come to read the text of LeRoi Jones's absence as the very sign of the incommensurability of the languages constructed in the name of race, Ed Dorn attaches his undeliverable postscript:

You talk of color?
Oh cosmological america, how well
and with what geometry
you teach your citizens

(232)

Of Slave Girls and Women

Two Epilogues

The language between us has had to serve both as the medium of transmission of the ideologies of race and as an implement for the dismembering of those ideologies. Our language has been seized upon to serve as a radical sign of immutable racial difference, but it has at the same time served, as it seizes us and moves within us, as the layering intertext of our shared subjectivities. White discourse has persistently posited the English language itself as racial. Not only does American writing bear within its history repeated denials of the abilities of African peoples to create literary art, it has often denied the humanity of black persons as speaking subjects by denying their ability even to pronounce and write English. So clichéd has this presumed incapacity become after centuries of white representations of black dialect that contemporary white authors need offer no explanation at all when referring to it. The narrator of Richard Powers's novel *The Gold Bug Variations* has among her varied duties as a public reference librarian the maintaining of a board where patrons may post inquiries. "A portion of board duty is always custodial," she observes depressingly, "disposing of 'Why can't Jigs talk English?'" (35). So powerfully persistent have been public assertions about black people and the English language that the librarian's grim duty of periodically removing these graphic tracings of racism is an instantly recognizable marker of the continuity of racist discourse for any experienced reader of American texts. Power over the dispensation of writing and speaking is one of the ultimate powers, and it has been guarded zealously by those who have impressed their racially organized hegemony upon the language itself. Rife with contradictions, this jealous custody of English as the very sign of whiteness has constantly to deny the truths of speaking and writing black people. Defenders of slavery in the past simultaneously argued that Africans were constitutionally incapable of exercising reason in writing and passed laws to bar black people from access to the knowledge of writing. In Willa Cather's *Sapphira and the Slave Girl*, the Reverend Mr. Fairhead, listening to a slave named Lizzie singing, "often wondered how it was that she sounded the letter 'r' clearly when she sang, though she didn't when she talked" (78–79). Our readings in American literature will turn up few such troublings of the discursive surface of racial and linguistic superiority, for as evident as it is that there must have been many such contradictory moments for white people over the ages, moments when the evidence of their eyes and ears sharply conflicted with what they had agreed to suppose about black people, it is equally evident that whites simply learned not to see, not to hear that which *their* language told them could never be. When forced to confront black eloquence, whites may mark that eloquence itself as such a departure from the self-evident as to prove the rule of black linguistic paralysis. How many black people have been told, with an air of wonder, that they didn't "sound black?" How many have been congratulated for being "so articulate?" Black Americans have had to learn that the language they produce, so intimately proceeding from and evidencing their own being, will be marked by whites as the sign of a primal lack, no matter how they speak. "Her speech I counted against her," remarks the narrator of *Sapphira and the Slave Girl* when she finally meets Nancy, the former slave girl of the novel's title (284). It is Nancy's failure to speak as she should, as a "black" speaker and as a southerner, that the narrator finds so annoying. That Nancy *is* a black person speaking is rather beside the point.

Both Willa Cather's *Sapphira and the Slave Girl* and Sherley Anne Williams's *Dessa Rose* are constructed with odd narrative folds at their conclusions that have the effect of reasserting a racially marked power over the narrative that has preceded. At the close of *Sapphira and the Slave Girl*, which has proceeded as a third-person narrative with an omniscient point of view, the reader is unexpectedly confronted with a first-person narrator who identifies herself as the author of all that has gone before. At the end of *Dessa Rose*, a novel structured upon the modernist principles of multiple and shifting viewpoints, mediated by the authorial voice of a linking third-person narrative, Dessa Rose speaks to the reader for a final time in her own voice and identifies herself as the author of her own narrative, a narrative spoken to and written down by her children, written counter to the efforts of white people to "read" her. *Dessa Rose* is yet one more American novel that ends in epilogue trailing out in ellipses. *Dessa Rose* and *Sapphira and the Slave Girl* end in an assumption of authority over their own language, and these assumptive epilogues embody the struggle over language that organizes the histories of race in American thought. Each epilogue ends in a clearly colored voice that says "This story is mine" and that offers the narrative as paradigmatic, as the story of representative and representing women.

"Her speech I counted against her."

The ending of Willa Cather's 1940 novel *Sapphira and the Slave Girl* is one of the most confounding in our literature. Toni Morrison has argued that the book "turns at the end into a kind of memoir, the author's recollection of herself as a child witnessing the return, the reconciliation, and an imposed 'all rightness' in untenable, outrageous circumstances" (*Playing* 27). Many have felt the sudden appearance of the narrator as an actor in her text as a violation of a sort of narrative contract Cather has made with her readers in the earlier chapters. Morrison describes *Sapphira and the Slave Girl* as "a book that describes and inscribes its narrative's own fugitive flight from itself" (*Playing* 19). Morrison's choice of words here is telling, as the epilogue to Cather's fiction (which was virtually an epilogue to Cather's life) inscribes the return of Nancy, who had left twenty-five years earlier in flight as a fugitive slave. *Dessa Rose*, by Sherley Anne Williams, also describes the flight of a fugitive into the safe margins of an American epilogue. But what is so outrageous about *Sapphira and the Slave Girl* is that Nancy, the unnamed figure of the novel's title, is returned at the end to a form of narrative bondage in which her life is played out and told before the gaze of the white writer, for the benefit of the white spectator, who is allowed by the narrative to remain in innocence even as Nancy and her narrative are bound over for the white reader's pleasure.

For Morrison, this final act "subverts the entire premise of the novel" (*Playing* 28), and yet, this novel's seeming betrayal of its own form reencodes a most basic unspoken premise operating in Cather's earlier chapters. Nancy must return at the end of her story to the white house of the newly revealed narrator because Cather cannot imagine the scene of meeting between a black mother and her daughter apart from that meeting's function as an object for the contemplation of the white gaze. Toni Morrison is surely right in her opinion that both the complexities and the problems of this text arise out of Cather's "struggle to address an almost completely buried subject: the interdependent working of power, race, and sexuality in white woman's battle for coherence" (*Playing* 20). As the novel's epilogue ends, what we hear is an unbelievable, perhaps incoherent testament from Nancy's black mother, Till, but this is followed immediately by another surprise appearance as Cather appends yet another note, a postscript, attempting to bring coherence to her novel by signing her name to the narrative and its sources. Even here the white author cannot permit the wholly imagined black speech of Till to be the final word, because Cather cannot imagine black people outside the context of enforced white coherence. In the realm of Cather's fictions, black people only have lives when witnessed by whites. No white writer can know empirically what black people say to one another when there is no possibility of white witness. Willa Cather, though, seems uninterested in devoting much textual energy to imagining how black people live for and with one another. It is true that African Americans have had to organize their lives beneath the power-wielding gaze of white surveillance, but it is also true that centuries of such living have seen the development of an expressive culture deep and rich as the continent itself. The Reverend Mr. Fairhead stumbles close to the discovery of black expressive life at the same time he discovers that Lizzie can pronounce the English *r* perfectly well when she wishes to sing it, but just as Fairhead is insufficiently curious to think further what this phonetic rupture might signify, Cather is unconcerned with black life save as it may exist for white witness.

One reason this text expends so little time imagining the full emotional lives of its African-American characters is that, like the white southerners depicted in the novel, Cather's narrative assumes that it is already possessed of surpassing and intimate knowledge of black mental life and motivation. Sapphira Dodderidge Colbert, as did so many slave owners, professes to a greater comprehension of black people than they have of themselves, except on those occasions when she wishes to make a point of the final incomprehensibility of black behavior. When Nancy expresses her concern about the mental wandering of the aged Jezebel, Sapphira cuts her off brusquely. "No need for you to be speaking up," Sapphira announces, asserting her authority by silencing Nancy. "I know your granny through and through. She is no more out of her head than I am" (89). Sapphira's daughter, Rachel Blake, though she has discovered the immorality of slavery in her own conscience, and though she conspires to spirit Nancy to freedom via the Underground Railroad, still presumes to the most intimate access to the thoughts of the black people she knows. As she sets about helping Nancy, rescuing Nancy's imperiled honor from the advances of Sapphira's nephew Martin Colbert, Rachel Blake contemplates the relationship between Nancy and Till and maps it with a self-confirming legend, a legend that has been supplied to her by white discourse, what Toni Morrison has called American Africanist discourse, a "shared process of exclusion—of assigning designation and value . . ." (*Playing* 7). That long-internalized apparatus of explanation affords Rachel the set of received descriptions that she believes to be her perceptions, insights she thinks she has gathered from direct experience of black life, and that Cather renders in free indirect discourse:

> She understood why Nancy did not go to Till for advice and pro-
> tection. Till had been a Dodderidge before ever she was Nancy's
> mother. In Till's mind, her first duty was to her mistress. . . .
>
> Nancy had come into the world by accident; the other relation,
> that with the Dodderidge's, Till regarded as one of the fixed condi-
> tions you were born into. Beginning with Jezebel, her kin had lived
> under the roof and protection of that family for generations. It was
> their natural place in the world. (219)

Cather's delineation of Rachel's thought here is devastating. Cather shows us in Rachel a woman convinced by the naturalizing and mystifying effects of racist discourse that she can speak the deepest, unspoken thoughts of black people, and equally convinced that those same naturalizing powers have indoctrinated black minds so completely that they find their relation of subservience to whites more "natural" than the "accidents" of their children's births. That Nancy's father is a "white" man renders her relation with her mother no more accidental than Till's status as property of the Dodderidge family, but such considerations don't seem to disturb the placidly patronizing surface of Rachel's maternal meditations upon the possibilities of black family. To Rachel, a supreme tragedy of slavery's powers of evil is that it is able to convince owner and owned alike that they are born to their status. Rachel believes that her mother and those her mother purports to own are all sincere in their acceptance of this relationship as the given of their lives. "No, it ain't put on," Rachel says aloud to herself. "She believes it, and they believe it. But it ain't right" (221).

The narrator of this novel, which is signed on its last page by Willa Cather, has also been taken up in the comforting embrace of the Africanist way of knowledge. It is the narrator, not one of her characters, who describes the "soft darky laugh" of Nancy (179), that inherently black laughter taken to be so identifiable a racial characteristic that it is mentioned in hundreds of texts written by white Americans. And in describing Till's childhood, it is the narrator who is at pains to show us just how natural Till's identification with those who own her is. Till, we are told, "was not, under any circumstances, a gay darky" (70). There must be some explanation offered for so unnatural a phenomenon as a "darky" who doesn't laugh, and we learn that as a very young child Till had witnessed the death of her mother when her mother's dress caught fire from a candle. It is understandable that a child in these circumstances might be traumatized, but what is particularly to be noted in this case is the manner in which the event comes, in the narrator's telling of it, to underscore once more the Africanist insistence upon superior knowledge of black being. The other black people at Chestnut Hill attempt to comfort little Till, but she is inconsolable and responds to their ministrations with terror. The slaves declare that she "had been struck dumb and would never speak again" (70). The narrator understands, however, both Till's terror of her fellow blacks and the likely falsehood of their diagnosis. Mrs. Matchem, the English housekeeper who was to become Till's teacher and model (and whose name seems to define her role in seasoning Till in slavery, matching slave to mistress), "took Till up to the big house and put her into a cot in her own room. There, away from the emotional darkies, she began to sleep naturally again" (70). In the narrator's understanding of the world it is in the nature of "darkies" to be emotional. But Till, who is never to be a "gay darky," can only achieve her "natural" night's sleep when she is removed from the terror of her compatriots, those who were first to offer her solace, and secluded in the bedroom of a white woman. Having had such an unnatural upbringing herself, she subsequently, according to Rachel, finds her relationship to her white mistress more natural, more a thing she was born to, than her relationship with the daughter born to her when a white man either seduced or raped her (and what would be the meaning of a woman's consent if she were not free to withhold it in the first place?).

Even as white discourse produces itself as already possessed of the secrets of the black heart, as having a more complete knowledge of Africans than they could ever have of themselves, that discourse must reassure itself of the basic irrationality of black actions. This total knowledge of a subject not considered worth knowing because lacking in reason leads the white characters in *Sapphira and the Slave Girl* to believe that the only conceivable motive for any black behavior is the one that comes to the white mind. If the white mind can conceive no motive, then the phenomena under consideration are taken as simple evidence of the childlike unreason of Africans. Cather sometimes works this to comic effect. In one of the novel's early scenes we learn, as evidence of Till's devotion to her mistress, that Till breaks in Sapphira's new leather shoes for her, saving Sapphira the discomfort new shoes would cause to her "dropsical" feet. At one point Sapphira steels herself for a first wearing of a pair of kid shoes Till has been limbering up for her, when Till tells her, "Now you just wear the cloth slippers and be easy, Miss Sapphy. Let me wear the kid shoes round the house a few days more an' break 'em in for you" (32). So thorough has been Till's inculcation with the values of the slave system that neither the reader nor Sapphira is allowed to suspect that Till may be manipulating the old woman for her own amusement, that her wearing of the better shoes a few more days may be her way of sartorial signifying against the mistress and her prerogatives. Cather does allow us a delicious moment of irony a few pages later. Sapphira, recoiling at the affront to her dignity when the slave Jefferson shows up to drive her about the neighborhood without any boots on his feet, exclaims to that same Till who has been wearing her new shoes, "I wish you could tell me why it's so hard to keep leather on a nigger's feet." Till replies in all apparent sincerity, "I jest don't know, Miss Sapphy" (34). This scene serves as a comic comment on the irrationality of an Africanist discourse that only sees evidence that conforms to that which is already "known," but it also underscores the extent to which slavery, and the author, have severed Till from ordinary empathy with Jefferson, to whom she has been "married" by her owners. Likewise in a later scene, Rachel Blake, ignoring the obvious import of all she has witnessed growing up in Virginia, finds some black actions inexplicable. At one point, the appearance of Mrs. Blake has saved Nancy from the more insistent advances of Martin Colbert, but he is unwilling entirely to give up the attempt of the moment. Having come upon Nancy while she is picking laurels, Martin is surprised to find Rachel with her. Knowing she will decline, Martin offers to give Rachel a ride behind his saddle. He then carries on his interrupted flirtation with Nancy before the indignant eyes of Mrs. Blake:

"Miss Nancy, maybe, would like to get home before her flowers wilt?" He had the brass to make this suggestion as he stooped to pick up his riding whip. "No? Then let me carry the basket to Aunt Sapphy while the flowers are fresh."

Nancy reluctantly handed him the basket. Mrs. Blake frowned,
wondering why she gave in to him. (174)

Few would wonder very long before imagining what consequences
Nancy had learned followed upon refusal of requests made by white
men to black women. Mrs. Blake's wonder is occasioned by her ability
to repress her own knowledge of the position Nancy is placed in by
Martin's request, and by her assurance that her continued presence
will be seen by Nancy as insurance against subsequent reprisals. In
this way does Rachel Blake maintain her innocence. These minor
acts accomplish more than merely acquainting us with the limitations
Cather has constructed for her characters; they also set the tone for
the novel's maddening later scenes in which black characters appear
to act only to accommodate white desire, those scenes at the end that
Toni Morrison feels subvert the entire premise of the novel.

It might be difficult to say with any precision what the major premise of the novel is. If Cather indeed set out to explore in fiction
"the interdependent working of power, race, and sexuality in a white
woman's battle for coherence" (Morrison, *Playing* 20), she appears to
have halted well short of any of the conclusions her materials might
seem to suggest. At the close of the book, the structures of power
relationships reckoned by race and gender are not only still intact,
but they remain essentially unquestioned. Slavery has ended by the
end of the book, and with it the moral interrogations set in motion
by the novel's plot have also ended. In its ending, *Sapphira and the
Slave Girl* produces a veritable apologia for post-Reconstruction re-
inscriptions of racial and gender oppression. This is a betrayal of
what went before in the novel only if we expect the characters to follow out the consequences of their questions about the *institution* of
slavery. For the most part they do not. In the end, Cather has contrived a narrative demonstration of the fact that it is possible to reject
the institution of slavery on moral grounds without rejecting any of
the essential assumptions of Africanist discourse, and without repudi-
ating the powers and privileges created by ideologies of racism, and
this is exactly what America did following the Reconstruction. The
failure of Cather's novel is ultimately the failure of the nation to pursue the questions set in motion in our early chapters. The novel's final
imposition of a sense of "all rightness" is of a piece with its implica-

tion in American Africanist thought. It must, as a novel written in 1940, condemn the immoralities of slavery per se, but it must also, as a novel that speaks an Africanist language, leave whole the present social configurations that were made possible by slavery.

Though the novel presents a relatively pastoral view of slavery in the present time of the narrative, Cather does, in the chapter titled "Old Jezebel," describe the terrors of capture in Africa and the sufferings of the Middle Passage. But even here Cather cannot seem to resist the clichés of Africanist discourse. A reader will gather that Nancy inherits some of her spirit from Jezebel. Cather wants us to know that the origins of that spirit are located in an uncivilized, half-human Africa. Jezebel and her fellow captives, we read, "came from a fierce cannibal people, and had not been broken in by weeks of discipline in the stockade" (91). Cather gives a detailed account of the rigors of the Middle Passage, drawing liberally from published sources. Having described the tightly packed " 'tween decks" where the naked Africans were forced to endure the rank atmosphere of the undrained quarters, Cather calls attention to the inhumanity of the traffic by stating calmly and straightforwardly that "the Captain of the *Albert Horn* was not a brutal man, and his vessel was a model slaver" (92). This skipper, who, like other captains described in the literature of the Middle Passage, never went near the slave deck because he couldn't stand the smell (93), stands to profit from a one-third interest in his own cargo and holds another kind of interest in Jezebel: "The skipper had a kind of respect for a well-shaped creature; horse, cow, or woman. And he respected anybody who could take a flogging like that without buckling" (94). This is the interest of a man who views Jezebel as a commodity, who sees that she may fetch a higher price than the others. In an act prefiguring the positions of Till and Nancy on Sapphira's farm, Jezebel is removed from her place among the other Africans and placed on the upper deck alone, with cast-off clothing from the whites and a tarpaulin for cover. There may be irony to be read in the fact that it is a Dutchman who first buys Jezebel in America, but it isn't long before she becomes the property of the Dodderidge family, brought to their farm the same year Sapphira is born. Here again Jezebel is separated from other Africans, at least symbolically in the power hierarchies of the slave system. She is made an overseer and even in old age metes out "justice" to the younger slaves. Bearing upon her back the scars of her passage, Jezebel becomes a symbol of slavery's evil and, in the minds of the whites at least, its inevitability. Reverend Fairhead regards her as an example of predestination. Among the other slaves, she becomes a reminder of what suffering really is, a reminder that serves the purposes of her owners, as she silences the complaints of the young. "You ain't no call to be comf'able," she tells one youth. "You settin' down de minute a body's back's turned. I wisht I could put dock burs in yo pants" (97).

So often, as in this passage, even Cather's efforts to describe the evil that slavery wrought are undermined when her words end up dividing and berating black people. Similarly, as her white characters grapple with the morality of the system they inhabit, they invariably end by shying away from the implied consequences of their own inquiries. So often Cather's characters end in a moral position not that far removed from that of the northern woman in the story who announces her disapproval of slavery but who, upon moving to Maryland, purchases two slaves because "in Baltimore there was no other way to get good servants" (207). If there is a major premise in *Sapphira and the Slave Girl* it may be the moral conclusion reached by Rachel Blake when she is still a child: "A feeling long smothered had blazed up in her—had become a conviction. She had never heard the thing said before, never put into words. It was the *owning* that was wrong, the relation itself, no matter how convenient or agreeable it might be for master or servant. She had always known it was wrong. It was the thing that made her unhappy at home, and came between her and her mother" (137). This is a difficult realization to formulate for someone like the young Rachel, who grew up within a community where such an idea, never put into words, would seem an impossible thing to think, but the terms of its very formulation also make possible the betrayal of this premise in Cather's epilogue, for this formulation implies the possibility that the "relation itself" might somehow be maintained in different form, without the ownership, exactly the situation at novel's end in the post-Reconstruction epilogue. Rachel's moral revelation leads to no far-reaching consequences, at least partly because the advent of slavery was never truly a moral decision in the first place. Rachel does not own slaves, but neither does she do anything substantive to hasten the end of slavery. She dares, at substantial risk, to assist Nancy's flight to freedom in Canada, but only to rescue Nancy from the individual fate that threatens her, the threat that Martin Colbert might rape Nancy with Sapphira's silent complicity. Rachel's act is bold, but she concerns herself with the moral safety of Nancy; she does not concern herself with the system of beliefs that endangers all black women, even after the abolition of slavery. Her father, Henry Colbert, struggles with the question of slavery throughout the text. He has become a slave owner through his marriage to Sapphira, and he has always been uneasy with the institution of slavery, but he continues to profit from it. He searches his Bible for clear guidance either for or against slavery, but he finds no help in that quarter. Further, he tends to subsume the moral question of holding human chattel within an untenable philosophy of obligation: ". . . Henry had often asked himself, were we not all in bonds? If Lizzie, the cook, was in bonds to Sapphira, was she not almost equally in bonds to Lizzie?" (110). A reader can almost hear the weight falling upon those words "almost equally"; they will not bear it. When Henry decides to conspire against his wife and facilitate Nancy's removal to Canada, he finally sees the difference: "Sapphira's darkies were better cared for, better fed and better clothed, than the poor whites in the mountains. Yet what ragged, shag-haired, squirrel-shooting mountain man would change places with Sampson, his trusted head miller?" (228–29). However, this is a reason to free all slaves, not just the one whose chastity is in most immediate peril. When, following Sapphira's death, Henry Colbert does free all his slaves, he meets the initial expense of putting them up at the town's hotel temporarily and assists them in securing employment. He does not calculate that share of the estate paid for with slave labor and compensate these newly emancipated African-American citizens. Afterward, he demonstrates that his act of compassion for Nancy is a token act and that he is far from becoming an abolitionist. "There are different ways of being good to folks," he assures his wife during her last days. "Sometimes keeping people in their place is being good to them" (268).

In reading the first eight books of *Sapphira and the Slave Girl* it is often difficult, because of Cather's extensive use of free indirect discourse as a narrative technique, to separate the racism of her characters from that of Cather herself. In the end it proves to be an unnecessary exercise. It is almost too much of a coincidence for those who study the history of racial discourse in America that the term

"coloured narrative" has come to be employed to describe the manner
in which a "narrative is seen to be 'coloured' by the speech of a character." In his comment upon this term, Jeremy Hawthorn contrasts
this mode of coloring with free indirect discourse, in which "it is the
speech which is coloured by the narrative voice" (71). The entire text
of *Sapphira and the Slave Girl* is colored white by the American Africanist discourse of the narrator, who, in the epilogue, signs a name
to her colored text, "Willa Cather." The novel inscribes, as Toni Morrison terms it, "the sycophancy of white identity" (*Playing* 19). The
startling epilogue is not truly a betrayal of the text that precedes it;
it is rather the unfolding of the textual assumptions that have served
as the foundation of consciousness for all the characters in the book.
Each white character claims total knowledge of black subjectivity and
finds in the text of Africanist subjectivity a reaffirmation of the sycophancy of white identity. When Henry Colbert considers purchasing
the slave Sampson from Sapphira and freeing him, Sampson responds
in a fashion that must have been reassuring to Henry, and to many
white readers in 1940: "[W]hen it was his turn to speak, he broke
down. This was his home. Here he knew everybody. He didn't want to
go out among strangers. Besides, Belle, his wife, was a slack worker,
and his children were little. He could never keep them in a city as
well off as they were here. What ever had put such a notion in Mis-
ter Henry's head?" (109). Cather clearly has not read Charles Chesnutt's hilarious satire of such assumptions in his story "The Passing
of Grandisson," for if she had, she could never recount this meeting
with just this coloration. As Morrison observes of Till's final speech
in this novel, "serviceable to the last, this Africanist presence is permitted speech only to reinforce the slave-holder's ideology" (*Playing*
28). Colbert's experience with Sampson early in the novel mirrors his
later experiences when he has difficulty ridding himself of the slaves
he has freed, and both episodes prefigure the incredible behavior of
Till and Nancy at novel's end. Henry Colbert falls in his fields, working "with the few negroes who begged to stay on at the Mill Farm
after the miller had freed all his wife's slaves," and it is they who
bear his body in his last moments into his house. What more touching
Africanist fantasy than this is to be imagined; the good master borne
aloft in his dying moments by those loyal slaves who begged to stay
on with him after emancipation? The text allows the reader not a

single glimpse of the options that were open to newly freed slaves, no hint of the considerations weighed by these black workers before they "begged" to remain with the man who had owned them. In a similar vein, Nancy's last thoughts as she heads north to a life in freedom are of her unfinished assignments in slavery. When Rachel notices a reticule Nancy has brought along, the soon-to-be free woman explains nervously: "Oh, Miz' Blake, the reticule ain't mine! Miss Sapphy give it to me yisterday, with three pairs a-her good silk stockings for me to darn. I did mean to darn 'em today, but some way I jist couldn't get down to it. I been kind-a flighty in the haid like. I'll mend 'em as soon as I get there, an' send 'em back by stage, or somehow" (232). Can any reader doubt that Nancy will complete that task? Scenes such as this may have more to do with underpinning the racial hierarchies and dogmas of 1940s America than with an artistic meditation upon our shared past. In Cather's inverted past, black workers who beg to stay with their masters meet a far happier fate than those like the unfortunate "Tap," whose story is delivered in the epilogue, who went to town before he was ready, when "he hadn't been able to stand his freedom" (290).

The obscenity of Cather's epilogue is that she writes a world in which even in freedom black life is determined by white desire. When twenty-five years have passed, Nancy returns, but her reunion with her mother takes place in the place of whiteness, in the home of the five-year-old white girl who has suddenly appeared and identified herself as the child who became the narrator of the book we are reading. "The actual scene of the meeting had been arranged for my benefit," she avers. "When I cried because I was not allowed to go downstairs and see Nancy enter the house, Aunt Till had said: 'Never mind, honey. You stay right here, and I'll stay right here. Nancy'll come up, and you'll see her as soon as I do'" (282). Toni Morrison's reading of this scene is as stark as it is astute: "Only with Africanist characters is such a project thinkable: delayed gratification for the pleasure of a (white) child" (*Playing* 27). In fact, everything in the novel has pointed to this unfolding of the plot before white eyes, everything has been determined by white insistence upon speaking for, and in the place of, black people, on speaking and defining their being.

When Nancy speaks, the narrator-as-a-child recoils: "It didn't seem a friendly way to talk. Her speech I counted against her" (284). There is a reverberating oddness about this complaint, for the returned Nancy speaks as the adult narrator writes, without the "friendly elision of syllables," a white writing and a speech not expected to proceed from the mouths of black people.

Much is made of ways of speech in this novel, speech as embodied sign of social status, speech as generator of community cohesion, speech as indicative of racial distance. The Colberts, even after decades of living in Back Creek Valley, Virginia, are markedly out of place. Slavery was not questioned in this margin of the Old Dominion, but "in that out-of-the-way, thinly settled district between Winchester and Romney, not a single family had ever owned more than four or five negroes" (22). It is the number of slaves owned as sign of wealth that marks the Colberts as foreign, but the accents they carry with them are also signifiers of their difference. Interestingly, in the case of Henry Colbert, Cather presents this as a mark of absence: "[H]is lack of a Southern accent amounted almost to a foreign accent" (5). Henry's practice of speaking English in the manner of the English settlers, a manner Cather describes as clear and decisive, is, like Nancy's acquired accent at book's end, perceived as an unfriendly way of speaking. "His wife also spoke differently from the Back Creek people," Cather comments. "But they admitted that a woman and an heiress had a right to" (5). Despite Nancy's rich heritage, despite the fact that she too is a woman, she obviously is not regarded as one entitled to cultivate an accent such as the one she possesses in the text of the epilogue. Cather seems to recognize some of the ironies implicit in the hierarchies of language constructed in intercultural contact. Filling in the history of the Dodderidge wealth Henry Colbert has married into, Cather describes the immensity of forestlands possessed by Lord Fairfax, a portion of which he deeded to Nathaniel Dodderidge. The features of those lands, Cather explains in an even tone, "had never been explored except by the Indians and were nameless except for their unpronounceable Indian names" (26). This passage is an exemplary instance of the ironies of "coloured narrative," as the description is colored by the assumption that words that cannot be easily pronounced by white people are unpronounceable. We must assume that the Indians did not go about assigning names to the landscape around them that they themselves could not pronounce.

The problem Nancy presents for the narrator-as-child is that Nancy has acquired pronunciations that should be beyond her capacities. Through the major portion of the text, Nancy speaks in what might be described as a Back Creek black: "Oh, I'm most drove out-a my mind, I cain't bear it no longer, 'deed I caint. I gets no rest night nor day. I'm goin' to throw myself into the millpawnd, I am!" (216). This is neither better nor worse than most contemporary representations of black speech in the writings of white authors. "Millpawnd" is intended to locate this pronunciation in the Virginia countryside, "cain't" is standard notation for one class of southern inflection, and the use of "drove" and "I gets no" displays the requisite untutored grasp of grammar. As is generally the case, Cather's representations of dialect are only partial and are inconsistent. Nancy apparently has no problems pronouncing the initial *th* sound in "throw," but elsewhere in the novel Cather has her black characters using the *de* and *dar* (204) of white people's standard black English. The scattering of typographic markers of linguistic difference never really serves the purpose of transcribing actual spoken language. It is a literary effect whose purpose is to characterize the person depicted speaking the dialect.

Upon Nancy's return, we are given very few instances of her new speech, only a one-sentence tribute to Rachel Blake and a few properly grammatical questions Nancy puts to her mother. When the narrator explains her reactions to Nancy's speech, she makes it a matter much like the neighbors' initial reactions to Henry Colbert's accent. While Henry has seemingly been marked by his inability, over decades, to acquire the speech of his surroundings, Nancy shocks because, over decades, she *has* acquired the speech patterns of her neighbors: "Whereas Mrs. Blake used to ask me if she should read to me from my 'hist'ry book' (*Peter Parley's Universal*), Nancy spoke of the his-to-ry of Canada. I didn't like that pronunciation. Even my father said 'hist'ry.' Wasn't that the right and easy way to say it? Nancy put into many words syllables I never heard sounded in them before. That repelled me. It didn't seem a friendly way to talk" (284). It is not, though, simply the fact that Nancy no longer speaks with the friendly elisions of the locals. After her twenty-five-year hiatus in Canada, Nancy no longer speaks in the dialect of her still living representation in the oral literature of the locale. As far back as our narrator can remember, she recalls going to sleep to the soothing lullaby sung to her by her white mother: *"Down by de cane-brake, close by de mill, / Dar lived a yaller gal, her name was Nancy Till"* (281). In the intervening years the absent Nancy has become a signifying figure in the folk culture of the community. In the lullaby's intertext, Nancy is transposed as the figure of a mythic blackness. The narrator's dismay upon hearing the returned Nancy speak is in part a function of her recoil from the living Nancy's violation of her representations in verse. The real Nancy comes back to speak an English that ruptures the signifying chains of racial difference and racial poetics.

For Nancy's mother, Nancy's new mode of speech represents a sort of linguistic apotheosis: "Nancy, dalin', you talks just like Mrs. Matchem, down at Chestnut Hill! I loves to hear you" (286). Readers might expect that Till would have more immediate reasons for loving to hear the sound of her daughter's speech after two and one-half decades, but in the racial calculus of this white-colored narrative her reaction is as predictable as the narrator's. Nancy's mastery of the forms of English speech as spoken by free Canadians brings her "accidental" relationship with her mother into alignment with the more "natural" relationship Till has had with her masters and with Mrs. Matchem.

This is part and parcel of that imposed sense of "all rightness" Toni Morrison finds in the novel's epilogue. At the close of the scene, the grown women "were called downstairs to the second table, to eat the same dinner as the family, served by the same maid (black Moses' Sally)" (286). The nature of the "all rightness" Cather imposes in her epilogue reveals the literary terrorism of white discourse. African Americans who do not, like "Poor Tap," attempt solo flight before they can "stand" their freedom may, like Till and like the former slaves who begged to stay on with their master, find happiness and fulfillment in their place. The more adventurous, if like Nancy they are light, intelligent, carefully guided by well-meaning whites, and separated from "emotional darkies" (Nancy is now the servant of an English family in Montreal, where she is married to a man who is half Scotch and half Indian), may seem unfriendly at first in their difference from other blacks but may serve their race by acting for whites as demonstration models of the ultimate improvability of the black heart. The "better" classes of black Americans may then just hope, in the happily ever after of Cather's epilogue, that they may one day be invited to an honored seat at the second table of the American feast, where they too may be served by a black maid. It is true that Cather gives the long-suffering Till the next-to-last word of the novel. It is also true that Till, ever serviceable as a token of the powers of white Africanist discourse, speaks *as* the servant who thinks first of her white mistress, even after that mistress has died, and unlike her daughter Nancy, the serviceable representative of a white writer's new Negro woman, Till still talks black.

"This *the childrens have heard from our own lips.*"

In her "Author's Note" to the novel *Dessa Rose,* Sherley Anne Williams speaks truth to the discursive power represented by such works as *Sapphira and the Slave Girl:* "Afro-Americans, having survived by word of mouth—and made of that process a high art—remain at the mercy of literature and writing" (ix). Cather's novel, for all its willingness to broach the legacy in race and sex of the Middle Passage in American consciousness, ends by being exactly the kind of oppressive discourse Williams describes. Black Americans have had to survive narratives of subjugation, have had to find ways to communicate with one another over the heads of, between the lines of white Americans speaking endlessly to themselves of white subjectivity. As Toni Morrison reads Cather's text, she sees what Dessa Rose herself sees: "That's what we was in white folks' eyes, nothing but marks to be used, wiped out" (185). Cather's writing is a black mark on the American slate of perpetual innocence; her Africanist discourse is a text to be read by those who construct their identities as white people, who color their narrative knowledge of the world white. *Dessa Rose* enacts a struggle for power in language that has proceeded from the time of the first publication of African-American words.

Black writing has always had to find ways to subvert the encompassing discourses of white mediation. The strategies of survival by word of mouth alluded to by Williams in her preface have had their parallels in the evolution of a poetics of black narrative. The palimpsestic, intertextual layerings of *Dessa Rose* replicate, as does Robert Hayden's "Middle Passage," the strategies of mastering authentication in the structures of the slave narratives and of early African-American fictions. The "Author's Note" itself could be read as an ironic reversal, one of several in the novel, of the history that the note adduces. One of the myriad ways in which African Americans have been at the mercy of literature is the practice of mediation itself. Beginning with Phillis Wheatley, hundreds of black authors saw their works ushered into the presence of a reading public, largely white, accompanied by approving prefatory notes from respected white citizens. Just as Willa Cather wouldn't quite allow her black character the last word in *Sapphira and the Slave Girl,* publishing practices in America for generations denied to black writers even the prerogative of the first words of their books. Before presenting the words of *Dessa Rose,* who will reappear in her own voice in the epilogue to authorize her narrative, Sherley Anne Williams addresses the reader in a note that delegitimizes white mediations of black life and language. After describing the two historical events upon which Williams has based her novel, she offers a "confession." "I admit also to being outraged by a certain, critically acclaimed novel of the early seventies that travestied the as-told-to memoir of slave revolt leader Nat Turner" (ix). The unnamed novel in question is obviously William Styron's *Confessions of Nat Turner.* That book, though, was actually published in 1967. Williams's chronological displacement of Styron's controversial book may be an accidental displacement of Styron's reputation, a sort of prefatory vengeance for the malign neglect with which white critics have so often treated black writing, and a vengeance that, in its carelessness with dates, parodies Styron's considerable carelessness with history. In his "meditation" on history Styron has produced a duplicitous text, not unusual in a novel. But if Styron's novel is a travesty, then it is the doubling of the travesty already accomplished in the first *Confessions of Nat Turner,* a pamphlet composed by (and copyrighted by) a white writer, Thomas R. Gray, in which Nat Turner's own words were in literal fact used against him in the mediated and recomposed narrative of his white author.

Sandra Gilbert and Susan Gubar's figuration of "the madwoman in the attic" as a trope for woman's presence, hidden, denied, and reformed, in British writing is already an ironic doubling back upon the master texts of England, for the titular madwoman is in fact a colonial subject representing, among other things, the denied reliance of British culture and prosperity upon slave labor. In the United States, one lesson provided by texts such as the 1831 *Confessions of Nat Turner* and Harriet Jacobs's *Incidents in the Life of a Slave Girl* is that the American historical text is predicated upon the denial of the black subject confined within the house of innocence, the black woman in the attic, the black man in the cell. When Toni Morrison asks "What are Americans always so insistently innocent of?" (*Playing* 45), these images provide one answer. American Africanist discourse is meant to speak *in the place of* black people and thus to immure them within a dank silence, to replace the speaking bodies of black people with white figurations of blackness, ensuring that the place where the texts of black consciousness are entombed will remain hidden. (This is the speech act conducted in our time by such insidious terms as "permanent underclass.") This Africanist discourse has become, in Morrison's formulation, "a disabling virus within literary discourse" (*Playing* 7). In the first section of *Dessa Rose*, Sherley Anne Williams reveals the laboratory in which this virus is replicated and circulated.

Dessa Rose is chained in a dark root cellar at the opening of her text, watched over and listened to by a white man, Adam Nehemiah, who is taking her words for his own use and profit. Few more powerful symbols are available for understanding the workings of race in American culture. There is a stolen blackness at the root of American experience, and there is a white narrative turning black words to the further subjugation of black people. As Thomas Gray, with the assistance of Nat Turner's white jailer, entered Turner's cell for the purpose of reconstructing Nat Turner's words to meet white expectations, so does Adam Nehemiah reconstruct the narrative of Dessa Rose from notes taken in the root cellar. The book he is writing he always refers to as *Roots*, perhaps Williams's sly way of signifying upon the white appetite for certain forms of heroic slave tales. The full title of Nehemiah's intended text links the enterprise of Thomas Gray and William Styron to Joseph Conrad's *Heart of Darkness*. Nehemiah's extended title is to be *The Roots of Rebellion in the Slave Population and Some Means of Eradicating Them* (Nehemiah thinks this "a compelling short title" [17]), a title that echoes the title of Kurtz's pamphlet on suppressing savage customs in Africa, with its footnote reading "Exterminate all the brutes!" (Conrad 66). Like the civilizing colonizers of Conrad's fiction, Nehemiah approaches his work with a missionary's righteousness. His work is a calling, a work with a capital *W.* "Ah, the work," he thinks to himself as he commences his labors. "*The* Work had begun" (26). His Work is a metanarrative of slavery. No slaveholder himself, he will explain the blackness of blackness, the "blackness of the darky heart" (250), to his white readers and will make of them more masterful masters.

What Williams achieves in the first section of the novel is an intervention to disrupt the metamastery of white narrative power, represented in the person of Nehemiah, by removing the object of white discourse. Like Nat Turner speaking in his cell to Thomas Gray, Dessa Rose speaks out of the darkness of the American language's root cellar as she awaits execution for her part in a slave uprising on a coffle. Her hanging has been delayed, like the reunion of Till and Nancy in *Sapphira and the Slave Girl,* to satisfy another white desire. She will not be hanged until she is delivered of the child she is carrying. The state intends her execution as a rhetorical act; she is to be an example; her's is to be a representative death by which the state's power to dispose of black life will be demonstrated. The state has no immediate interest in Dessa's soon-to-be-born child but awaits delivery to placate the outraged owner of the slave coffle, Wilson. In the same way that the state will represent its power by taking Dessa's life, Wilson will demonstrate the power of property, the power of individual white people to own absolutely the bodies of black human beings, by taking Dessa's infant. Nehemiah hopes to exercise textual power. "Pray God this darky don't die before I get my book" (27), he writes, in his own hand. His book, his guide to metamastery, will be the published demonstration of white power to determine the meaning of black existence. In writing Nehemiah's journal, Sherley Anne Williams reverses the act by which William Styron travestied the already travestied speech of Nat Turner, reverses the act by which, in her epilogue, Willa Cather represents the meaning of black life as the meaning of black life for white people. Williams inscribes white desire for narrative power over blackness, and then she prevents her character's white mastery of its own text by removing and revoicing the black woman at its center.

In that act she also reasserts black authorship in American history by reauthoring the intertexts of historical consciousness. It is Independence Day, a fact Nehemiah's journal notes "in wearied surprise" (69), the Fourth of July, 1847, when Nehemiah finds that his narrative has been undone, that he has no end, that he will be prevented from reaching the conclusion of his text on the eradication of rebelliousness among slaves because his captive rebel, the sole source for his volume, has vanished without a trace from her root cellar. Nehemiah will spend the rest of the novel attempting to recapture his captive speaking subject, to reassert the anticipated conclusion necessary to the white reader's sense of all rightness. The irony as we read in the contemporary context of Nehemiah's thoughts is one thing; the intertextual irony asserting itself within the reading of Nehemiah's notes is another all together. Reading Williams's novel within the fuller text of African-American writing, we may see that Dessa's departure is also the enacting of an answer to the title question of Frederick Douglass's 1852 speech "What to the Slave is the Fourth of July?" (There are multiple allusions to Douglass throughout the novel.) Perhaps more fundamentally, the date of Dessa's escape also may be read as a revision of the "original" *Confessions of Nat Turner*. Thomas Gray's account reports that Turner and his fellow rebels had at first planned their uprising for the Fourth of July, an answer before the fact to Douglass's question. For a number of reasons including Turner's taking ill, the commencement of violent rebellion was postponed, but in Williams's intertextual revision of the *Confessions*, Nat Turner's original plan is memorialized by the successful escape of Dessa Rose, engineered by black people moving in the self-assured midst of the vigilant whites.

At one point prior to Dessa's escape, Williams has Nehemiah pause to consider the seeming outlandishness of the "facts" he has been recording in his journal. "Had he but the pen of a novelist—And were darkies the subject of romance, he thought sardonically, smiling at his own whimsy" (35). The sardonic pen of the novelist who writes these words alerts us to a reading of this novel as the destruction of white romance, the undoing of the Africanism of such novels as *Sapphira and the Slave Girl* as well as Styron's and Gray's purportedly less fantastic romances. (So purple does Williams's prose become in scattered passages that a reader's only defense may be to take those lines as acutest parody of the language of novels like *Gone with the Wind* and *Mandingo:* "His tongue left trails of liquid fire along her flesh. He eased between her thighs, entering that nameless deep, filling that lonely cavern. Will-less, she gathered around him; the day exploded into a thousand nights and endless stars" [167–68].) Not only do certain features of *Dessa Rose* closely parallel *Sapphira and the Slave Girl*, such as propertyless Terrell Vaugham's acquisition by marriage of Dessa Rose and all the other slaves on his three farms, but parts of Williams's text seem to supply what Cather had been unable to imagine in her final novel. It is at times as if a door had suddenly been opened in the narrative of *Sapphira and the Slave Girl* affording the reader a clear view of signifying acts unreadable to Willa Cather. The black characters in Cather's narrative invariably appear *in* character, as white people would expect them to appear. In *Dessa Rose* we see black characters *acting in character* for the white gaze, as when Dessa determines to mask herself in conversations with Nehemiah, a decision clearly recalling Paul Laurence Dunbar's poem "We Wear the Mask." "She now kept her face vacant (better to appear stupid than sassy)" (54). A reading of the passages in *Dessa Rose* that concern Jemina, the slave of Dessa's jailer, produces a veritable explication of the deeper structure of life concealed by Africanist descriptions in Cather's characterization of Till. Jemina quickly becomes Dessa's means of speaking past Nehemiah's notes, and Jemina is the key to Dessa's passage beyond the walls of her imprisonment. Nehemiah, however, like Amasa Delano in Melville's "Benito Cereno," sees, when he interrogates Jemina, only that which the categorical structures of racist discourse have prepared him to see: "Hughes' darky was, of course, incoherent—when was a nigger in excitement ever anything else?—but we finally pieced together, between the darky's throwing her apron over her head and howling, 'Oh, Masa, it terrible; they was terrible fierce,' and pointing to her muddied gown to prove it, what must have happened" (70). What "must have happened" is, naturally, thanks to Jemina's acting out what is expected of her, which to Nehemiah is as much proof as the deliberately muddied gown he is shown, not at all what Nehemiah believes to have happened.

In a text that is so centrally concerned with reauthoring the text of America's racial history, enunciation, in both its quotidian and theoretical senses, comes to serve as a primary signifying apparatus. Adam Nehemiah would, had his text in progress not been preempted by Dessa's removal, have enunciated in her place, would have represented her and her speech as he would have them to be for white readers. Like Henry Colbert, Nehemiah's own speech sets him apart from other whites, but unlike Colbert, Nehemiah cultivates this linguistic apartness assiduously. It is one of those things that gives him access to the metacritical levels from which he writes. He holds Sheriff Hughes in near contempt, partly because "the fellow spoke English little better than a negro" (19). This sign of Nehemiah's whiteness, his adept pronunciations of English, marks him in Dessa's estimation, though, as an alien: "'You a *real* white man?' she asked, turning back, as the thought struck her. 'For true? You don't talk like one. Sometime, I don't even be knowing what you be saying. You don't talk like Masa and he a real uppity-up white man, but not like no po buckra, neither'" (65). Nehemiah, who has prided himself on speaking English better than the most well-to-do white people, is greatly offended at the thought that his language places his whiteness in question. He angrily assures Dessa, "I *teach* your master and his kind how to speak" (65), but quickly learns that his status as a teacher does not elevate him in Dessa's eyes above other white people.

In the later portions of *Dessa Rose*, enunciation, naming, and the powers of language become the metaphoric apparatus Williams uses to confront more profoundly than Cather ever did those intersections of race, sex, and power so quickly elided in *Sapphira and the Slave Girl*. Freed from bondage in the root cellar, Dessa is free to exercise power in language, to assign value to the signs of her world. At its most playful level, this provides her the opportunity for free play in the field of language, where she can transpose signs from one signifying system to another, bringing them alive with new meanings. When Harker introduces her to his modest collection of French words, he explains to her: "'Negro' meant black man; 'negress' was black woman; 'blank' was white. I laughed at that, thinking about Miz Lady. She could sure look like it wasn't nothing shaking behind that face" (201). Loosed from the strictures of race and language enforced by slavery, Dessa Rose arrives at a site of radical reinscription in the margins of the slave state, a place where no sign really means what it appears to mean from the outside. Following her rescue, Dessa Rose joins other African-American fugitives at the farm of Ruth Elizabeth Sutton. Like Cather's Henry and Sapphira Colbert, Bertie and Ruth Elizabeth live in a remote area "where there [are] few slave holders and few of those who [own] more than two or three slaves" (108), but, with Bertie away on a conveniently interminable journey, Sutton Glen

becomes a signifying inversion of Sapphira Colbert's farm. At Sutton
Glen a white woman nurses a black infant, the supposed slaves oper-
ate the farm and make all the important decisions, and the mistress
of the house falls in love with a black man. It is as if Sutton Glen were
a region in which the laws of gravity did not apply. Here Dessa is free
to speak for herself.

Across the course of the novel, Dessa Rose and the mistress of Sutton Glen contend with each other over the forces of the language that
speaks race to them, and they eventually reach a point, on their way
to the freedom of the frontier, where they can speak to each other as
equals, where they can speak outside the constraints of traditionally
gendered and racialized language, beyond the reach of the root cellar's chains, and where they may begin to make their own mark on the
language. As is so often the case with historical romance, as was true
of *Sapphira and the Slave Girl*, *Dessa Rose* meditates upon history as a
way of meditating upon the present conversations between black and
white women. By transposing contemporary debates about women's
emancipation back into an imagined antebellum narrative, Sherley
Anne Williams provides an intertext for reimagining the possibilities
for white women and black women to find each other.

The movement toward a truly free speech between black and white
begins in a contest upon the terrain of naming. It begins as Dessa
abruptly challenges the narrative Ruth is telling of her own past. As
Ruth recounts her memory of a dress made for her by her mammy,
Dessa interrupts, as she had never been able to before that day when
she interrupted the text of ownership by striking back against her
owners: "'Wasn't no "mammy" to it.' The words burst from Dessa.
She knew even as she said it what the white woman meant. 'Mammy'
was a servant, a slave (Dorcas?) who had nursed the white woman. . . .
[G]oaded by the white woman's open-mouthed stare, she continued,
'Mammy ain't made you nothing!'" (124). Dessa's eruption arises
within the signifying space between two disjunct systems of enunciation. When Ruth speaks the word *mammy*, she adopts a relationship
to black womanhood invented by slavery and perpetuated by racism,
and her words are intended to naturalize that relationship in the same
way that Till's relation to the Dodderidges had been naturalized in
the discourse of Rachel Blake. When Dessa speaks the word *mammy*,

she refers to her biological mother. She knows what the white woman means, and that is why she protests. That white meaning is a slur upon the relationship intended by her own usage, a white imposition upon Dessa's use of the language imposed upon her.

One intertextual chain operating in this scene clearly reaches to the debates over Adrienne Rich's essay in her 1976 collection *Of Woman Born*, in which she adopts the black woman who was her childhood nurse as her black mother. That debate over Rich's textual claim of a woman who could not speak back to her, which Rich summarizes and responds to with care in the later republication of *Of Woman Born*, in turn stands forth as a symbol of the difficulties black and white women have faced in their efforts to move more closely together toward a feminist politics that does not subsume the problems of racism in America beneath an idealized and imposed gender unity. The contest over the word *mammy* in *Dessa Rose* figures the struggle of white women to account for and contend with the continuing realities of white privilege. Williams composes a comic conversation among the women at Sutton Glen that compresses an analysis of this centuries-long refusal of most white people to acknowledge their power within a racially determined social structure: "Ada tell you in a minute, white woman ain't got no excuse to be so trifling when all it take is they *word*. Aunt Lefonia and Emmalina had said about the same thing. They didn't have too much patience with white womens amongst theyselfs—though they never let on about this before any mistress; before mistress they was good slaves" (190). Dessa Rose sees at once what neither Ruth nor Sapphira had ever conceded, that the names they imposed upon black people were meant to suppress those people, that the name *mammy* even repressed the given "slave" name of the temporary mother.

Sherley Anne Williams's deft orchestration of the themes of naming and the politics of speech is one of the novel's finer formal accomplishments. Ruth's slow coming to consciousness of her reluctance to relinquish white prerogatives, and thus her coming to nominal understanding with Dessa Rose, in many ways begins with Dessa's challenge to Ruth's memories of her mammy. Ruth's claim to a mother-daughter relationship founders, not only on the rock of her realization of the one-sidedness of her claim, but also upon her recognition of her own failure to be a proper daughter to the black mother she cannot, in the heat of argument, name. Dessa forces this moment to crisis:

> "What was her name then?" Dessa taunted. "Child don't even know its own mammy's name. What was Mammy's name? What—"
> "Mammy," the white woman yelled. "That was her name." (125)

Pressed to provide the most elementary daughter's knowledge of a mother, Ruth can only speak from a position of white discursive power, naming a function that the black woman must fill. So long as she reserves to herself, as a white person, this power to speak words that black women must serve, she and Dessa Rose will have no common ground to speak of.

Dessa's triumphant challenge forces Ruth to reconsider for the first time the full significance of her power to own a nominatum. Through most of the narrative Ruth is called "Rufel" by the other characters, and only occasionally does she attempt to reassert her given name. "Miz Rufel," we learn, "was a slave-given name, discarded by white people when they reached adulthood" (103). In the normal course of antebellum affairs Ruth would have been expected to outgrow the name she was called by her African nurse in the same way she would have been expected to outgrow the need for the nurse herself. Now, whenever she wishes to reclaim her authority as a white person, she attempts to force black people to name her again by *her* position. "Shaking, Rufel screamed, 'My name is "Mistress" to you!'" (103). Her pleas are inefficacious in every instance. The reader's consciousness of her is colored by the narrative's habitual use of her slave-given name. For once white readers are taught to call things by the names slaves gave them. The continued use of Ruth's childhood nickname also seems to denote at some level the state of arrested development imposed upon women within the patriarchal hierarchies of slavery.

The black characters keep up a game with Ruth's name meant to establish her real position in their estimation. In addition to "Rufel," the names she is given include "Miss Lady" and "Miss Ruint." From childhood, Ruth assured herself with what she had learned to believe about the ability of black tongues to negotiate English phonetics. "The darkies never could get her name straight, slurring and garbling the syllables until the name seemed almost unrecognizable" (131). When

Dessa forces Ruth to retrieve Dorcas's name from behind the function name she has been forced to bear under slavery, Ruth's grounding assumptions about the given world of racial definition are sundered. "Seeing with an almost palpable lucidity how absurd it was to think of herself as Mammy's child, a darky's child" (132), Ruth begins to hear, as if for the first time clearly, how she was being called out by black people. In the first stage of her thinking she sees what it must mean to be called out of your name: "Had Mammy minded when the family no longer called her name? Was that why she changed mine? Rufel thought fearfully. Was what she always thought loving and cute only revenge, a small reprisal for all they'd taken from her?" (137). Ruth finds it impossible to accept the idea that she has gone through life answering to the vengeance of the black woman she called "mammy." She cannot believe that Dorcas didn't love her, but neither can she know, now that she has begun to question her social universe, what it means to be loved in a system that enforces motherly affections, that requires black women to love white women. If Ruth decides to believe that Dorcas loved her, it can bring her little pleasure to know that she was cared for by someone who had no choice. She wants "desperately to believe that Mammy had loved her not only fully, but freely as well" (147).

It isn't difficult to imagine the trifling image Ruth presents to Dessa Rose at this point, a white woman whose simple words have carried ultimate power in the past reduced to rage and confusion at the thought that a black woman doesn't love her. Williams's text parodies the ways that white speech has travestied its own most valued words by insisting upon speaking them in a situation in which they will not permit them to signify. Dessa remembers how her friend "Cully could have you dying about his old master trying to raise him as a slave *and* like a son—teaching him to read but not to write, to speak but daring him to think" (181). This travesty of familial language and values explains why the tragedy of *Sapphira and the Slave Girl* is inevitable. Nancy's father *was* a white man, but Henry Colbert could not truly act fatherly toward Nancy without destroying the equilibrium of slavery. Nancy would have to pay for the luxury Henry allowed himself in taking his paternalism to heart.

Ruth finally fastens upon a saving fiction by which she refigures her own renaming as an act of freely given love: "Maybe this was what Mammy had felt when she had changed Ruth Elizabeth's name, that somehow she had snuck a little piece of the child for herself, had marked at least some part . . . with something of her own making" (160). This marks the beginning point of Ruth's willingness to accept black people's command of language, to share the right to describe the world we live in. She must still earn by her actions the respect and love of the black people she will work with, but it is at this moment of accepting the name given her by a black woman as a sign of freely given love, the name given her against the spirit of patriarchal law, that she earns the right to be called by the name she chooses for herself, the name that signs her accession to adulthood. She remains a slow learner of the realities of slavery and discourse, but she chooses to be a learner. For her part, Dessa Rose accepts the humanity of Ruth in that moment when she sees that Ruth's power as a white woman is vulnerable to subjugation by men. Having helped Ruth escape an attempted rape, Dessa realizes: "The white woman was subject to the same ravishment as me; this the thought that kept me awake. I hadn't knowed white mens could use a white woman like that, just take her by force same as they could with us" (220). There is a doubleness in this realization. In seeing that Ruth's whiteness will not save her from assault, Dessa sees again the brute nature of power. White men do not oppress black people and rape women *because* they are white, or *because* they are men, but because they have the power to do so. That power has expression in other than racial terms; otherwise any white man could get away with raping any white woman. Power in America has been lodged in whiteness and in maleness and in wealth, and it has been a tragedy of American history that most white people have been unwilling to refuse the piece of power offered to them on condition that they accept it as white people. For Dessa this too is a first step; she tells us, "I didn't know how to be warm with no white woman" (220). Yet each woman has begun to learn to read the other in the fullness of her own text, not ignoring color or the experience of race, not viewing the other's race as a subset of her own humanity, not reading the other simply as a version of the self, but reading the names they offer to each other: " 'Ruth,' 'Dessa,' we said together" (256). In this ending the black woman does not exist solely so that the white woman may name her experience, as is the case at the close of Willa Cather's *Sapphira and the Slave Girl*. At the end of Sherley Anne Williams's *Dessa Rose*, the black woman and the white woman set out to describe a territory in which they can speak to each other freely in the fullness of their languages.

The triumph of Dessa Rose is that she escapes the textual determinations Africanist discourse has prepared for her, a text she has exceeded all along. When Adam Nehemiah reappears and tries to reestablish what he thinks of as his God-given right to name the world, his text is taken out of his hands. He insists violently upon the prerogatives of his metaknowledge and attempts to enlist the law in the enforcement of his text's long-delayed conclusion. "I know it's her," Nehemiah shouts, trying to employ force to make Dessa conform to his description of her, trying to force her by law back inside his narrative. "I got her down in my book" (254). Dessa escapes his book as effectively as she had escaped her chains in the root cellar of American writing. Nehemiah is left sputtering impotently: "Science. Research. The mind of the darky" (255). When he finds his incantations no longer have power to transform material reality, when he sees that a white woman has joined with Dessa to effect her transcendence of his textual prison, he is reduced to the final, feeble mantra of outraged patriarchy: "All alike. Sluts" (255).

From first page to last ellipses, *Dessa Rose* is a novel that reenacts black taking of textual power. Dessa Rose refuses Adam Nehemiah her last words, and in so doing she refuses the finality of the confessions of Thomas Gray and William Styron. The self-freed slave whom Dessa loves, Harker, invents out of the same powers of his own mind, the mind that American Africanist discourse denies him, a system of graphic marks as a "way of understanding where we had to be and what we had to do" (212). In the act, he repeats Frederick Douglass's unlawful inscriptions, his writings between the lines of the master, that end by displacing the mastery of the master's texts. In Sherley Anne Williams's novel, the rich intertextual inventions of African-American thought overwhelm the efforts of white writing to enclose black experience within the clichéd lines of an oppressive romance, a romance that would end in the "all rightness" of continued white power. Dessa Rose steps forward in the novel's epilogue and claims

Sherley Anne Williams as one of her writing children, by authorizing the words of her text.

> *This why I have it wrote down, why I has the child say it back. I never will forget Nemi trying to read me, knowing I had put myself in his hands. Well,* this *the childrens have heard from our own lips. I hope they never have to pay what it cost us to own ourselfs.* (260)

After Words

The darkness had materially increased,
relieved only by the glare of the water
thrown back from the white curtain
before us.
—Edgar Allan Poe,
"Narrative of Arthur Gordon Pym"

The drama's done. Why then here does
anyone step forth?—
—Herman Melville, *Moby Dick*

Oh, we have paid for our children's place
in the world again, and again . . .
—Sherley Anne Williams, *Dessa Rose*

    Ethiopians speak
sometimes by simile . . .
—Phillis Wheatley, "America"

. . .

Works Cited

Adams, John Quincy. *Argument of John Quincy Adams before the Supreme Court of the United States, in the Case of the United States, Appellants, vs. Cinque, and Others, Africans*. 1841. *The Amistad Case*. New York: Johnson Reprint, 1968.

Appiah, Kwame Anthony. *In My Father's House: Africa in the Philosophy of Culture*. New York: Oxford UP, 1992.

Ashbery, John. *Rivers and Mountains*. New York: Ecco, 1977.

———. *The Vermont Notebook*. Santa Barbara, Calif.: Black Sparrow, 1975.

Attali, Jacques. *Noise: The Political Economy of Music*. Trans. Brian Massumi. Minneapolis: U of Minnesota P, 1985.

Baker, Houston. *Modernism and the Harlem Renaissance*. Chicago: U of Chicago P, 1987.

———. *Singers of Daybreak: Studies in Black American Literature*. Washington, D.C.: Howard UP, 1974.

———. *Workings of the Spirit: The Poetics of Afro-American Women's Writing*. Chicago: U of Chicago P, 1991.

Balibar, Étienne, and Immanuel Wallerstein. *Race, Nation, Class: Ambiguous Identities*. Trans. Chris Turner. London: Verso, 1991.

Banks, Russell. *Continental Drift*. New York: Harper & Row, 1985.

Baraka, Amiri (LeRoi Jones). *The Autobiography of LeRoi Jones/Amiri Baraka*. New York: Freundlich, 1984.

———. *Black Magic: Poetry, 1961–1967*. New York: Bobbs, 1969.

———. *Black Music*. New York: Morrow, 1967.

———. *Blues People: Negro Music in White America*. New York: Morrow, 1963.

———. *The Dead Lecturer*. New York: Grove, 1964.

———. *Home: Social Essays*. New York: Morrow, 1966.

———. Introduction. *The Moderns*. Ed. LeRoi Jones. New York: Corinth, 1963. ix–xvi.

———. *The LeRoi Jones/Amiri Baraka Reader*. Ed. William J. Harris. New York: Thunder's Mouth, 1991.

———. *The Motion of History and Other Plays*. New York: Morrow, 1978.

———. Personal interview. Washington, D.C., Feb. 27, 1979.

———. *Preface to a Twenty Volume Suicide Note . . . .* New York: Totem/ Corinth, 1961.

———. *Selected Poetry of Amiri Baraka/LeRoi Jones*. New York: Morrow, 1979.

———. *The System of Dante's Hell*. New York: Grove, 1965.

———. *Tales*. New York: Grove, 1967.

Baraka, Amiri, and Diane di Prima, eds. *The Floating Bear: A Newsletter: Numbers 1–37, 1961–1969.* La Jolla, Calif.: Laurence McGilvery, 1973.

Barber, John W. *A History of the Amistad Captives.* 1840. New York: Arno and the *New York Times,* 1969.

Benét, Stephen Vincent. *John Brown's Body.* 1927. New York: Rinehart, 1954.

Bentson, Kimberly W. *Baraka: The Renegade and the Mask.* New Haven: Yale UP, 1976.

Bernstein, Charles. "Professing Stein/Stein Professing." *Poetics Journal* 9 (1991): 44–50.

Bérubé, Michael. *Marginal Forces/Cultural Centers: Tolson, Pynchon, and the Politics of the Canon.* Ithaca, N.Y.: Cornell UP, 1992.

Bhaba, Homi. Interview. *Emergences* 1 (1989): 63–88.

———, ed. *Nation and Narration.* London: Routledge, 1990.

Blackburn, Paul. *The Collected Poems of Paul Blackburn.* Ed. Edith Jarolim. New York: Persea, 1985.

———. *In, On, Or About the Premises.* New York: Grossman, 1968.

Brooks, Cleanth, R. W. B. Lewis, and Robert Penn Warren, eds. *American Literature: The Makers and the Making.* 2 vols. New York: St. Martin's, 1973.

Brooks, Gwendolyn. *Blacks.* Chicago: David, 1987.

Brooks, Peter. *Reading for the Plot: Design and Intention in Narrative.* New York: Vintage, 1985.

Brown, Sterling A. "Slim in Hell." *The Last Ride of Wild Bill and Eleven Narrative Poems.* Detroit: Broadside, 1975. 37–40.

Buhle, Paul. *C. L. R. James: The Artist as Revolutionary.* New York: Verso, 1988.

Burt, E. S. "Developments in Character: Reading and Interpretation in 'The Children's Punishment' and 'The Broken Comb.'" *The Lesson of Paul de Man.* Ed. Peter Brooks, Shoshana Feldman, and J. Hillis Miller. *Yale French Studies* 69 (1985): 192–210.

Canot, Theodore. *Adventures of an African Slaver As Told to Brantz Mayer.* Ed. Malcolm Cowley. New York: World, 1928.

Cather, Willa. *Sapphira and the Slave Girl.* 1940. New York: Vintage, 1975.

Clark, Vèvè. "Developing Diaspora Literacy and *Marassa* Consciousness." *Comparative American Identities.* Ed. Hortense Spillers. London: Routledge, 1991. 40–61.

Clifton, Lucille. *Good Woman: Poems and a Memoir.* Brockport, N.Y.: BOA Editions, 1987.

———. *Next: New Poems.* Brockport, N.Y.: BOA Editions, 1987.

Coleridge, Samuel Taylor. *Coleridge's Verse: A Selection.* Ed. William Empson and David Pirie. New York: Schocken, 1973.

———. *The Collected Works of Samuel Taylor Coleridge 2, The Watchman.* Ed. Lewis Patton. London: Routledge & Keegan Paul, 1970.

———. *The Poetical Works of Samuel Taylor Coleridge.* Ed. James Dykes Campbell. New York: Macmillan, 1895.

Conrad, Joseph. *Heart of Darkness.* Ed. Ross C. Murfin. New York: St. Martin's, 1989.

Coolidge, Clark. *At Egypt.* Great Barrington, Mass.: Figures, 1988.

————. "from Comes through in the Call Hold (Improvisations on Cecil Taylor)." *Village Voice Jazz Special* June 26, 1989: 9–10.

————. "a constant retrogression and this is not memory." *Poetry: Conversations in the Workshop with Contemporary Poets.* Ed. Lee Bartlett. Albuquerque: U of New Mexico P, 1987. 1–18.

————. *The Crystal Text.* Great Barrington, Mass.: Figures, 1986.

————. *Mine: The One That Enters the Stories.* Berkeley, Calif.: Figures, 1982.

————. *Own Face.* Lenox, Mass.: Angel Hair, 1978.

————. *Polaroid.* Berkeley, Calif.: Big Sky, 1975.

————. *Quartz Hearts.* San Francisco: This, 1978.

————. "Registers (People in All)." *Temblor* 10 (1989): 59–67.

————. *Solution Passage: Poems 1978–1981.* Los Angeles: Sun & Moon, 1986.

————. *Sound as Thought: Poems 1982–1984.* Los Angeles: Sun & Moon, 1990.

————. *Space.* New York: Harper & Row, 1970.

————. "*Talisman:* An Interview with Clark Coolidge." Ed. Edward Foster. *Talisman: A Journal of Contemporary Poetry and Poetics* 3 (Fall 1989): 16–46.

Creeley, Robert. *The Collected Poems of Robert Creeley: 1945–1975.* Berkeley and Los Angeles: U of California P, 1982.

Cullen, Countee. "Heritage." *The New Negro.* Ed. Alain Locke. New York: Boni, 1925. New York: Atheneum, 1968. 250–53.

Dante Alighieri. *The Divine Comedy.* Trans. C. H. Sisson. Chicago: Regnery Gateway, 1981.

Davis, Charles T. "Robert Hayden's Use of History." *Modern Black Poets: A Collection of Critical Essays.* Ed. Donald B. Gibson. Englewood Cliffs, N.J.: Prentice, 1973. 96–111.

Davis, Miles. *Miles: The Autobiography.* With Quincy Troupe. New York: Simon & Schuster, 1989.

Deleuze, Gilles. *Foucault.* Trans. Sean Hand. Minneapolis: U of Minnesota P, 1986.

Deleuze, Gilles, and Felix Guattari. *Kafka: Toward a Minor Literature.* Trans. Dana Polan. Minneapolis: U of Minnesota P, 1986.

————. *A Thousand Plateaus: Capitalism and Schizophrenia.* Trans. Brian Massumi. Minneapolis: U of Minnesota P, 1987.

Deren, Maya. *Divine Horsemen: Voodoo Gods of Haiti.* New York: Dell, 1972.

Derrida, Jacques. *The Other Heading: Reflections on Today's Europe.* Trans. Pascale-Anne Brault and Michael B. Naas. Bloomington: Indiana UP, 1992.

di Prima, Diane. *Pieces of a Song: Selected Poems.* San Francisco: City Lights, 1990.

Donnan, Elizabeth. *Documents Illustrative of the History of the Slave Trade to America.* 4 vols. 1935. New York: Octagon, 1969.

Dorn, Edward. *The Collected Poems: 1956–1974*. Bolinas, Calif.: Four Seasons Foundation, 1975.

Douglass, Frederick. *My Bondage and My Freedom*. Ed. William L. Andrews. Chicago: U of Illinois P, 1987.

———. *Narrative of the Life of Frederick Douglass*. 1845. *The Classic Slave Narratives*. Ed. Henry Louis Gates, Jr. New York: Mentor, 1987. 243–331.

Dove, Rita. *Grace Notes*. New York: Norton, 1989.

Dow, George Francis. *Slave Ships and Slaving*. 1927. New York: Dover, 1970.

Eliot, Thomas Stearns. *The Complete Poems and Plays: 1909–1950*. New York: Harcourt, Brace & World, 1971.

Empson, William. Introduction. *Coleridge's Verse: A Selection*. Ed. William Empson and David Pirie. New York: Schocken, 1973. 13–100.

Equiano, Olaudah. *The Interesting Narrative of the Life of Olaudah Equiano or Gustavus Vassa, The African. Written by Himself*. 1814. *The Classic Slave Narratives*. Ed. Henry Louis Gates, Jr. New York: Mentor, 1987. 1–182.

Farnsworth, Robert M. *Melvin B. Tolson 1898–1966: Plain Talk and Poetic Prophecy*. Columbia: U of Missouri P, 1984.

Feinstein, Sascha, and Yusef Komunyakaa, eds. *The Jazz Poetry Anthology*. Bloomington: Indiana UP, 1991.

Fetrow, Fred M. *Robert Hayden*. Boston: Twayne, 1984.

Fredman, Stephen. *Poet's Prose: The Crisis in American Verse*. 2d ed. Cambridge: Cambridge UP, 1990.

Frost, Robert. "Birches." *The Poetry of Robert Frost*. New York: Holt, 1969. 121–22.

Fruman, Norman. *Coleridge: The Damaged Archangel*. New York: George Braziller, 1971.

Gardner, Drew. "The Cover." *Hambone* 10 (Spring 1992): 89–98.

Gates, Henry Louis, Jr. *Figures in Black: Words, Signs, and the "Racial" Self*. New York: Oxford UP, 1987.

———. *The Signifying Monkey: A Theory of African American Literary Criticism*. New York: Oxford UP, 1988.

Ginsberg, Allen. *Collected Poems: 1947–1980*. New York: Harper & Row, 1984.

Gleason, Philip. "American Identity and Americanization." *Concepts of Ethnicity*. By William Petersen, Michael Novak, and Philip Gleason. Cambridge: Harvard UP, 1982. 57–143.

Gray, Thomas. *The Confessions of Nat Turner*. Baltimore: Thomas R. Gray, 1831.

Guattari, Felix, and Toni Negri. *Communists like Us*. Trans. Michael Ryan. New York: Semiotext(e), 1990.

Haeger, J. H. "Coleridge's Speculations on Race." *Studies in Romanticism* 13.4 (1974): 333–57.

Hale, Mike. "The Politics of Modern Literature." *San Jose Mercury News Arts & Books* July 28, 1991: 24.

Hansen, Chadwick. "The Metamorphosis of Tituba, or Why American

Intellectuals Can't Tell an Indian Witch from a Negro." *New England Quarterly* 47 (1974): 3–12.

Harris, William J. Introduction. *The LeRoi Jones/Amiri Baraka Reader*. Ed. William J. Harris. New York: Thunder's Mouth, 1991. xvii–xxx.

———. *The Poetry and Poetics of Amiri Baraka: The Jazz Aesthetic*. Columbia: U of Missouri P, 1985.

Harvey, Irene E. *Derrida and the Economy of Difference*. Bloomington: Indiana UP, 1986.

Hawthorn, Jeremy. *A Concise Glossary of Contemporary Literary Theory*. London: Edward Arnold, 1992.

Hawthorne, Nathaniel. "Chiefly about War Matters." *The Complete Works of Nathaniel Hawthorne*. Boston: Houghton, 1909. 12.

Hayden, Robert. *Collected Poems*. Ed. Frederick Glaysher. New York: Liveright, 1985.

Henderson, Stephen. *Understanding the New Black Poetry*. New York: Morrow, 1972.

Hoover, Paul. *The Novel*. New York: New Directions, 1990.

Hudson, Theodore R. *From LeRoi Jones to Amiri Baraka: The Literary Works*. Durham, N.C.: Duke UP, 1973.

Hughes, Langston. *The Big Sea*. New York: Knopf, 1940.

———. *Selected Poems*. New York: Knopf, 1959.

———. "To a Negro Jazz Band in a Parisian Cabaret." *Crisis* Dec. 1925: 67.

Jacobs, Harriet A. *Incidents in the Life of a Slave Girl*. Ed. Jean Fagan Yellin. Cambridge: Harvard UP, 1987.

James, C. L. R. *At the Rendezvous of Victory: Selected Writings*. London: Allison & Busby, 1984.

———. *The C. L. R. James Reader*. Ed. Anna Grimshaw. Oxford: Blackwell, 1992.

———. *Mariners, Renegades, and Castaways: The Story of Herman Melville and the World We Live In*. 1st ed., New York: C. L. R. James, 1953; 2d ed., Detroit: Bewick Editions, 1978; 3d ed., London: Allison & Busby, 1985.

JanMohamed, Abdul, and David Lloyd. "Introduction: Toward a Theory of Minority Discourse." *Cultural Critique* 6 (1987): 5–12.

Jefferson, Thomas. *Notes on the State of Virginia*. New York: Harper & Row, 1964.

Johnson, Barbara. "Rigorous Unreliability." *The Lesson of Paul de Man*. Ed. Peter Brooks, Shoshana Feldman, and J. Hillis Miller. *Yale French Studies* 69 (1985): 73–80.

Johnson, Charles. *Middle Passage*. New York: Atheneum, 1990.

———. *Oxherding Tale*. Bloomington: Indiana UP, 1982.

———. *The Sorcerer's Apprentice: Tales and Conjurations*. New York: Atheneum, 1986.

Johnson, James Weldon. *Along This Way*. 1933. New York: Penguin, 1990.

――――. *The Autobiography of an Ex-Colored Man.* 1912. New York: Hill & Wang, 1960.

――――. *Black Manhattan.* 1930. New York: Atheneum, 1968.

Jones, Hettie. *How I Became Hettie Jones.* New York: Dutton, 1990.

Kallen, Horace. *Cultural Pluralism and the American Idea: An Essay in Social Philosophy.* Philadelphia: U of Pennsylvania P, 1956.

Kermode, Frank. *The Sense of an Ending: Studies in the Theory of Fiction.* Oxford: Oxford UP, 1967.

Kerouac, Jack. *The Subterraneans.* New York: Grove, 1981.

Kristeva, Julia. *Revolution in Poetic Language.* Trans. Margaret Waller. New York: Columbia UP, 1984.

Kutzinski, Vera M. "Changing Permanences: Historical and Literary Revisionism in Robert Hayden's 'Middle Passage.'" *Callaloo* 9.1 (1986): 171–83.

Levy, Eugene. *James Weldon Johnson: Black Leader, Black Voice.* Chicago: U of Chicago P, 1973.

Lieberman, Laurence. "Review of *Harlem Gallery.*" *Hudson Review* Autumn 1965: 456–58.

Lowe, Lisa. "Rereadings in Orientalism." *Cultural Critique* 15 (1990): 115–43.

MacAllister, Archibald T. Introduction. *The Inferno: A Verse Rendering for the Modern Reader.* Trans. John Ciardi. New York: Mentor, 1954.

Mackey, Nathaniel. "Other: From Noun to Verb." *Representations* 39 (1992): 51–70.

――――. "Poseidon (Dub Version)." *Wilson Harris: The Uncompromising Imagination.* Ed. Hena Maes-Jelinek. Mundelstrup, Denmark: Dangaroo, 1991. 116–26.

Mariani, Paul. "Williams' Black Novel." *Massachusetts Review* 14 (1973): 67–75.

Marshall, Paule. *Praisesong for the Widow.* New York: Putnam's, 1983.

Melville, Herman. *Mardi: And a Voyage Thither.* New York: Signet, 1964.

――――. *Moby Dick or, the Whale.* Ed. Harrison Hayford, Hershel Parkes, and G. Thomas Tanselle. Chicago: Northwestern UP, 1988.

――――. *Piazza Tales.* Ed. Egbert S. Oliver. New York: Hendricks, 1948.

Mesher, David R. "The Remembrance of Things Unknown: Malamud's 'The Last Mohican.'" *Studies in Short Fiction* 12.4 (1975): 397–404.

Morrison, Toni. *Beloved.* New York: Knopf, 1987.

――――. *Playing in the Dark: Whiteness and the Literary Imagination.* Cambridge: Harvard UP, 1992.

――――. *Song of Solomon.* New York: Knopf, 1977.

Nelson, Dana D. *The Word in Black and White: Reading "Race" in American Literature, 1638–1867.* Oxford: Oxford UP, 1992.

Nicosia, Gerald. "Kerouac at the Brandeis Forum: The Origin of 'The Origins of the Beat Generation.'" *The Jack Kerouac Collection.* Santa Monica, Calif.: Rhino Records, 1990. 24–25.

O'Brien, Flann. *At Swim-Two-Birds.* New York: New American Library, 1976.

O'Hara, Frank. *The Collected Poems of Frank O'Hara.* Ed. Donald Allen. New York: Knopf, 1971.

Olson, Charles. *Call Me Ishmael.* San Francisco: City Lights, 1947.

———. *The Collected Poems of Charles Olson.* Ed. George F. Butterick. Berkeley and Los Angeles: U of California P, 1987.

———. *The Maximus Poems.* Ed. George F. Butterick. Berkeley and Los Angeles: U of California P, 1983.

———. *A Nation of Nothing but Poetry: Supplementary Poems.* Ed. George F. Butterick. Santa Rosa, Calif.: Black Sparrow, 1989.

O'Neill, Eugene. "The Emperor Jones." *The Plays of Eugene O'Neill.* New York: Modern Library, 1982. 173–204.

Osterud, Nancy Grey. *Bonds of Community: The Lives of Farm Women in Nineteenth-Century New York.* Ithaca, N.Y.: Cornell UP, 1991.

Patton, Paul. "Marxism and Beyond: Strategies of Reterritorialization." *Marxism and the Interpretation of Culture.* Ed. Cary Nelson and Lawrence Grossberg. Chicago: U of Chicago P, 1988. 123–39.

Poe, Edgar Allan. *Complete Stories and Poems of Edgar Allan Poe.* New York: Doubleday, 1966.

Pound, Ezra. *Pound/Zukofsky: Selected Letters of Ezra Pound and Louis Zukofsky.* Ed. Barry Ahearn. New York: New Directions, 1987.

Powers, Richard. *The Gold Bug Variations.* New York: Morrow, 1991.

Rampersad, Arnold. *The Life of Langston Hughes, Volume II: I Dream a World.* New York: Oxford UP, 1988.

Rawley, James A. *The Transatlantic Slave Trade: A History.* New York: Norton, 1981.

Rodefer, Stephen. "I inhabit the language the world heaps upon me." *Talking Poetry.* Ed. Lee Bartlett. Albuquerque: U of New Mexico P, 1987. 184–208.

Rukeyser, Muriel. *Willard Gibbs.* Garden City, N.Y.: Doubleday, Doran, 1942.

Said, Edward. *Culture and Imperialism.* New York: Knopf, 1993.

San Juan, Epifanio, Jr. *Racial Formations/Critical Transformations: Articulations of Power in Ethnic and Racial Studies in the United States.* Atlantic Highlands, N.J.: Humanities, 1992.

Sartre, Jean-Paul. *Nausea.* Trans. Lloyd Alexander. New York: New Directions, 1964.

Schmidt, Peter. *William Carlos Williams, the Arts, and Literary Tradition.* Baton Rouge: Louisiana State UP, 1988.

Shapiro, Karl. Introduction. *Harlem Gallery.* By Melvin B. Tolson. New York: Twayne, 1965. 11–15.

Simone, Timothy Maliqalim. *About Face: Race in Postmodern America.* Brooklyn, N.Y.: Autonomedia, 1989.

Spanos, William V. *The End of Education: Toward Posthumanism.* Minneapolis: U of Minnesota P, 1993.

──────. "The Uses and Abuses of Certainty: A Caviling Overture." *boundary 2* 12.3–13.1 (1984): 1–17.

Spillers, Hortense, ed. *Comparative American Identities: Race, Sex, and Nationality in the Modern Text*. London: Routledge, 1991.

──────. "Who Cuts the Border? Some Readings on 'America.'" *Comparative American Identities*. Ed. Spillers. 1–25.

Spivak, Gayatri C. "'Postmodernism,' 'Poststructuralism,' 'PostMarxism,' 'Postanalytical Philosophy,' 'Postpedagogy': Where is the 'Post' Coming From?" Lecture delivered at the Modern Language Association Convention. Chicago, Dec. 29, 1985.

Stein, Judith. "Defining the Race, 1890–1930." *The Invention of Ethnicity*. Ed. Werner Sollors. New York: Oxford UP, 1989. 77–104.

Stevens, Wallace. *The Palm at the End of the Mind: Selected Poems and a Play*. Ed. Holly Stevens. New York: Knopf, 1971.

Stowe, Harriet Beecher. *Uncle Tom's Cabin or, Life among the Lowly*. Ed. Kenneth S. Lynn. Cambridge: Harvard UP, 1962.

Taylor, Cecil. Liner notes to *Live at the Cafe Monmartre/Nefertiti, the Beautiful One Has Come*. Notes by Nat Hentoff. Rec. Nov. 23, 1962. Arista-Freedom, AL 1905, 1975.

──────. "Scroll No. 1." Liner notes to *Indent*. Rec. 1973. Arista-Freedom, AL 1038, 1977.

Tolson, Melvin B. "All Aboard!" Ts. Library of Congress, Washington, D.C.

──────. *Caviar and Cabbage: Selected Columns by Melvin B. Tolson from the Washington Tribune, 1937–1944*. Ed. Robert M. Farnsworth. Columbia: U of Missouri P, 1982.

──────. *A Gallery of Harlem Portraits*. Ed. Robert M. Farnsworth. Columbia: U of Missouri P, 1979.

──────. *Harlem Gallery*. New York: Twayne, 1965.

──────. Letters to Allen Tate. Ts. The Allen Tate Papers. Box 50, Folder T. Princeton University, Princeton, N.J.

──────. *Libretto for the Republic of Liberia*. New York: Twayne, 1953. New York: Collier, 1970.

──────. The Melvin B. Tolson Papers. Library of Congress, Washington, D.C. (There are ten containers in this collection. The folders in them are not numbered sequentially. References to these papers within the text will cite the container number.)

──────. "The Negro Scholar." *Midwest Journal* 1.1 (1948): 80–82.

──────. "The Odyssey of a Manuscript." *New Letters: A Magazine of Fine Writing* 48.1 (1981): 5–15.

──────. "A Poet's Odyssey: Melvin B. Tolson." Interview with M. W. King. *Modern Black Poets: A Collection of Critical Essays*. Ed. Donald B. Gibson. Englewood Cliffs, N.J.: Prentice, 1973. 84–95.

──────. Reading at the Library of Congress. Tape Recording. Oct. 18, 1965. Washington, D.C.

Walcott, Derek. *Omeros*. New York: Farrar, 1990.

Ward, Jerry W. "The System of Dante's Hell: Underworlds of Art and Liberation." *Griot: Official Journal of the Southern Conference on Afro-American Culture* 6.2 (1987): 58–64.

Watkins, Evan. "Intellectual Work and Pedagogical Circulation in English." *Theory/Pedagogy/Politics: Texts for Change*. Chicago: U of Illinois P, 1991. 201–21.

West, Cornell. *Race Matters*. Boston: Beacon, 1993.

Wheatley, Phillis. *The Collected Works of Phillis Wheatley*. Ed. John Shields. New York: Oxford UP, 1988.

Wideman, John Edgar. *Fever*. New York: Holt, 1989.

———. *Hurry Home*. New York: Harcourt, 1970.

———. *Philadelphia Fire*. New York: Holt, 1990.

———. *Reuben*. New York: Holt, 1987.

Williams, Pontheolla T. *Robert Hayden: A Critical Analysis of His Poetry*. Chicago: U of Chicago P, 1987.

Williams, Sherley Anne. *Dessa Rose*. New York: Berkeley, 1987.

Williams, William Carlos. *The Collected Poems of William Carlos Williams, Volume I: 1909–1939*. Ed. A. Walton Litz and Christopher MacGowan. New York: New Directions, 1986.

———. *The Collected Poems of William Carlos Williams, Volume II: 1939–1962*. Ed. Christopher MacGowan. New York: New Directions, 1988.

———. *Imaginations*. Ed. Webster Schott. New York: New Directions, 1970.

———. *Interviews with William Carlos Williams: "Speaking Straight Ahead."* Ed. Linda Wagner. New York: New Directions, 1961.

———. *In the American Grain*. New York: New Directions, 1956.

———. *Many Loves and Other Plays*. New York: New Directions, 1961.

———. *Paterson*. New York: New Directions, 1963.

———. *The Selected Letters of William Carlos Williams*. Ed. John C. Thirwall. New York: McDowell, Obolensky, 1957.

Williams, William Carlos, Fred Miller, and Lydia Carlin. *Man Orchid*. *Massachusetts Review* 14 (1973): 77–117.

Wright, Jay. *Boleros*. Princeton, N.J.: Princeton UP, 1988.

Wright, Richard. *12 Million Black Voices: A Folk History of the Negro in the United States*. New York: Viking, 1941.

Index